CASSELMAN'S CANADIAN WORDS

A COMIC BROWSE THROUGH WORDS AND FOLK SAYINGS INVENTED BY CANADIANS

BILL CASSELMAN

McArthur & Company

Toronto

First published by Little, Brown and Company (Canada) Limited
This edition published in 1999 by McArthur & Company

CANADIAN CATALOGUING IN PUBLICATION DATA

Casselman, Bill, 1942–
        Casselman's Canadian words: a comic browse through words and folk
        sayings invented by Canadians

ISBN 1-55278-034-1

1. Canadianisms (English). *2. English language — Etymology. I. Title.
II. Title: Canadian words.

FC23.C37 1999   422   C-99-930479-8
F1006.C37 1999

Cover and text design by Kyle Gell
Printed and bound in Canada

McArthur & Company
322 King Street West, Suite 402, Toronto, Ontario, Canada M5V 1J2

10 9 8 7 6 5 4 3 2 1

This book
is dedicated to
Eleanore Hand
for her love
&
encouragement.

TABLE OF CONTENTS

MICKY

RUBBY

IMAX™

Canadian words and phrases so new they have not
yet appeared in dictionaries

CAMAS

From aboriginal myths to cheesy tourist come-ons,
we get spooked by Ogopogo and the chilling
Gougou.

TUQUE

TOGGY

Synonyms for drunk. Canadians have more for this
word than for any other adjective—so many we've
arranged them from A to Z.

HOSER

From Pablum to Imax to canola, from Skidoo to
Nanaimo bar, we brand it Canuck.

SLINK

From an edible lichen called rock tripe to wappa-
too and *flèche d'eau*, Canadian plants have interesting names and uses.

FUNGY

KUTIA

Let us don an assean of stroud with a toggy and a
"Canadian shoe" to boot.

GASPÉ

A few words from your humble scribe

Scarborough means Harelip's Fort. There's a 200-foot woman waiting for you in the coastal waters off New Brunswick. Her name is Gougou. No triflers, please. In Kitchener, you may eat a lard-sparrow. The opposing team at a Montréal Canadiens hockey game might be called *une bunch de bommes*. Canadian computer freaks dwell in Nerdvana.

I have old Canuck words for you, new ones minty from today's headlines, naughty place names, and folksy sayings. Danish mañana appears in this sentence: *He doesn't ride the day he saddles*. Immigrants from Denmark brought this bit of folk speech to the lower mainland of British Columbia. It's a direct translation of a Danish saying that aptly defines one who procrastinates.

I heard a farmer near Morrisburg, Ontario, scolding a young hired hand who had made an error operating a tractor. He said, "I swear, boy, I've seen more brains in a sucked egg." The practice of sticking a finger through the top of a fresh egg and sucking out the yolk and the white has largely disappeared from rural eating habits. But the expression still makes a potent comic insult.

I have sayings. I have words.

'Zounds! I was never so bethumped with words
Since first I called my brother's father dad.

So says Philip the Bastard in Shakespeare's *The Life and Death of King John*.

But which words are uniquely ours? Where do these Canadianisms come from? Why would every reference book in Canada claim that *insulin* is a term invented in Canada? Banting, Best, & Collip were certainly the worthy discoverers of insulin, but they said they invented the word, too. Inside you'll discover the real story. Pablum, a well-known Canadian baby food, was named after Roman horse feed, as a joke. But in American Ralph Nader's salute to our achievements, *Canada Firsts*, Ralph and his staff of Naderettes tell us, and I quote exactly, "the name is derived from the Greek *pabulum* for food." Well now, it's not Greek and it does not mean food. And the sentence quoted is poor English. Otherwise, Ralphie, perfecto! By the way, fellah, thanks for spelling Canada correctly.

The researcher for the Nader book obviously copied the mistake about *pabulum* being Greek for food from *Colombo's Canadian Quotations* where it appears on page 80 of the 1974 edition.

Am I a crabby etymological fussbudget when it comes to accurate citation from the ancient tongues? You bet your tattered toga. Get it right or get it out.

What's the correct term for those crisply decorated Ukrainian Easter eggs? *Pysanky*. Why would W.B. Hamilton in *The Macmillan Book of Canadian Place Names* say that Gimli, Manitoba, is "named after the home of the gods in Norse mythology." Er, not really, W.B. Check my entry for the correct answer.

Say, that's awfully snotty of you, Bill. Correcting a scholar and Ralph Nader, both apparently too pooped to check basic facts. Who am I to wax so pompous? Shucks, folks, I'm just a writer who has been studying Canadian English and Canadian folk sayings for most of my life, with the help of correspondents all across Canada. Some of my helpers are mentioned by name in the text. Others show up in the bibliography. Unlike, it seems, some of the experts, we've done our homework. And we have questions. Why would a decent, God-fearing country use the Mi'-Kmaq words for chafed testicles to name a national park?

Why was Canada almost called Efisga? Why is Lachine, P.Q., a sarcastic insult? True, these may not be the questions that try men's souls. But they are piquant inquiries nonetheless.

All my life long, dictionaries have been my boon and my bane. When I was very young, my father would never define new words. He always said, "There's a book for that." In our house there were a *Tiny Tot's Picture Dictionary*, a *Junior Dictionary*, and the *Oxford English Dictionary* in thirteen volumes. I first learned to read sitting on the big padded arm of my father's living room chair. Dad would point to headlines in the *Globe and Mail* and ask me to sound out the words, with his help. When I arrived in Grade One, I knew how to read. One day in Grade Four, after I had corrected the spelling of a word my teacher had chalked on the blackboard, she turned to the class and said, "I'm sure we'd all like to thank Bill Casselman, the only dictionary that wets the bed." As I began to learn that day, not everyone appreciates exactitude.

Etymology, the study of the roots of words, is not an exact discipline. Surprisingly though, it attracts Pecksniffian precisians of the minutest scholarly scruple. Onomastics, the study of the names of people, places, and things, is an even wispier endeavour. The sandpaper of time has in many cases smoothed away what is left of the original name or place or word root, and all that can be done is read, research, know the language involved, and make an educated guess—that black sheep of Academe. The obdurate certainty of the autodidact has no place in etymology. Digging for word history, one relies on centuries of patient spade work by great linguists. Guesses are many, hits few, revisions constant. Luckily, Canadian place names are relatively new, mere babes in the onomastic woods, and thus for the most part their origin is clear. But if mistakes sprout here, help me weed them.

Throughout this book are Canadian folk sayings like *He had a smile on him like poison come to supper*. Many of these expressions see print here for the first time. They are emotional parts of our familial and national life. Scholars have, for the most part, looked upon these wise saws and comical figures of Canadian speech as the babble of peasants, and left them out of their studies, with the dismissive suffix of a guffaw. That's a snobbish mistake. In a future volume, I will correct it. Any reader who knows zippy old sayings or Canadian folk words not included here should kindly send them to me at the address given later. If I can use them in my next book, I will happily give you credit. Always include where and from whom you heard the word or saying. And tell me what you think it means.

We Canadians are always asking who we are. My friend, broadcaster Jack Farr of Winnipeg, tells the definitive story about this. A cannibal chief captured a Frenchman, a Canadian, and an American. He was a civilized cannibal. So many of them are. The chief offered each of the victims a last wish before they were eaten. The Frenchman wished for a sumptuous meal, divinely prepared, superbly served. The cannibal chief agreed. Next the Canadian had his last wish. He wanted to be given a short period of time to make a little speech about what it means to be a Canadian. The cannibal chief agreed. Finally he came to the American, standing beside the large iron pot, and asked him, "Do you have a last wish?" The American said, "Yes, can I please be eaten before the Canadian makes his speech?"

Casselman's Canadian Words. The title is not merely immodest; the choice of words and phrases **is** personal. I picked terms that delighted me, or ones whose origins surprised me. And I have included a study of some words not strictly of Canuck origin. As you peruse the words we Canadians have added to the polysyllabic trove of English, you really will find they add up to a linguistic portrait of who we are. The picture is not entirely flattering. There is genocide, racism, war. But take together all the Canadian words we have used to name ourselves, our places, and our fellow creatures, and you will find that our words say: We were here. We did this. We spoke thus. Perhaps we can improve?

A professor of linguistics I knew used to ask in self-mocking delight, "What could be more exciting than to watch one syllable roll down through the centuries?" Why, short of watching Don Cherry's collars rise, nothing!

205 Helena Street,
Dunnville, Ontario, Canada N1A 2S6
June, 1995

ACKNOWLEDGMENTS

Getting happily published is rare—so gnarled misanthropes with eyes like peach pits (authors) have told me. Well, *habent sua fata libelli* 'even books have their fate,' and preparing this one for publication has been a delight. My thanks go first to Jeff Miller, Publisher, Trade and College Divisions, Copp Clark, for his intelligence, enthusiasm, and friendliness in quelling all the little paranoias that pop up in a neophyte's head. His constant encouragement meant a lot to me. For bringing my work to the attention of Jeff Miller, I thank my agent, Daphne Hart of the Helen Heller Agency. Daphne's warmth, smarts, and brio are a unique medley. Pamela Erlichman edited the book with meticulous tact, and her knowledge of what constitutes clear copy saved me from many infelicities. The first furtive rootings of research began at the Dunnville Public Library and I thank the staff there for their courtesy and assistance. Librarians in the Language & Literature division of the Central Reference Library of Metropolitan Toronto were very helpful. At the Public Archives of Canada in Ottawa I selected the historical lithographs and engravings to illustrate the book. The archivists there went beyond the call of ordinary duty in making certain I was exposed to the great riches of the collection, and I am grateful for the extra time they gave me. Kathryn O'Hara of CBC Radio's *Later the Same Day* gave a friendly ear and early support to this project. Her creative attention helped spur further research.

Finally, I could not have written this book without the help of dear friends who read and commented on early drafts. Thank you, Barry Dickson, Darren Hagan, and Keith Thomas.

THE GREEK ALPHABET

It's all Greek to me, and it can be to you too!

'Fess up, Casselman. Why did you show Greek roots using the Greek alphabet? To strut and vaunt and show off a tatterdemalion classical education? To sow confusion among otherwise agile readers? No, indeed. Check out the word *alphabet*. It's made up of the first two letters of the Greek alphabet. Watch out for those gamma rays! Did you join Phi Beta Kappa at college? Consider the words the New Testament puts into the mouth of Christ, "I am Alpha and Omega" 'I am the first and the last.' The Greek alphabet is everywhere in English. Think of the delta of a river, then look at the Greek capital. Every letter of the Greek alphabet is used in scientific notation, in mathematics, physics, and chemistry. What's the value of π?

Every language looks best dressed in its native script. Greek words look best in Greek letters. Besides, only a dozen or so Greek letters are different from our Roman alphabet. A few minutes of study and practice writing out the forms will be repaid many times over. It will assist if you look at the Cyrillic script in which Russian is written. When he was composing an alphabet for Slavic languages, St. Cyril easily borrowed from his native Greek letter-hoard.

Even Greek letters that differ from ours can begin to seem familiar when seen in familiar words. Ψυχολογία is not that far from psychology. So, when you meet the Greek alphabet in this book, don't skip over it, work through it. There is ample reward.

alpha		A	α
beta		B	β
gamma		Γ	γ
delta		Δ	δ
epsilon		E	ε
zeta		Z	ζ
eta		H	η
theta		Θ	θ
iota		I	ι
kappa		K	χ
lambda		Λ	λ
mu		M	μ
nu		N	ν
xi		Ξ	ξ
omicron		O	o
pi		Π	π
rho		P	ϱ
sigma	Σ	σ	ς
tau		T	τ
upsilon		Y	υ
phi		Φ	φ
chi		X	χ
psi		Ψ	ψ
omega		Ω	ω

Canadian words so new they are not yet in most dictionaries

Artist's conception of the first computer

A living language spits out new words like a sizzling Uzi. Yet the active life of most new terms can be measured in nanoseconds. New phrases are lucky to last a day, like those short-lived insects that hatch in the morning, breed in the afternoon, and die by nightfall.

From the very first computer, which was quite literally manual, to last week's super-chip, new words spew in digital frenzy from computer technology. A few have caught my attention. I liked Nerdvana, so I tossed it into this chapter. But it's only my guess that such a pun will last. Seedy ROMs is another pert coinage. Cyberpunks seem firmly established, loitering and swaggering on the literary corner.

But don't blame me if some of these neologisms have hit the lexical dumpster even as you read them. Such is the nature

SOME NEW WORDS ARE FORMED BY ANALOGY

↓

Hardware

↓

Software

↓

Liveware
(humans who compute)

↓

Bugware
(error-ridden software)

↓

Dataware

↓

Vapourware
(software announced by a
company but never published)

↓

Wankware
(pornographic software)

↓

Wetware
(synonym for liveware)
&
We await the creation of
wimpware, which we shall
purchase immediately!

of neology, even in Canada. For words are the living tissue of any language. Just like our skin cells, words have a life, wear out, and slough off. Then new verbal tissue takes their place.

But, fleeting as most new words are, some coinages stick in the craw of a language; speakers like the fresh word and use it and spread it; such persistence earns the wordlet a place in a dictionary, perhaps at first just a dictionary of slang. Then berobed, crowned, and bearing the high sanction of wide usage, the trembling verbule is ushered by coaxing editors into the august repository of the *Oxford English Dictionary*, there to repose in referential glory for eternity. Verbule, for example, is a modest Latinate coinage of mine and means 'little word.' New words are the mountain streams that keep the mighty river of a living language flowing. And fresh terms spring up wherever tongues wag, in the gutter, in the laboratory, at the writer's desk, or beside a computer terminal.

Analogy is one of the most fertile formers of fresh verbiage, as you can see in the box on the left. *Hardware* has been in use in English since 1515 when it referred to useful items of ironmongery like nails and files. In the computer business it refers to the machines—the computers, printers, scanners, and external CDs that now festoon our desktops. Since the first commercial computer programs were issued on floppy disks, a natural coinage by analogy was—*software*.

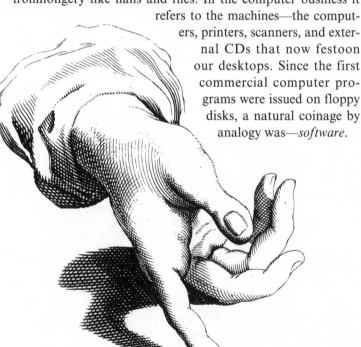

CASCADIA

A hot new Canadian buzzword. You hear it in bars where Ottawa trendoids gather to congratulate themselves on how cool they are. You hear it in Howe Street watering-holes where sincere penny-stock promoters in taupe Armani suits romance Vancouver grannies over white wine coolers. And it's part of the latest Canadian bar game: Break-up. Break-up works like this: Whoever at the table comes up with the most realistic scenario for the break-up of Canada is bought a free drink by the other players. Yes, as separatist rumours fly across the fretful pasture-lands of our dominion, Canuck paranoia explodes, like a thermometer in a malaria ward.

Cascadia fills out headlines in British Columbia newspapers. It's part of the daily vocabulary of British Columbians who are interested in stronger economic ties with the American states of Washington and Oregon. Some British Columbia residents even favour political union with the United States. May ghostly fathers of confederation seize them!

Cascadia is the name of the putative area, which would include the states of Washington and Oregon and the province of British Columbia, based on the fact that it encompasses roughly the watershed of the Cascade Range, a part of the Rocky Mountains cordillera that runs right up into southern British Columbia. The name may have been suggested by Cascadia State Park in Oregon. Cascadia is on the lips of many Vancouver businesspeople who have complained for years that B.C. federal tax money flows, not back over the Rockies to British Columbia, but into the hands of all the have-not provinces.

There's a scrap of folk wisdom that says, if you really love something, you can set it free. I don't know. I do know that, in the midst of constant separation anxiety, being a Canadian this decade is about as much fun as working the night shift at a pet crematorium!

CYBERPUNK

American critic Gardner Dozois first coined this term to label the work of Canadian writer William Gibson, author of *Neuromancer*, *Count Zero*, *Mona Lisa Overdrive*, and *Virtual Light*. Cyber is short for cybernetics, the scientific study of automatic control systems, including the human nervous system. American mathematician Norbert Wiener of MIT coined the word in 1948 in his pioneering book *Cybernetics*. Κυβερνήτης, *kybernetes*, is Greek for 'a pilot, a helmsman, a steersman.' To get cyberpunk, add punk from the world of eighties pop music. Hollywood films like *Robocop* and *Terminator* popularized the concept of the cyborg, a blend of cybernetic and organism, referring to any mix of man with machine. Then *cyber* became a fertile prefix for computer game buzzwords in the nineties. Cyberspace is a synonym for virtual reality. Other cyberwords, all of them possibly verbal ephemera, include cybernaut, cybergeek, cyberpolice, cybernet, and cybergame. The Greek root *kybern* is akin to the Latin root *gubern*, which gives a word like *gubernator* 'helmsman, leader,' and that was slowly transformed into French *gouverneur* and then into English *governor*.

GUMBY GOES TO HEAVEN

Gumby goes to heaven is the derogatory title of what many consider Canada's worst piece of public art. Effectively blocking the view up University Avenue in Toronto, Gumby is a lozenge of sculptural kitsch purporting to commemorate the Canadian air force. Its correct title, *Per ardua ad astra*, is the motto of the Royal Air Force and means in Latin 'through difficulties to the stars.' The sculpture depicts a human figure, evidently in the throes of anorexia nervosa, bearing in its upstretched arms an airplane. The real Gumby was a Plasticine™ slab, animated by single-frame cinematography into a smiling and vaguely moronic cartoon character of early American television, and then repopularized in the 1970s by Eddie Murphy during his stint on the NBC comedy show, *Saturday Night Live*. Gumby as a nickname stems from gumbo, a Louisiana chicken or fish soup thickened with the vegetable okra. In Angolan Bantu *ngombo* is the word for 'okra.' Gumbo then acquired the secondary meaning of any fine clay soil that becomes impassable after a rain. Gumbo also came to mean thick, sticky mud, and this mud's slight resemblance to Plasticine™ suggested the character's name.

INTER-CROSSE

This no-contact version of lacrosse, without the injury-producing violence, was invented in 1982 by Quebecer Pierre Filion, among others. It is a new Canadian sport that has become popular all over the world, and is now played in more than thirty-two countries. It's on the sports curricula at more than five hundred Quebec schools. The lacrosse ball is now a hollow rubber ball, and the sticks are plastic, not wood. Iroquois peoples invented lacrosse to train native warriors in agility and aggression. We have quite enough of the latter in sports, so inter-crosse is a timely invention, well-liked by the kids who play it, and by their parents. Lacrosse is simply *la crosse*, Canadian French for the hooked stick used to play the game.

NERDVANA

Jack Kapica, of the *Globe and Mail*, coined this shameless pun on nirvana, in a 1994 column about the sterile world of computer users who surf every night on the Internet. In the same article he used another new pun to describe the bleakness of the user's face, bathed in the ghostly light on a monitor screen, alone and palely keyboarding. Such a person was, wrote Kapica, in *Cyberia*.

NEUROMANCER

Canadian fiction writers have not been prolific coiners of new words. But one winner of the highest prizes in science fiction writing, Vancouver's king of cyberfiction, William Gibson, is no slouch in the neology department. *Neuromancer*, the title of his first novel, well illustrates Gibson's playful word-making. Neuromancer is formed on the analogy of necromancer, one who foretells the future by consulting the black arts. Μαντεία *manteia*, is the ancient Greek word for 'divination.' Νεκρός *nekros*, is Greek for 'dead.' Thus a necropolis is a city of the dead, a cemetery. Neuron means nerve. Neuromancer is one who foretells the future by reading neurons, the nerve cells of the human brain. Sci-fi writers like Gibson have also been called neuromantics, punning both on the title of his trail-blazing novel and on romantics.

NUNAVUT

Nunavut was created by act of parliament in 1993 as a new Canadian territory, slated to be fully operational by April 1999, and made up of land in the eastern arctic that used to be part of the Northwest Territories. Nunavut will hold one-fifth of Canada's land. In the Inuktitut language the word means 'our land.'

SEEDY ROMS

A pun to describe sexually graphic CD-ROMs, the phrase was coined by Katherine Kelly and John Karmazyn in the *Toronto Star* (4 August 1994). In another little felicity of language from the same article, they described the typical lone male consumer of such computer sex as a "Don-Juan-a-be," punning again, this time on street slang "wannabe," meaning a no-talent aspirant to celebrity, the kind of guy who would want to dally with Virtual Valerie. What's around the bend in this new world of cybersex, porno-tainment, and interactive erotica? Consider

WANKWARE

teledildonics, a VR system featuring plastic bodysuits, head-gear, and gloves, that permits two people thousands of miles apart to "like get tactile, dude!" *Tele* is the Greek word-forming element meaning 'far away,' and a dildo is an artificial penis. A related new word is wankware, coined in imitation of software. It is software on CD intended for masturbatory, not educational purposes. The term was noted in the November, 1994 issue of *Wired* magazine, but appeared earlier on Canadian computer bulletin boards. To wank in current British slang means to masturbate. A wanker is one who does so.

Scum-sucking monsters from a cold Canadian hell

Y ou are alone walking in the cold winter twilight. Quite alone. What was that movement? Over by the stand of birches. Nothing really. Just the Wendigo. A cannibal fiend that will disembowel you and plan a midnight snack of unusually proteinaceous spaghetti. Canada has a splendid host of ghoulies and ghosties. Sure, they may not have had Dracula's press agent. They're new fiends, but they're hard workers. Here are a few of my favourite things that go bump in the night. May they grab your attention, not your throat.

Sasquatch and Ogopogo? Bunch of wimps, dude! This Halloween, let's go searching for Gougou, she who dwells on a very mysterious island in the Gulf of St. Lawrence. According to Samuel de Champlain and his local Mi'-Kmaq sources of

GOUGOU

1603 A.D., Gougou is a colossal woman, roughly 200 feet tall, whose chief pastime is wading through the waters off Canada's east coast and catching unwary mariners, plucking them from their boats and canoes, stuffing them into a big leather pemmican pouch, and then later, when she's peckish, yanking them out and gnawing on them as children might a Christmas candy cane. Pretty scary, eh, boys?

If one were offering a psychoanalytic approach to the origins of Gougou, and if one were—to quote one of James Joyce's more egregious puns from *Finnegans Wake*—"jung and easily freudened," one might say Gougou represents the archetype of the female sea monster, the vast, oceanic, devouring uterus that waits to reclaim what she has earlier spewed forth in the act of birth. The oral aggression of the monster is, of course, a psychic stand-in for the vulval and labial aggression that males both desire and fear, the literally unfathomable Ur-pudendum of male nightmare. Or maybe Gougou is just a big, spooky, misunderstood giantess, like Madge at the back of the typing pool who sits at those three desks.

NANABOZHO

Nanabozho is the trickster hero of Ojibwa myth, a mighty giant who created the world and the humans and then turned to stone and flung himself into Lake Superior just off present-day Thunder Bay where he lies as a series of islands called The Sleeping Giant.

NOISE GHOST

The Noise Ghost is an Inuit poltergeist, an arctic auditory phenomenon of incorporeal guile. This spirit noisemaker may announce his visitation by curling around a northern house on a quiet night and making a small but high-pitched hissing. It seems to be circling the house now, the hiss rising to an unearthly whistle. It gets closer and closer to the frightened people inside the house. It shrieks as if it is inside your heart. Wise elders, however, know the ancient words that will silence the Noise Ghost.

OGOPOGO

Ogopogo, monster of Lake Okanagan, British Columbia, is a creature whose *absence* would strike fear in the heart of any Okanagan tourist operation. The name sounds aboriginal, but is in fact a nonsense word taken from a British music hall song of the Edwardian era. It was dubbed Ogopogo in 1912. Local

Salish people once believed in a flesh-eating lake creature, long before whites arrived in the beautiful valley. The Salish call him *Naitaka*, Demon of the Lake. People who claim to have actually seen the beast say he seems friendly. Right. People said the same thing about Bob Rae.

SASQUATCH

Se'sxac is a word for bogeyman in Halkomelem, a language of the Salish peoples of southern British Columbia. Bigfoot is a tall, hairy humanoid who has a knack for appearing at the precise moment when human cameras are out of focus. Clever, eh? Various blurry homemade movies exist of furry apelike droolers crashing through rain forest scrub. Some Salish people believe in these 8-foot creatures who are said to have gorilloid noses and long arms.

SIKUSI

A monster that is now a trademark, Sikusi began mythological life as a giant ice worm who was sometimes helpful to humans, and sometimes played tricks on hunters. *Sikku* is one of the words for 'ice' in Inuktitut. The trademarked doll is 18 inches long, covered with fur, and decked out with wee horns and a lascivious tongue. It was created for possible commercial rivalry with the successful Ookpik doll of the sixties by some Inuit women of Tuktoyaktuk in the Northwest Territories. "Tuk" is near the mouth of the Mackenzie River, on a little peninsula jutting out into the Beaufort Sea.

TORNIT

Only some of the Tornit have a place in a chapter about monsters. Tornit or Tornait is the Inuktitut plural of Torngak, a supernatural spirit or a devil. And to the great spirit, Torngarsuk, is due only reverence. It is said he lives with his mother in a secret place where it is always summer and no night ever dares to snuff out a perpetually shining sun. But one abode of evil spirits is Tuurngatalik Island off southern Baffin Island, whose name in Inuktitut means 'place of evil spirits.' Other denizens of Inuit mythology are the Tunit, a people who inhabited the north before the Inuit. Anthropologists call them people of the Dorset or Thule culture. Legend says they were taller than the Inuit and fought with them. On Baffin Island, however, the Tunit or Tunik were evil dwarves.

WENDIGO

Witiku is Cree for 'evil spirit' or 'cannibal.' Early English speakers heard Witiku as Wendigo. Many Algonkian-speaking peoples, like the Cree, believe in it. The Wendigo (or Windigo) can possess any male, especially during a fever or an attack of madness. Often it invades the human heart as a lump of ice. The victim's face may turn black with frostbite. He may be able to fly through winter nights in search of new prey, his own species. Any man who goes on a solo hunt and never returns may have fallen victim to a Wendigo. Eating human flesh, even in an emergency, may be a sign that a starving hunter has "turned Wendigo." Such a wretch will be shunned by all members of his group, and probably driven from the camp. For once the Wendigo has tasted human flesh, he will yearn to feed again.

If possession by Wendigo is confirmed, a shaman must be summoned to exorcize the horror—a tricky procedure, for it entails trying to melt the lump of ice that has frozen the victim's human heart. Boiling fat has been poured down a throat. A raving victim has been plunged into boiling water. One of Canada's astute ethnologists, Dr. Diamond Jenness, in *The Ojibwa Indians of Parry Island* offered this insight into the psychological origins of the Wendigo myth: "The most dreaded of all supernatural beings that are evil or hostile to man is the 'Windigo,' a personification of the starvation and craving for flesh that so often befell the Ojibwa in the last months of the winter."

A brooding body of water ringed by desolate shores in Algonquin Park bears the name, Windigo Lake. A lone canoeist, paddling in the crisp air of a September morning, may even think the lake picturesque. But, on a cloudy day, from the middle of Windigo Lake, one can scarcely see anything on shore that is shuffling hungrily toward the water's edge.

MARCH 28, 1860

"Thickfoot's brother had killed his grandson, a boy ten or twelve years of age, being apprehensive that the boy was becoming a Wendigo."

Extracted from the files of the *Nor'Wester*, a newspaper of the Red River Settlement.

He's got his snowsuit on and he's heading north

That figure of speech from northern Manitoba is a vivid metaphor for the state of being stiff as a pine plank with drink. There are more synonyms for the adjective *drunk* than for any adjective in English. At last count approximately three thousand words and phrases indicate a certain liquorous befuddlement. One of the first word-students to make a list of drunken synonyms was Benjamin Franklin, who collected about three hundred in his *Drinkers' Dictionary* of 1733. Among Ben's faves were: *he's had a thump over the head with Samson's jawbone* and *he be as good-conditioned as a puppy*.

Canadians have contributed to the staggering number of booze terms, too. Among the Canuck words we'll discuss in this chapter are: Calgary redeye, callibogus, hootch, micky, moose milk, and rubby.

One area of northern ingenuity we do not cover here is new recipes. It is said a Canadian concocted the first banana-peach schnapps. I have not discovered the name of this person. But when I do find it, vigilantes shall ride by night, and the vengeance exacted shall be dire.

THE TIPSY ALPHABET

But first we present a tipsy alphabet of drunken synonyms. All phrases have been reported used in Canada. Many are not, however, of purely Canadian origin. The British navy birthed many of the following nautical nifties. FUBAR is the child of the American Army during World War II. It means *fouled up beyond all recognition.*

Of course, in this age of political correctness, the sombre drones of temperance remind us that there is nothing funny anymore, anywhere, ever, on earth. Being drunk is bad. After heavy drinking, men often cannot perform sexually, and this temporary and unpleasant state has been dubbed, in a Canadian phrase, brewer's droop. If you drink, don't drive. Certainly that is a very commonsensical admonition. All that said, my final word to the abstemious bluestocking is a quotation from the novel *Tom Jones* by Henry Fielding, in which the learned English judge and novelist makes this observation: "It is said strong drink dulls a man. And so it will. In a dull man."

A   anchored in sot's bay

B   burns with a low, blue flame

C   cocked to the gills

D   decks awash
     ding-swizzled

E   embalmed

F   flying one wing low
     fried on both sides
     FUBARed

G   got a brass eye
     got his snowsuit on and he's heading north

H   he couldn't find his ass with both hands

I   in his cups
inter pocula (Latin, literally 'among the cups')
in an interpoculary stupor [my own phrase]

J   jug-bitten

K   knows not the way home

L   listing to starboard
lit to the gunnels
loaded to the Plimsoll mark
lost his rudder

M   main-brace well-spliced
moist around the edges

N   not able to see through a ladder

O   out in left field with a catcher's mitt on

P   paintin' his nose
put to bed with a shovel

Q   quilted

R   rosy about the gills

S   saw Montezuma
slightly slew-eyed
sniffed the barmaid's apron
stewed as a fresh-boiled owl
stiff as a carp
swacked

T   three sheets to the wind and the
        other one flapping
tight as the bark on a tree
topped off his anti-freeze
trifle maudlin

U   under the affluence of incohol
up the pole with no grease

V   vulcanized

W   wam-bazzled
     wrapped up in warm flannel

X   x'ed in both eyes (from the way cartoon
     characters were shown to be blotto)

Y   yappy as a dead dog

Z   zorked, zozzled, and zissified!

CALGARY REDEYE

So ends our tipsy alphabet. So begin our Canuck booze words. Calgary redeye is beer mixed with tomato juice. I've never figured out how it could give you a red eye. Surely it would have to at least reach one's stomach; and its taste often prevents that particular digestive catastrophe.

CALLIBOGUS & SPRUCE BEER

Recipes differ for callibogus, a Canadian Maritime drink, but it's usually spruce beer fortified with rum or whisky, sometimes with a dollop of molasses added. The origin of the word is lost. Native peoples taught white settlers to prevent scurvy by drinking spruce tea, made from boiling tender young spruce shoots that were high in vitamin C. Whites then added yeast and molasses to ferment this mild antiscorbutic into the more potent spruce beer. And later, to confect a brew that might flatten a lumberjack, someone thought of adding strong spirits.

DAILY TOT

The daily tot was a ration of dark rum given to every serving member of the Canadian navy from 1910 to 1972, when Canada's puritanical and temperance-minded busybodies finally caught up with this pleasant custom borrowed from the British navy. It could scarcely have been the cause of intemperance since the sailor's daily portion was a scant 75 millilitres. Tot was English dialect for a small child, then came to mean a child's cup, hence a small portion.

MICKY

It's micky or mickey. Since the middle of the last century, we've been tucking small flasks of liquor under the buffalo robe for that Saturday afternoon at the college football game, or, later in the season, a sleigh ride on a snowy evening. Here is yet another boozy addition to drinking English created by Canadians from Mickey Finn, which was nineteenth-century slang for an Irishman and a synonym for knock-out drops. When a drunk got too bothersome, the bartender slipped a few drops of chloral hydrate into the guy's whiskey. Thus mickey-finned, the boozer collapsed in a short faint, during which his carcass could be carried out of the beverage room to a waiting snowbank. Hospitality, thy name is Canada. And note that beverage room and beer parlour are Canadianisms.

MOOSE MILK

Ought we to fret that so many Canadian words concern quaffing spirits? Up north, moose milk is homebrew or rum and milk. A more piquant potion is concocted in the Maritimes. Recipes for moose milk vary, but one lollapalooza contains emulsified fiddleheads and clam juice, liberally diluted with cheap wine. Perhaps Chateau Moncton? Last week was a fine vintage. Fiddleheads are the spring-fresh fronds of the ostrich fern, plucked before they unravel to the forest sun, and consumed as a delicacy, often by boiling and buttering.

RUBBY

The rubby or rubbie is another of our verbal contributions to the bibulous fraternity of booze-hounds. This unfortunate derives his label from an unhealthy habit of drinking rubbing alcohol. He can buy it in drugstores on Sunday, when most Canadian liquor stores are closed. It is worth pointing out that rubbing hooch is highly toxic. It is **not** the same alcohol that's in booze. And it will curdle your gizzard quicker than Bob Rae used to sing "The Face on the Bar Room Floor," with accompaniment.

Enjoy that new, lemon-fresh, litigiously defended, that-i-stole-from-my-brother-in-law, industrial-strength neology, now!

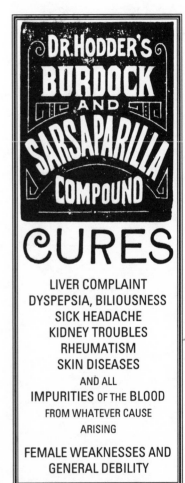

DR. HODDER'S BURDOCK AND SARSAPARILLA COMPOUND

CURES

LIVER COMPLAINT
DYSPEPSIA, BILIOUSNESS
SICK HEADACHE
KIDNEY TROUBLES
RHEUMATISM
SKIN DISEASES
AND ALL
IMPURITIES OF THE BLOOD
FROM WHATEVER CAUSE
ARISING

FEMALE WEAKNESSES AND
GENERAL DEBILITY

I nventors, engineers, amateurs, doctors, entrepreneurs, and bustling commerce in general have all packed our stockroom of brand-name Canadian words. My wee inventory of this vast treasure follows. May it pay tribute to the spirit of enterprise that made us what we are today in Canada: employees.

ACTH

ACTH or Adreno-Cortico-Tropic Hormone is an important pituitary hormone that acts on the adrenal glands which secrete corticosteroids that affect many of the body's chemical processes. It was named and first isolated at McGill University by Dr. James B. Collip, a brilliant biochemist born in Belleville, Ontario. Earlier in his career, Dr. Collip had assisted Doctors

Banting and Best in purifying insulin and in its commercial preparation. Although Dr. Collip did not share in the Nobel Prize for the discovery of insulin, his contribution was so important that he did share in the money portion of the Nobel.

ANIK

Anik A-1 was our first geostationary communications satellite launched from Cape Canaveral in 1972 and carried to its orbit by an American rocket. Symbolism, anyone? The word is Inuktitut.

BARR BODY

The Barr body is named after its discoverer, Dr. Murray Barr, an anatomist at the University of Western Ontario. Inside the cell nucleus, chromatin is the carrier of the genes. In 1949 Dr. Barr was the first to identify the chromatin involved in sex typing, later called the Barr body. Within the cell nucleus, it is a marker of genetic femaleness, being composed of a dense mass of inactivated X chromosomes. It is thus one of the genetic items sought in the analysis of a sample taken from a pregnant woman by amniocentesis. Fetal cell debris floating in the amniotic fluid can be analysed, and the presence of Barr bodies tells the parents that the fetus is female.

BRICKLIN

In the saga of sad-sack flivvers, here is Canada's very own Edsel. Aided by copious Canuck bucks from the government of New Brunswick, an American moneybags named Malcolm Bricklin produced a few cars in 1973, and then, in 1975, *mirabile dictu*, the company went bankrupt. Mr. Bricklin did not though.

CABOTEUR

Caboteur is a French, then an English, term for a Canadian boat or its captain. A caboteur is a vessel that plies the coast and does not often venture out into open sea. It was named after early explorer John Cabot.

CANADA DRY

Canada Dry Ginger Ale was patented in 1907 by J.J. McLaughlin, a pharmacy graduate of the University of Toronto. The product is now owned by Cadbury-Schweppes of England who market it all over the world.

CANADARM

Canadarm, the remote manipulator system for the space shuttle, was named and developed by Canadian scientists at the National Research Council between 1975 and 1981. Still to be explored are more earth-bound uses for Canadarm such as underwater pipeline repair and computerized public throttling of certain politicians.

DEEP ROVER

Deep Rover is a Canadian one-person submarine that can dive to a depth of one kilometre and stay submerged for seven days. Constructed by Can-Dive Ltd. at Dartmouth, Nova Scotia, in 1984, the first Deep Rover was used by Petro-Canada for its oil drilling off the coast of Newfoundland.

DEWLINE

In the mid-fifties the building of the Dewline, a 3,000-mile line of networked radar stations and small airports for jet fighter planes, "opened up" Canada's extreme north to influences from southern civilization, not all of them beneficial. Canada and the United States feared transarctic Soviet invasion, by rockets and Russian bombers. To intercept such threats they constructed a Distant Early Warning line.

FISH LADDER

In 1870, James Wyeth King of Shubenacadie, Nova Scotia, patented The King Fish Ladder, which allowed fish swimming upstream to spawn to pass waterfalls and dams more easily. The invention was a particular boon to some salmon streams on the east and west coasts.

IMAX ™

This trademarked method of filming and projecting giant movie images was invented in 1968 in Toronto by Grahame Ferguson, Robert Kerr, and Roman Kroitor. The original name stands for eye-max, the maximum that human eyes can view on a screen. Imax™ was first used at the Canada pavillion during Expo 70 in Osaka, Japan. Following Omnimax, their latest format coup is called Solido, a 3-D image projected on a large dome in which the audience sits, so that gigantic moving images fill their entire visual field.

INSULIN

The name of this pancreatic hormone is often claimed as a Canadian word, but yes, there was hanky-panky afoot back in 1921, when four scientists at the University of Toronto—Banting, Best, MacLeod, and Collip—first isolated the chemical. That year when they published their research in the *American Journal of Physiology* they wrote: "We suggest the name insulin." Nine years earlier, Sir Edward Schaefer, a noted British physiologist, had suggested the existence of the chemical and had named it insulin, from its secretion in the islets of Langerhans in the pancreas. *Insula* is Latin for 'island.' An islet is a small island. And Banting, Best, MacLeod, and Collip, worthies all, told a small fib. Although people with diabetes all over the world are grateful for the discovery of insulin, it was a bit tacky of the Ontario scientists to take another man's verbal invention, and try to fob it off as their own creation.

KEROSENE

A Canadian discovered kerosene and the kerosene lamp. Dr. Abraham Gesner first demonstrated his product at a public lecture on Prince Edward Island in 1846. His early experiments in the fractional distillation of coal appear in a book entitled *Treatise on Coal* (1860). Dr. Gesner coined the word from the Greek word for 'wax' *keros*, and a common scientific ending *-ene* applied to names for alcohols and other chemical distillates.

NELVANA

Nelvana of the Northern Lights was a superheroine of Canadian comic books during World War II. Adrian Dingle of Toronto drew the strip from 1940 to 1945. In her long cape, Nelvana came to the rescue of her Inuit brothers. Today, Canada's leading producer of animated TV and film cartoons calls itself Nelvana Productions.

PAINT ROLLER

If you've just repainted the breakfast nook in a nutritious flat latex mustard, give a thought to Norman Breakey of Toronto who conceived this device in 1940. But no Canadian company would touch it, and Breakey died broke, while several American companies infringed his patent and made big bucks.

SKIDOO

The Skidoo is a Canadian invention, also called an autoboggan and a motor toboggan. It is basically a sled with front skis and a rubber belt on the back with deep treads mounted on a rotor turned by a gasoline engine. Synonyms and commercial variations abound, among them skidoo, snow-bug, snowmobile, Snow Cruiser, and skiscooter. The Skidoo was invented in 1959 by Joseph-Armand Bombardier, who as early as 1922 created the very first operational snowmobile. The word *toboggan* is a borrowing through early French *tabagane*, from the Mi'-Kmaq word *tobagan*, which means 'hand-sled.'

SLICKLICKER

The slicklicker is a machine for cleaning up oil spills, invented and named by chemist Richard Sewell in 1968 at the research laboratories of the Canadian Department of National Defence. After incorporating their own company, Sewell and his brother built and sold slicklickers until they stopped production in 1981. Many other producers now manufacture oil-spill cleaners.

SMITH BROS.

Smith Brothers cough drops are throat soothers invented by a restaurant owner in St. Armand, Québec, one James Smith. After his death, when his two sons William and Andrew took over the cough drop business, they put engravings of their own bearded selves on the box as a trademark. Many suckers of cough drops thought the two hirsute worthies were inventions of an advertising artist, and that their names were Trade and Mark.

STANDARD TIME

Canadian scientist Sandford Fleming at a public Toronto lecture in 1879 announced his idea to divide the world into twenty-four time zones, each with its own standard time. Railways, then whole countries, then by 1900, most countries of the world, adopted his system. In 1897 Queen Victoria knighted Fleming for his timely invention.

SUPERMAN

Sometimes an attributive mania overtakes us Canadians as we search for Canadian firsts. It is true that it was Toronto-born Joe Shuster who created the comic strip *Superman* with an American buddy, Jerome Siegel, in Cleveland, Ohio. It first appeared in *Action Comics* in 1938, with Clark Kent working for *The Daily Star*, later changed to *The Daily Planet*. But several histories of comic books also give Shuster credit for the hero's name. Maybe on Krypton, fellahs. Not on this planet.

In 1903 George Bernard Shaw translated a term he had been reading in the writings of the German philosopher Nietzsche, *Übermensch*, and he used it in the title of his play, *Man and Superman*. The German means literally 'overman.' Shaw translated *over* into Latin to achieve the punchier superlative, *Superman*.

The monotony of botany banished

☞ OR ☜

A garland of Canadian plants

The John A. Macdonald "moth" pollinates the flower of Confederation

From the crimson dye of *sang dragon* to flesh-devouring bog-dwellers, Canadian plants are beautiful, odd, and useful. Jack-in-the-Pulpit is very good for teenage acne. Prickly pear cactus leaves, despined, may be roasted in hot ashes, should you find yourself foodless in southern Alberta. The first French name for poison ivy was *l'herbe à la puce* or fleawort. But early French settlers said the name was far too mild.

Nature may well be the bounteous apothecary, but be warned: don't eat or apply internally or externally any wild plant unless you have correctly identified it and know its properties. With that premonitory injunction clearly in mind have we traipsed the sward of our green world and brought back, for your delectation, the following specimens.

ANEMONE

A "STEARN" REBUKE

Professor William T. Stearn, probably the world's leading expert on botanical Latin, in *Stearn's Dictionary of Plant Names for Gardeners* (1992) says there is no connection between anemone and the wind, and that anemone stems from a Greek version of the Semitic mythological hero Naaman (Adonis), from whose spilled blood sprang up a red anemone.

Only a person who has never seen ripe anemone seeds being carried off by the wind could postulate such a derivation, supported as it is in Stearn's text by one obscure Dutch linguist with absolutely no textual proof.

The Canada anemone of our eastern provinces, *Anemone canadensis*, can be cultivated in gardens, although it is an intrusive little rooter that quickly invades garden space set aside for showier plants. Better perhaps to enjoy its white flowers in the wild as nodding tokens of late spring. The Canada anemone likes wet meadows and is comfy on the banks of creeks and forest brooklets.

A common name is wind flower, a translation of its ancient Greek name, ἀνεμώνη, which literally means 'daughter of the wind' and is so called because its plumed seeds parachute on autumn winds, born aloft and billowy as sea foam, as they disperse to new sites.

A prairie anemone is the Pasque Flower or *Anemone patens*, which is the official flower of Manitoba. Pasque is one Norman French spelling of the Old French word for Easter, *Pasches*, ultimately through ecclesiastical Latin *pascha* to Koine Greek πάσχα to Aramaic *paskha* to its origin in the Hebrew word for passover, *pesach*.

So why Pasque Flower? Well, some ponderous tomes of botanical wisdom say it's because in England it blooms approximately around Easter (actually in England it's a different but related plant, *Anemone pulsatilla*). One very famous writer on plants, John Gerard, even claimed in *The Herball, or General Historie of Plants* published in 1597 that *he* named the plant due to its Easter flowering. But a bit of riffling through other, more objective ancient herbals uncovers the news that Pasque Flower gave a juice from its sepals that was used as a green dye for painted Easter eggs in many European countries. Canadians brought up on the prairies know that downy seedheads of Pasque Flowers being combed by a stiff breeze mean autumn is truly here and winter's but a stubbled field or two away.

ARCTIC WILLOW

Arctic willow is *Salix arctica*. There are dozens of species of ground-hugging dwarf willows in our north and they hybridize freely. Staying low and clustered together is a protective strategy to keep out wind and freezing cold, making dwarf willows among the prostrate plant forms that grow in more elevated arctic regions.

The bark of this scrawny, mat-forming shrub (about 3 inches high) contains the antirheumatic glycoside, salicin. Willow bark was imported into ancient Egypt to treat fevers and aches. More than 2,400 years ago Greek physicians prescribed extract of white willow for gout. Many of the first peoples of North America chewed its bark to alleviate toothache. The Montagnais of eastern Canada brewed a rich tea of arctic willow leaves and drank it to reduce headaches. The active ingredient, salicin, breaks down in the stomach into salicylic acid.

In the 1840s European chemists synthesized, i.e., created artificially in a laboratory, salicylic acid and it became a widely used antirheumatic. Doctors and patients noticed that it also brought quick relief from fevers, aches, and smaller pains of the body. Unfortunate side effects did include nausea and general gastric discomfort. Then in 1899 the Bayer Company, a German pharmaceutical firm, instructed its chemists to try to find a synthetic derivative of salicylic acid that might not have such unpleasant side effects. They found a previously synthesized one called acetylsalicylic acid and began to market it under the name Aspirin, the "a" for the acetyl radical, and "spirin" because salicylic acid had been first isolated from spirin found in certain species of the garden shrub *Spiraea*.

A long trip indeed, from willow bark to Aspirin, the most used synthetic drug ever created. New synthetic drugs have and will take over some of Aspirin's functions, but it still packs a healing wallop as an anti-inflammatory, analgesic, and antipyretic (reducing fever).

Arrowhead, duck potato, *flèche d'eau*, tule, or wapatoo. Leaves shaped like an arrowhead give this plant its name in botanical Latin, *Sagittaria*. The Roman word for 'arrow,' *sagitta*, also hits the target in Sagittarius, the sign of the zodiac that means 'the archer' in Latin, referring originally to the constellation. The two common species in Canada are the more southerly *Sagittaria latifolia* with its *lata folia* or broad leaves, and the more northerly *Sagittaria cuneata* with cuneate or wedge-shaped leaves. Arrowhead tubers grow in the muddy guck of shallow streams and marshes across Canada, where wild geese, ducks, beavers, and muskrats chomp them with gusto. Observing the animals feasting on tubers, native peoples found wapatoo could provide good food even in the winter. Adult aboriginal people used digging sticks to harvest arrowhead tubers, but children jumped into the streams and found tubers by squishing them between toes in the warm muck and yanking

WORDS FROM THE ALGONKIAN ROOT *WAP* OR *WAB* 'WHITE'

- *Wabamun* in Central Alberta is Cree for mirror, literally 'white glass'
- *Wampum* is short for *wampum-peag* 'white strings' of beads made from shells for decorative & monetary use (*wap* 'white' + *umpe* 'string')
- *Wapiti* is Cree for 'elk,' compare *wapita* 'it's white' referring to the elk's light-furred rump
- *Wapun* means dawn in Cree 'the white time'; compare Wabanakiyak, the correct name of the Abenaki people meaning 'people of the dawn, of the east'
- *Wapus* or *wabus* meaning rabbit 'the white animal'; hence, Wabasso™ linen and Wabush in Labrador West District—Naskapi for 'rabbit place'

ARROWHEAD
OR
WAPATOO

them loose. Wapatoo is then boiled or roasted in hot ashes. Wapatoo is Chinook Jargon, borrowed from an Algonkian language where *wap* or *wab* is the root for 'white.' Wapatoo means 'white food.'

BASSWOOD

Basswood, *Tilia americana*, is a hardwood tree of the Linden family that native peoples and early settlers sought out for its tough bark that ripped off easily in strips. Coureurs-de-bois called it *bois blanc*. Aboriginal women boiled basswood bark in thin strips, pounded it until flexible, rolled it on their laps, and made many kinds of hemplike rope and even thread to sew up moccasins. The wood could be carved, and basswood is used today for interior wood trim since it is light and easily worked. As a wind-pollinated tree, basswood is one of many arboreal culprits implicated in hay fever allergies.

BEECHDROPS

Beechdrops is a common parasitic plant of Ontario, and anywhere else beech trees thrive. With no chlorophyl of its own, beechdrops absorbs food from the roots of beech trees, hence its botanical name *Epifagus* from the Greek ἐπί meaning 'on' and the Latin *fagus* 'a beech tree.' Note that, although it is plural in form, the word most often takes a singular verb. This dun-coloured and low-growing plant is often overlooked by the botanizing wanderer through a stand of beeches, even when its pallid flowers open in late summer. Beechdrops Pond is an official place name in Algonquin Park, Ontario. The term itself is not of Canadian origin but was coined by early settlers in Virginia who were clearing beech copses and noticed the flowers.

BIRCH

The white birch of eastern North America is also called canoe birch or paper birch, the latter common name being reflected in its botanical binomial, *Betula papyrifera*. A summer resort in Alberta has the birchy name of Betula Beach. When walking through a stand of silver birches, most kids have ripped off the shaggy bark and written secret messages on it. Birch bark was not only used to build light, watertight canoes. Some migratory Algonquins carried birch bark in large portable rolls that could be quickly fixed over a twig frame for shelter on the trail.

BLOODROOT

Canada bloodroot is *Sanguinaria canadensis*. Its name in Algonkian languages is *poughkone*, often Englished as puccoon. The French is *sang dragon* 'dragon's blood.' *Sanguis* is Latin for 'blood.' All its names refer to the red dye that could be extracted by making a powder of the dried root of this member of the poppy family native to eastern North America. White pioneers learned from first nations to make a red dye for clothing and woven baskets. Puccoon also produced a ceremonial face paint.

It blooms late in April or early in May, with a single, short-lived, waxy, white flower, and does best in the rich soil of shaded woods. By midsummer the plant has completely died down. There is a bloodroot with a double flower that can make an attractive addition to the shade garden, if care is taken with soil preparation.

Bloodroot was called tetterwort by the very earliest English visitors to North America. Tetter is an Old English word for any of various skin diseases like ringworm, impetigo, and eczema. Extract of *Sanguinaria* was used in the eighteenth and nineteenth centuries to treat warts and nasal polyps. A British doctor, J.W. Fell, read about the native peoples along the shores of Lake Superior who treated skin cancers with red sap of bloodroot and he tested it to his satisfaction in the 1850s.

In Russia, bloodroot is a folk remedy for skin diseases, too. The Rappahannock people of eastern North America made tea from bloodroot as a specific against rheumatism. And other eastern tribes applied the crimson roots of *Sanguinaria* directly to decayed teeth as a remedy for toothache. Members of the poppy family contain many physiologically active substances that we may learn to extract and use. For example, biochemists have isolated an alkaloid called sanguinarine from bloodroot, but any therapeutic efficacy is so far much in dispute.

CAMAS

Camas, camass, commas, kamass, or quamash—there are more spellings for this once staple food bulb than you can shake a digging stick at. Its botanical tag is *Camassia quamash*. Pacific coast peoples once used to harvest the bulbs of this blue-flowered member of the lily family and bake them immediately in ground ovens. They could be eaten hot, or dried and stored for winter rations. Another name for the plant was bear grass, because black bears would grub for the tasty bulbs in the summer. Humans, however, harvested them in the plump-bulbed autumn.

Camas is the Chinook Jargon descriptive that came from the Nootka adjective *kamas* 'sweet.' Tribes on the prairies used a western relative, *Camassia hyacinthina*, for the same alimentary purpose. The original Nootka name for the place that became Victoria on Vancouver Island was *Camosun* 'place where we gather camas.'

There is one fly in the paradisal ointment here—isn't there always?—and that is death camas, a nasty little plant that sometimes grows with camas and has bulbs similar in appearance, but it never has a blue flower. Death camas blooms a sickly white. *Zygadenus venenosus* is highly toxic to humans and other animals. Care had always to be taken at harvest. Indeed native peoples usually weeded out death camas when it flowered among the food camas. In 1878 there was a camas war in Oregon territory when the U.S. Army fought Nez Percé people, after white settlers had let their pigs loose in the camas prairies that Nez Percé had used for centuries as natural gardens.

Several species including *Camassia cusicki* and *Camassia quamash* make good garden subjects, planted like tulips in the fall and left undisturbed until overcrowding occurs. In its natural setting in British Columbia camas likes mountain meadows that are wet in the spring and dry up by midsummer.

COLUMBINE

Our common eastern columbine is *Aquilegia canadensis*, whose ruby bells chime with nectar sweet enough to summon hummingbirds, moths, bumblebees, and butterflies: all long of tongue and deft of theft, when it is a question of the honeyed drop at the end of each flower spur. Honeybees who have no long tongues to probe simply chew through the spur to lap up the nectar. A child—this child anyway—picks one flower, plucks the spur, and presses it expectantly against the roof of his mouth.

Out west is British Columbia's blue columbine, and high up in the Rockies blows the yellow columbine. Almost seventy species of aquilegia thrive in North America.

The only contentious tidbit of lore surrounding columbine and aquilegia is the origin of these two names. Many a learned word-book states that the generic aquilegia stems from the Latin *aquila* 'eagle,' from a supposed similarity of the flower spur to the claw of an eagle. Now the adjective from *aquila* is *aquilinus*, 'eaglelike.' We know it from long, hooked noses, which English may term *aquiline*. For aquilegia to have anything to do with eagles it would mean that for this one and only time in all the history of borrowing Latin words into English and French an "n" becomes a "g." Well, that's utter flapdoodle, piffle, and poppycock! It never happened. It's against all the many rules of consonantal transmutation in the Romance languages. Yes, there are rules for the form that words take as they pass from Latin into French or into Spanish or Italian; these are not rules from heaven, but rules extracted by logic and common linguistic sense from multiple examples. We know *père* stems from Latin *pater*, just as *mère* comes from *mater*. We know because we know what happened to intervocalic Latin "t" when spoken in street Latin by certain Gallic peoples. It got dropped, folks. Just like "tt" in *bottle* when pronounced in Cockney English. The "t" gets replaced by a glottal stop.

So back to aquilegia. Here is a choice sample of a learned dictionaryism, concocted over a dusty volume one midnight by some hapless word-nut and lazily passed down through the years from dictionary to dictionary without a single text that illustrates or proves or suggests the likelihood of the etymology. There is an etymologically sensible origin, it so happens, in the ancient Roman adjective *aquilegus*. As an adjective it means 'drawing water,' just as the spur in the flower of the columbine collects its sweet droplet of nectar. The source is apt, possible, clear, and compelling to reason. But you won't find that derivation in any dictionary I know of.

By far the silliest and most spurious etymology hovers about the word *columbine*. Now check out this real doozie. *Columba* is the Latin word for 'dove.' And, yes, *columbinus* is the adjective meaning 'of or like a dove or pigeon.' Fine. Why is the flower so named? Well, let's quote one edition of *Webster's New International*: "from the fancied resemblance of its inverted flower to a group of five pigeons." Isn't that cute? Their teeny pigeon heads turned inward to drink at the minuscule fountain of the nectar droplet in the spur of the flower. What a load of codswallop! Just picture it. A person is walking through a meadow, notices the flower, examines it, and says, "Just like five doves turned inward to drink!" Odd. When I examine a columbine, as I so often do each morning while skipping down my garden path, I see five stegosauruses doing the lambada on a proton.

Once again, a commonsensical and cogent hypothesis exists. The Latin adjective *columbinus* gave rise to many female proper names in Romance languages, the most familiar being French *Colombine* and Italian *Colombina*. In the *commedia dell'arte*—the rollicking, improvising farce of the late Italian Renaissance—Colombina was a stock character, the mistress of Harlequin, in early days played by a hussy in outrageous jester's motley, played for laughs. In fact, one particular joke, used even later by the French writer of comedies, Molière, involves setting up her entrance. She is praised for her modesty, her chastity, the demure manner of her dress. Then on comes Colombina, a flirt and a tart dressed as gaudily as the company's meager resources will allow.

Could this flower not have been named for her? In all European languages, it is quite common to label flowers with female names and properties. Think of marguerite, of maidenhair fern, of *Belle Angèlique*, etc. Far-fetched? It may be useful to recall that, in the Victorian language of flowers, the columbine was the symbol of folly, because its flower looked all loose and jangly like a jester's cap and bells. In the very exuberant vocabulary of Renaissance Italian, *una colombina* came to mean a woman who was one's lady love. So the word referred to a lovely woman and was easily transferred to a lovely flower. No need at all to conjure five frumpish pigeons cooing petulance and sipping nectar.

CORPSE PLANT

Corpse plant, ghost flower, or more commonly, Indian pipe, are names of *Monotropa uniflora*, a pale saprophyte whose single, spooky-white flower nods downward and looks just like a pipe that a ghost might smoke. Without chlorophyll, this 3- to 9-inch saprophyte gets nourishment from the fungus that grows on decaying humus strewn in the spectral gloom of dense conifer stands. In North American folk medicine of the early nineteenth century, the juice of Indian pipe stems used to be squeezed directly on inflamed eyes, just as the modern sufferer in search of soothing eyewash might reach for a plastic bottle of Visine™.

DOGWOOD

Two species merit Canuck attention, dwarf dogwood and its tree-high cousin the splendid Pacific dogwood, which is the floral emblem of British Columbia.

Cornus canadensis or dwarf dogwood carpets moist, shady woodlands and logged-over areas all across Canada. In the autumn its leaves turn a deep bronzed plum colour, and it fruits in glistening clusters of orange-red drupes that result in dogwood's other common name, bunchberry. The prim symmetry of massed dwarf dogwood makes it one of Canada's most attractive wild flowers. An involucre of creamy-white bracts surrounds each flowerhead like the starched and fluted ruff of an Elizabethan collar, giving the little plant the air of a modest courtier awaiting regal attention in some verdant chamber of nature.

Cornus nuttallii is for me the star tree of the Pacific coast, especially at summer's start when these larger tree forms of Pacific dogwood are spangled with starry white bracts that can measure 5 to 7 inches across. The cherry and purple leaves as a background to the thousands of orange-red berries make the tree an autumn stand-out, too. The specific part of the botanical name honours Thomas Nuttall (1786–1859) who was one of the pioneer botanists of the North American west.

But why is so fetching a family of plants saddled with that drudge of a name, dogwood? One local folk etymology of British Columbia says dogwood began life as *dagwood*, not from the comic strip about Blondie and Dagwood, not from the 1940s Dagwood sandwich, but from lumberjack's jargon of the nineteenth century where a dag was a wedge or skewer made from any very hard wood like that of Pacific dogwood. That does not quite account for the fact that we have dogwood as a word in print in England in the year 1617, referring to a closely related species of the British Isles, long before dag shows up in British Columbia history as lumberjack slang. The real origin of dogwood is more prosaic, but interesting.

For a creature often called man's best friend, the dog has suffered much abuse, both physical and linguistic. For five hundred years, *dog*, prefixed to an English word, has denoted something worthless or contemptible. The fruit of a British species, *Cornus sanguinea*, was called dogberry as early as 1551, possibly because the fruit was unfit for humans, but might feed a dog. In his comedy *Much Ado About Nothing* Shakespeare creates the prototype of the stupid official and dubs him Dogberry. English abounds in expressions of canine unworthiness. To lead a dog's life was to pass through this vale of tears as a miserable lickspittle. Dog Latin was low, illiterate or spurious Latin. Dog-drunk speaks for itself. Dogwood appeared as a word long after dogberry and dogtree had been established. Dogwood stuck as a term, even when the hardness of the wood made it very far from useless. It was for centuries the standard wood from which butchers' pricks were made.

Prick was the word for meat-skewer. Watchmakers cleaned out the pivot-holes in clockwork with it. And its smooth grain made it highly suitable for toothpicks.

FIREWEED

Saturday, August 17 is Discovery Day in Yukon Territory, recalling the big strike of 1896 that began the Klondike Gold Rush. A sprig of fireweed often decorates posters and advertising concerning Discovery Day because the pink-blossomed fireweed, *Epilobium angustifolium*, is the official flower of the Yukon. ἐπίλοβον in Greek means 'on the pod' and refers to the placement of the flower in this genus and the way it sits on top of a long ovary that later becomes a thin seed pod or capsule. When the pod dehisces after midsummer, it sends delicate aerial flotillas of silky-winged seeds out across thousands of northern acres. The specific adjective *angustifolium* means 'with narrow leaves.'

Native peoples of the north liked the sugary pith of fireweed obtained by splitting a young stalk and scooping it out. Elk and deer browse in fireweed fields; and the dark, sweet-smelling honey that results makes it worth putting beehives near fireweed. Beekeepers also plant fireweed close to apiaries because the honey produced is of superior taste. French Canadian voyageurs called it *l'herbe fret* and cooked it as greens. In Russia, fireweed leaves are brewed for kapporie or kapor tea.

When invasive as on cleared or logged-off land, it sometimes bears the name mooseweed. Its most common name signifies that fireweed is among the first plants to bloom on land after a burn-over. Campers in our north may brew up a refreshing backwoods tea by pouring hot water over the tender young leaves of fireweed. The tea is light green and sweetish. Just make sure you have correctly identified fireweed before tea time, so that there may be an after-tea time.

Among other names for this herbaceous perennial are great willow-herb, blooming Sally, French willow, and rosebay (after its flower colour).

GARRY OAK

Garry oak is a Pacific coast tree and the only species of oak native to British Columbia. *Quercus garryana* was named for a Hudson's Bay Company official, Nicholas Garry (1781–1856). Its range stretches down the American west coast, but the tree's sparse stands make it of little value as a commercial lumber tree, and therefore perhaps guarantee that it might be with us on earth for some little time to come.

GROUNDNUT

Groundnut, *Apios americana*, is a member of the pea family, and its dark red or brown flowers resemble those of sweet pea. They thrive in damp ground from Nova Scotia to Ontario. Mi'-Kmaq people prized the sweet tubers of this plant, which have a chestnut flavour, and they call it *sequbbun*. Early white settlers in the Maritimes shared the taste. The Nova Scotia town and river, Shubenacadie, is a French and English attempt at a Mi'-Kmaq phrase that means 'sequbbun (groundnuts) grow here.' The plant is also called Micmac potato, bog potato, and travellers' delight. The botanical genus name is Greek, ἄπιος 'a pair,' because the tubers on an individual rhizome seem to grow in pairs. One healthy plant may have ten or twelve tubers.

HEPATICA

No better introduction to this early little beauty exists than that by our pioneer writer Catherine Parr Traill. In *The Backwoods of Canada*, published in 1836, she wrote: "The hepatica is the first flower of Canadian spring: it gladdens us with its tints of azure, pink, and white, early in April, soon after the snows have melted from the earth. The Canadians call it snow-flower, from its coming so soon after the snow disappears." Two species brighten eastern Canadian woodlands, *Hepatica acutifolia* and *Hepatica americana*. *Hepar* is Latin for 'liver' from the mottled, liverish colour and the shape of the leaves that come only after the pale purple flowers have faded. The earliest British settlers thought of it as—Noble Liverwort. Indeed.

JACK-IN-THE-PULPIT

Jack-in-the-pulpit, *Arisaema triphyllum*, the familiar little arum of our moist woods, takes its generic name from Greek for 'blood arum' because certain European species have reddish spots on the leaves. The specific, *triphyllum*, also Greek, refers to its three leaves.

French-Canadian lumberjacks encountered the plant in Québécois woodlands and thought the spathe that bends like a little pointed flap over the "jack" or spadix looked more like one of their implements, a hand-held log-hook or *gouet*, hence the French name, *gouet à trois feuilles* 'hook with three leaves.'

Iroquois peoples named it *kahahoosa* 'papoose cradle,' because it looked like the backpack Iroquois women used to carry their babies.

Indian turnip was a pioneer name for the plant. The corms of jack-in-the-pulpit can only be eaten well cooked. Consumed raw, they burn the tongue, mouth, and throat, and are highly poisonous. Scottish settlers called it Devil's Ear. Medical records contain case histories of those who ate jack-in-the-pulpit raw and died from a hideously painful gastroenteritis. Colonists in early Virginia dubbed it American wake-robin, but that name has no practicality as a folk term because it was used to refer to at least six separate plants, all of different plant families, including the trillium.

KINNIKINICK

Kinnikinick means 'mixture' in Cree and Ojibwa, specifically a smoking mixture that might contain dried bearberry leaves, dried sumac leaves, red-osier dogwood bark, and tobacco. This very pungent Indian tobacco was smoked in a pipe.

The red fruit of the bearberry is much munched by bears, too, hence its common name, and its botanical label: *Arctostaphylos uva-ursi*. *Arcto-* means 'bear.' *Staphyle*, σταφυλή is 'berry' in Greek. *Uva ursi* means 'grapes of the bear' in Latin. The combined English, Greek, and Latin of the botanical nomenclature appear to make clear the ursine connection, eh?

Grouse browse bearberries. Deer delight in them. Gardeners looking for a crisp groundcover ought to ponder their use. The tiny flowers look like white bells with pink rims, and the dense mats of leathery, evergreen leaves are most attractive.

Offering tobacco leaves to the spirit of the river

LABRADOR TEA

Labrador tea, *Ledum groenlandicum*, an evergreen shrub of the heath family, has been a staple infusion of northern peoples since the first humans crossed from Asia to America some 12,000 to 20,000 years ago, give or take a day. One *Ledum* species is circumpolar, so anthropologists posit that first peoples may have brought knowledge of its refreshing and medicinal properties with them. The tea is made by lightly steeping cleaned, crushed, dried leaves. Arctic explorer Sir John

Franklin in his 1823 *Narrative of a Journey* reported that the tea smelled like rhubarb. It acted as a mild digestive and perked up one's appetite. The Hudson's Bay Company for a time imported the leaves into England where they enjoyed popularity under the peppy name of Weesukapuka! Canadians spelled it in a variety of ways, usually referring to the plant as wishakapucka, their attempt at the Cree term, *wesukipukosu* 'bitter herbs.' The leaves might also be added to kinnikinick as part of the standard native smoking mixture.

Mayapple possesses the pleasingly plosive appellation of *Podophyllum peltatum.* The first part of the botanical name is Greek for 'foot-leaf.' The basal leaf does have a long, footlike stem. *Peltatus* is classical military Latin for 'armed with a pelta.' The pelta was the sturdy little shield, shaped like a half moon, carried by the Roman infantry whose armourers borrowed it from the πέλτη shield of the ancient Thracians. The mayapple's two large leaves resemble such a shield.

MAYAPPLE

The leaves and roots are poisonous. The ovoid yellow fruit of the mayapple is edible only when it is ripe. Before it ripens, the fruit may be quite dangerous to consume. Like many common names of plants, mayapple is a slight misnomer, since the yellow fruit does not appear until later in the summer. But, having ripened enticingly, the mayapple sent pioneers and even visiting explorers into dizzy dithyrambs of praise. Here is W. Ross King, author of *The Sportsman and Naturalist in Canada* (1866): "a delicious and refreshing wild fruit . . . about the size of a bantam's egg . . . presents a mass of juicy pulp and seeds, not unlike pineapple in flavour." Steady on, old man.

Ripe fruit can be "done up" as preserves and added to jams and jellies, too. Many moderns who have tasted it say mayapple berries are bland, acidic, and too pulpy. Although there are many dangerous folk remedies connected with extracts of mayapple, such as its unadvised use as a purgative, pharmaceutical investigation has led to the clinical use of podophyllin, a resin from the mayapple, and its less toxic derivatives like epipodophyllotoxin. In 1977, podophyllin was the drug of choice in the treatment of venereal warts. American medical literature reports that the Penobscot peoples of Maine treated certain cancers with an extract from the rhizome of the mayapple. And so the search goes on.

PICKEREL WEED

Many an angler of eastern Canada has squatted in a boat patiently hoping that a pickerel weed marsh in the calm summer waters of a shallow cove will live up to its name—soon! Canada's sweetest eating fish does frequent stands of pickerel weed named to commemorate Giulio Pontedera, an eighteenth-century professor of botany at the University of Padua. *Pontederia cordata* has rootstocks that creep through the mud, one large heart-shaped (Latin, *cordatus*) leaf, and many blue florets on a big phallic flowerspike that pokes into bloom late in summer. Pickerel lay their eggs on the submerged stalks of the plant. Owners of aquatic and bog gardens use pickerel weed as an ornamental, although the blue flowers are quite short-lived. It's a relative of the much more widely grown aquatic ornamental, water hyacinth. In the American south the plant is called wampee, and in Florida, it's alligator wampee, for gators love to lurk and slumber in hideaways of disguising foliage that *Pontederia* provides.

PIPSISSEWA

If you've ever taken a swig of good, tongue-startling, home-made, palate-corrugating root beer (not the homogenized, limp-bubbled suds of commercial root beers), then you know the refreshing, wintergreenlike taste of Pipsissewa. The word comes from the language of a people inhabiting northeastern Canada, the Abenaki. In their language, Abnaki, *kpi-pskw-àhsawe* means 'flower of the woods.' Its name in botany is *Chimaphila umbellata*. The generic is Greek, χειμοφιλός 'winter-loving'—because the leaves stay green all the year round. The specific refers to the umbel or loose terminal cluster of little waxy heathlike flowers of pink hue that bloom in the summertime in dry evergreen woodlands. Nowadays oil of wintergreen is synthesized, but its chief active ingredient, methyl salicylate, is found in Pipsissewa leaves. Outdoorsy folk still chew the leaves for their minty brio, and the plant is widely used in herbal remedies.

PITCHER PLANT

Sarracenia purpurea, also called Whip-poor-will's boots, Indian Cup, and *petits cochons* or piggywigs, is the floral emblem of Newfoundland. Pitcher plant is the stout little carnivore of Canada's peat-quilted swamps and jelly-earthed bogs, where it traps insects in leaves modified to hold water. The slippery sides of each pitcher are lined with downward-pointing hairs that help insects slide into the pitcher but prevent them from escaping. Trapped without mercy, they fall

exhausted back into the water, drown, and their decomposed bodies provide essential nutrients for the plant. The special Canadian connection is the genus name. *Sarracenia* commemorates Dr. Michel Sarrazin (1659–1734), Canada's first professional botanist. He came out to *La Nouvelle France* in 1685 to become surgeon-major to the colonial army, and later co-wrote one of our pioneering botanical works, *L'Histoire des plantes de Canada*.

PRICKLY PEAR CACTUS

On the dry banks of old coulees in southern Saskatchewan and Alberta, on the dry hills of British Columbia's interior, even on some dry islands in Georgia Strait, the prickly pear cactus blooms in early summer. Among the toxic cat's cradle of prickly spines sit sensual cups of translucent yellow sepals, seemingly spun of buttery silk. These cactus flowers really do look like sexual organs, and of course they are, as they beckon insects into their vulval bowls with the promise of nectar, and send them on their way with a freight of pollen, male microspores eager to egg-on any friendly ovum in the area. But sweet as the flowers are, prickly pear spines penetrate shoe leather quick as steel needles. They hide under snow too and stiletto straight through a ski boot. But if you skin the stubby leaves and carefully pluck out the spines, you can eat the leaves after roasting them in the bottom of a hot campfire. The spiky name of the plant is *Opuntia polyacantha. Poly-acantha* is Greek for 'many-thorned.'

PRIMROSE

The Canadian primrose, *Primula mistassinica*, is now rare in the Pacific and western areas of its range. A hardy little primula that likes cool wet feet, it welcomes a June morning with a compact umbel of purply pink flowers that have vivid yellow eyes. The plant was discovered in the spring of 1786 in the eastern part of its range in northern Quebec. The year before, Louis XVI, petulant monarch of France, had fallen into a regal mope because his gardens at Versailles had begun to bore him. "One more clump of *fleur-de-lys* and I'll eat my wig!" he may have pouted to France's greatest botanist of the day, André Michaux. So he shipped the obedient and delighted Michaux off to the New World to collect more inspiring specimens. One such gem Michaux found beside Lake Mistassini in Québec, named by the local Montagnais for the great stone that sat in the middle of the lake. *Mista-assini* means 'big rock' in Montagnais. Michaux called it a fairy primrose because it was smaller than the French species he knew.

In botanical Latin the genus was first termed *primula veris* 'first little thing of spring' for *primula* is a diminutive of *primus* 'first.'

A popular folk belief of gardeners is that all primulas cause skin irritation if one touches the leaves. No. Only varieties of the species *Primula obconica* do this, through glandular hairs on the underside of the leaves. The heads of these hairs contain a quinone called primin that will indeed irritate human skin but usually only in persons particularly prone to dermal allergies.

Shakespeare enjoyed the sound of the word, as in Act 2 of *Macbeth* where the porter's famous hell speech concludes, "I had thought to have let in some of all professions that go the primrose way to the everlasting bonfire." In *Hamlet*, the chaste Ophelia advises her brother Laertes against "the primrose path of dalliance."

PURPLE MOUNTAIN SAXIFRAGE

Purple mountain saxifrage is termed in botany *Saxifraga oppositifolia*, the specific denoting that this is the only saxifrage that has opposite leaves. *Saxifraga* is Latin for 'stone-breaker' since it likes to root in patches of gravelly soil in arctic rock clefts and is at home in limestone scree as well. Whether or not a cumulative effect of such rooting is to actually split a large stone remains to be proved. It's more likely that early botanists simply noted its preferred site.

Ancient books of herbal lore say it's saxifrage because an extract of the plant was once used to break up gallstones! Today a doctor is more likely to suggest extracorporeal shock-wave lithotripsy (ESWL) in which sound waves conducted through water disintegrate the stones and the debris is washed out of the system.

Back in nature's rock garden, an older English name for saxifrage is rockfoil, and not because it "foils" rocks. This foil is an Englishing of the French word for 'leaf,' *feuille*, itself from Latin *folium*.

A Spanish word for saxifrage was used by the sixteenth-century Spanish botanist Monardes to name an unrelated tree of our eastern seaboard, the sassafras.

Saxifrage cushions miles of tundra and clings in flat mats not more than 2 inches high to elevated rocks in all the arctic regions that ring the top of the world. Hikers in the Swiss Alps know saxifrage as do backpackers through the Scottish highlands. The purple-pink flowers are tiny but so bright that they are never overlooked by northern hunters. Tiny, too, are the fat, stubby leaves with their waxy outer cell layer to conserve water and protect against drying by wind and cold. Many a northern plant fancier would place this little circumboreal charmer high on their floral Top Ten Hits list.

ROCK TRIPE

Rock tripe is a translation of the Canadian French coinage *tripe de roche*, here meaning 'rock guts.' Native peoples first showed whites how to eat this emergency food, which they called *wakwund*. Voyageurs often scraped this edible lichen directly off the rocks from their canoes, and sometimes carved their initials in the blank rock wall so exposed. It is not highly nutritious, but it does fill the stomach of a starving wretch until he or she finds their fellows, their fate, or some real food.

Lichen is a symbiotic partnership between a fungus and an alga. The fungus supplies the outer form of the lichen, the alga supplies chlorophyll so photosynthesis can take place. Rock tripe belongs to the genera of lichen called *Gyrophora* and *Umbilicaria*.

Here's what explorer Samuel Hearne said about rock tripe in 1795 in *A Journey from Prince of Wales' Fort*: "There is a black, hard, crumply moss, that grows on the rocks . . . and sometimes furnishes the natives with a temporary subsistence, when no animal food can be procured. This moss, when boiled, turns to a gummy consistence, and is more clammy in the mouth than sago; it may, by adding either moss or water, be made to almost any consistence. It is so palatable, that all who taste it generally grow fond of it. It is remarkably good and pleasing when used to thicken any kind of broth, but it is generally most esteemed when boiled in fish-liquor."

Tripe started life at the back of the butcher shop. It's tissue from a cow's first or second stomach used as food. Tripe came into the English word-stock from Norman French after 1066 and all that. The French borrowed it from Provençal *tripa* and cow-stomach-eating troubadours heard it first in Italy as *trippa*. English extensions of the meaning followed, and tripe meant guts, then tripe was a worthless person, food, or thing.

ROSE POGONIA

Rose pogonia, adder's-mouth, or snakemouth, is a startling pink orchid of peat bogs in eastern North America. It may with difficulty be grown in a bog garden with a hefty pH of 4 or 5. Πώγων is the Greek word for 'beard' and refers to the exquisite crests and fringes of its yellow, purple, and white labellum or lip. The genus name is a botanist's attempt at a feminine form of the Greek diminutive, *pogonion* 'little beard.'

The *pogon* root also gives rise to two obscure and silly English words—pogonophoric 'wearing a beard' and pogonotrophy 'the growing of a beard.'

In its full botanical binomial, *Pogonia ophio-glossoides*, the specific is a Greeking of another old common name, snake's-tongue.

Rose pogonia spreads through the squelchy sphagnum of bogs by means of underground rhizomes. Thus, an itinerant bog-trotter, bored with yet another stand of rotten stumps, may suddenly have his heart lifted by coming upon a mass of pogonia all in bloom on a hot summer afternoon. Even the miasma of a fetid swamp may be disbursed, as the subtle spice of pogonia fragrance dances in the air.

It seems to me that pogonia would make an excellent proper name, perhaps most suitably in the title of the yet-to-be-written blues song, "Pogonia, You Is My Woman Now."

It is noteworthy—so here's a note on it—that a plant family like orchids, which gives us so many strangely handsome flowers, has a name that is derived from the common Greek word for testicle. European plant-namers first called it *orchis* because the roots of several species of southern European orchids seemed to resemble human testicles. The root shows up, too, in English medical words like orchidectomy or surgical removal of the testes. Just a thought.

SALMONBERRY

Salmonberry, *Rubus spectabilis*, recently gave its name to a Canadian movie starring Alberta's k.d. lang. In *Salmonberries* the frisky warbler of pop songs played a provocative but beguiling role. So, too, did the sweet red berries of this shrub that belongs to the huge Rose family of plants.

Rubus is a randy genus where species interbreed at the drop of a pollen grain, so that there are hundreds of named varieties. *Rubus* is one of the Latin words for 'red,' and is an old botanical name for any bramble bush. The Latin root pops up in the English word *ruby* and in learned adjectives like *rubefacient* 'causing redness.'

Flowers are rosey red. The specific, *spectabilis*, means 'showy.' Its juicy fruits look like big raspberries and are eaten ripe or made into a delicious jam. The common name was first used along the banks of the Columbia River where native peoples had a favourite dish that consisted of the very young, tasty shoots of the plant eaten with dried salmon roe. Indeed, salmonberry's home range is the Pacific coast, and it thrives west of the Rockies where it was called ollalie in Chinook Jargon.

Skunk cabbage comes in a western and in an eastern Canadian type. Both are swamp plants of similar habit but of entirely different genera.

SKUNK CABBAGE

In the thick-aired gloom of a rain forest bog one spies the bold, yellow sword that is the spathe of western skunk cabbage poking up as early as February. *Lysichitum americanum* takes its generic name from Greek where it means 'loose chiton.' Now, the chiton was one ancient Greek equivalent of a tunic. It could be made of homespun cotton, of sturdier and more expensive linen, or, on a prostitute, it might be of the flimsiest gauze. If an Athenian citizen or a slave in the fifth-century city wore too loose a chiton, local prudes would tsk-tsk and declare it an outer sign of an inner moral laxity. Wearing a loose chiton meant the wearer could simply flip it up over his or her head for a quickie nooner in the boscage by the portico. After such a carnal connection, one nipped into any nearby temple of Athena for a thirty-second prayer to the virgin goddess, and, all sins absolved, went merrily on one's way, sandals flip-flopping on the paving stones. Western skunk cabbage is not such a tart, but it does emerge in the cool of February with its spadix coyly sheathed in a yellow all-covering tunic. This tunic or spathe later opens, to reveal the flower-bearing rod of the spadix within.

Some plant books label western skunk cabbage as "evil-smelling" and "with a foul stench." I lived in British Columbia for three years in the 1970s, most happily in a cottage on

Beach Grove Road near Tsawassen. One day in early spring I took the ferry to Vancouver Island, and went tromping and swamping for a day or two in Pacific Rim National Park. I certainly saw vast platoons of serried skunk cabbages in fenny glades a few yards from the Pacific waves. They did not smell skunky at all. The odour that *lysichitum* gives off probably imitates the sex pheromones of several swamp insects that pollinate the plant. The aroma is one of fresh, primal fertility, of the vernal surge of life. Why, I immediately began to hum the opening bars of Stravinsky's *Rite of Spring*, and kept looking over my shoulder expecting the arrival of husky Neanderthal maidens all in a circle pounding out their ring dance and some guttural hymn to wet fecundity.

Bears wolf down—so-to-speak—the whole plant, rootstock and all. The root can also be roasted, dried, and pounded into a good flour, much like its Polynesian relative, taro.

Eastern skunk cabbage does stink, as its name makes plain, *Symplocarpus foetidus*. The Latin adjective *foetidus* gives us fetid in English. The generic means 'with connected fruit' referring to the aggregate fruit formed from joined ovaries. Eastern skunk cabbage often is the first flower of spring in eastern Canadian wet places. The spathe that at first encloses the spadix is not yellow like the western version but a mottled brown-purple. Both skunk cabbages do belong to the capacious plant family, Araceae.

CALCIUM OXALATE: A WARNING

While we are discussing arums (members of Araceae), it is appropriate to mention a common toxin that plants of this family contain. Calcium oxalate accumulates in the fleshy parts of arums like their leaves and stems. The microscopic structure of a calcium oxalate crystal is nasty. One might say its crystal resembles a long needle made of minuscule razor blades. What happens when calcium oxalate crystals become embedded in mucous membranes that line the human mouth and throat? Pain, irritation, and swelling produced by the irritation, and then hysterical apprehension that the victim is choking—are frequent symptoms of ingestion.

These effects of calcium oxalate give a common name to a houseplant called dumbcane, found in many houses with small children and pets. Dumbcane ought to be banned from greenhouses and plant stores. It contains massive accretions of calcium oxalate. Fortunately for many peoples who depended on the roots of arums for flour-making food, a great deal of crystalline oxalate is dissolved when plant parts are boiled in hot water. Though not a Canadian plant, dumbcane or *Dieffenbachia seguine* is a real pest. Perhaps I am hypersensitive because, as a small child, I watched a playmate gag and choke after chewing a big dumbcane leaf. I always wished the jerk who sold it to his mother had partaken of it.

SNOW LILY

Snow lily is the giant dogtooth's violet of our Pacific mountains. It is frequently called glacier lily, too, and took that name because of its abundance in Glacier National Park near Golden, British Columbia, not too far from Banff. *Erythronium grandiflorum* is the name in science from ἐρυθρός, Greek for 'red,' referring to the one Eurasian species that has pink to purple flowers. The specific is botanical Latin for 'big-flowered.'

The plant has a plenitude of common names, including Adam-and-Eve, and in California, chamise lily. Glacier lily may be called fawn lily, because its leaves are like dappled flanks of fawns. One older, not-very-appropriate English name is adder's tongue. A peppier North American nickname is yellow avalanche lily, which at least is a mnemonic for this plant's big, clear-yellow flower that pokes through the shawl of melting snow on many a spring slope.

The bulbs of snow lily have in the past been dried and stored for winter food, but since the literature of veterinary science reports that bulbs of some dogtooth violet species have poisoned chickens, don't be too eager to try this. Siksika people of the west used snow lily root to treat some skin disorders.

TEASEL

To most farmers, teasel is a pesky weed. To the artsy craftsy set on a woodsy jaunt to collect specimens for a dry autumn bouquet, the sight of the tall burrs incites the cry, "Oh, look, Alexandra, teasel! We'll dry it, spray it pink, and festoon it with metallic spangles, to represent raw nature, pink in tooth and claw." *Dipsacus sylvestris* is a striking example of a totally inappropriate botanical name. The specific *sylvestris* is a Latin adjective whose full meaning is 'found in dense woods.' The teasel grows in open spaces where it receives the full sun it needs. *Dipsacus* is a transliteration into botanical Latin of a Greek word, διψακός, found in the writings of Galen, a second-century Greek physician whose texts ruled medical literature for almost 1,000 years. His works were treated as sacred canons of medical orthodoxy, and the slavish adherence to Galen's every word held back medical research quite literally for one whole millennium.

Dipsa is a Greek word for 'thirst.' *Dipsacus* does *not* mean 'thirst,' although you will find it so translated in hundreds of sloppy explanations that purport to offer derivations of botanical names, penned usually by authors with not one iota of knowledge of classical Greek. In Galen's works, the context makes clear, the ancient physician used the word to refer to the ravening thirst that accompanies critical stages of some forms of diabetes. The assertion by most horticultural encyclopedias that the plant was called *Dipsacus* because its leaf axils may hold a bit of water, and it thus staves off thirst, is preposterous. The droplet of water in such an axil would not dampen the arse of a gnat. The truth is that the reason for teasel being named *dipsacus* has been lost. If one had to make a guess, quite unattested by any textual proof, one might hazard that it was termed *dipsacus* because the ancients once used it to treat diabetes.

We do, however, know solid facts about teasel. It was called teasel because it was used to tease up the nap in wool by certain medieval English clothmakers. The dried burrlike flowerheads of teasel with their armament of stiff bracts and spines were collected and nailed to a long board. The board was then drawn over the newly spun and "walked" wool. This was called "fulling the cloth." Later the teasels were fastened to a spindle that could be turned by hand as cloth was fed under the spindle. Now it so happened that just as the cloth trade peaked in medieval England, a great many English surnames were receiving their final form. The surname Fuller refers to a founding ancestor named after his occupation. He fulled the wool by teasing up the nap with teasel. Sometimes he also put sizing in cloth and used a fine clay called Fuller's Earth to do so. Commercial gardens of the European species, *Dipsacus fullonum* (Latin 'teasel of the fullers') were often planted near woollen factories.

Do you remember Little Tommy Tucker? Well, that's where the surname Tucker comes from, too. A tucker teased cloth. And Little Tommy is a remembrance of the child labour encouraged for hundred of years in English woollen mills.

TRILLIUM

The great white trillium, *Trillium grandiflorum*, is the floral emblem of Ontario. A common colonial name was wake-robin, because it blooms in spring. But much more frequently, in earlier diaries and pioneer letters home, the trillium was simply called a lily. In Nova Scotia, settlers called it moose-flower, according to the 1868 *Canadian Wild Flowers* by Catharine Parr Traill. One species on the west coast is *Trillium ovatum*, or western wake-robin.

The genus has more than thirty species, all of them with three-part leaves and flowers, hence the first root in the botanical name. The great eighteenth-century Swedish botanist and founder of systematic botanical taxonomy, Carolus Linnaeus (1707–1778), may have named the genus; and so the *Oxford English Dictionary* suggests that trillium is a Latinizing of the Swedish word for 'triplet' *trilling*. Maybe. There's no written proof of that. A member of the lily family, trillium might also be a shortening of *tri* and *lilium* 'three-part lily.' On the right, a bouquet of columbine, trillium, and dog's-tooth violet.

WATER LILY

Nymphaea odorata is the common, white water lily of eastern North America. Many-petalled, sweetly odorous, and of exquisite symmetry, the flowers open early in the morning on the still waters of quiet ponds and waveless inlets. Their fragrance attracts to the floating pads of their leaves damsel-flies and all manner of tiny fauna like toadlets and turtles. The genus name echoes nymph, a Greek root whose prime and sensuous meaning is 'young maiden.' One race of semi-divine nymphs, the naiads, took particular joy in haunting brooks and sylvan streams. Nymphs were the guardian spirits of fountains, rivulets, and creeks.

A very close relative of our white water lily is *Nymphaea lotus*, the sacred floral symbol of divinity in ancient Egypt and Greece. There, in sandy hieroglyphs, reposing on a lotus pad shines Ra, sun god of the old Nile. Or Ra appears springing up from a lotus blossom. The ancients believed the lotus represented intellect, for the flower of human thought rises from the muddy clay of our mortal bodies, just as the water lily's beauty has its origin in the muck of a river bottom. Various plants in history have been called lotus. Hindu mythology's plant is a water lily of the genus *Nelumbo*. The same *Nelumbo* is the sacred lotus of China. The Lotus-Eaters of Homer may have munched on *Ziziphus lotus*, a North African shrub whose fruit was edible.

Our white water lily spreads its seeds by means of a neat adaptation. Water lily seeds dwell in a capsule of air-filled, spongy tissue. The capsule breaks free of the lily pad and bobbles lazily downstream—sometimes for miles—before the spongy air spaces slowly fill with water so that the heavy capsule sinks to the bottom, settling into fertile muck to root. The seeds of some Eurasian water lilies were taken to quell the tumult of sexual desire, and thus were termed anaphrodisiacs.

WILD GINGER

Our wild ginger, *Asarum canadense*, clings to the damp humus of shady forest hummocks. Its dense kidney-shaped leaves usually hide the brownish-purple flower that grows at ground level to facilitate pollination by crawling insects. Wild ginger spreads also by a creeping rhizome.

First peoples taught early white settlers to peel the root for use as a spicy flavouring. To pep up pioneer baked goods, wild ginger root was boiled with sugar as a bread and pastry spice. Many Algonquin tribes of eastern Canada made a wild ginger tea to relieve jumpy heartbeat, although today cardiac arrhythmias are best treated by a doctor. Other native North Americans steeped the roots and poured the liquid into the ear to treat minor earaches. A pioneer toothpaste of powered black alder and black oak bark was made palatable by adding an equal portion of ground-up wild ginger root. On the west coast, a Pacific species, *Asarum caudatum*, provided a spring tonic tea when Skagits people and their neighbours to the north boiled the leaves of wild ginger.

Many groups of first North Americans also used high concentrations of the root extract as an emmenagogue, that is, an agent to promote menstruation. As they did of many plants so used, native healers also thought wild ginger extract could induce abortions if given in sufficient strength and dosage. Needless to say, none of these ancient remedies should be taken—if ever—except under competent medical supervision.

From wild ginger modern science has extracted aristolochic acid, which has some antimicrobial effect, and from the root comes a broad-spectrum bactericide of limited use in some prescription cough medicines. A final caution about wild ginger root is that some of the essential oils have caused cancerous tumours in laboratory tests.

WOLF WILLOW

Wolf willow, *Elaeagnus commutata*, a member of the oleaster plant family, is also called silverberry bush because of the silvery sheen of its leaves, flowers, and fruit. A former specific was *argentea* 'silvery' in Latin. A hardy shrub that flourishes all across our prairies, wolf willow especially likes the dry banks of rivers and streams. The greyish-silver colour of the shrub gave good camouflage to the prairie wolf, hence its common name. Silvery, yellow-lined flowers give off a sickly sweet and powerful aroma in early summer. This shrub makes a useful windbreak for a prairie field, and is easily grown in dry sites, reaching 3 to 12 feet.

Native American women showed pioneer women how to make bead necklaces and bracelets from the hard, brown nuts obtained after boiling off the mealy flesh of the silverberry. Wolf willow nuts were also strung on buckskin clothes to decorate them and to weigh down the buckskin fringes so they would hang straight.

The genus name, *Elaeagnus*, seems to contain two Greek roots that mean 'holy oil,' and perhaps a sacred lotion was extracted once by unknown southern Europeans from a plant of the oleaster family, although due caution would have been practised, because so many oleanders and other members of the oleaster family of plants teem with toxins. But *Elaeagnus* is a hideous generic name for all that, unpronounceable to most on first sight, difficult to spell, its Greek mangled and twisted by its semiliterate coiner. For the record, the stems are: ἔλαιον, Greek for 'olive oil' and then becoming a general word for any oil + ἀγνός, Greek for 'pure, chaste, holy.'

For an unsentimental glare at the hardships of home-steading in southern Saskatchewan, I do recommend a 1955 novel by Wallace Stegner called *Wolf Willow*. Stegner, who won the Pulitzer Prize, blends historical fact with what are clearly family memories as he displays how a frontier pickaxes the human soul chip by chip.

For the apparel oft proclaims the Canuck

C lothing terms created by Canadians cascade from the mild silliness of Wonderbra™ to the practicality of mukluk. Pioneer garb demanded warmth and durability. Modish yuppie parkas in designer colours came only with the boom in outdoor cavortings by the newly well-to-do middle class of the fifties and sixties.

From its first white settlement, Canada did supply fashionable furs to Europe. The greed to get those beaver pelts back to Paris and London spurred the brisk penetration of the virgin wilderness, and the resulting constant push westward and northward for fresher and more bountiful fur supplies opened up our country. So here, fling open the trunk, and see what words of haberdashery Canadians have added to English.

AMAUT

An amaut is Inuktitut for a fur-lined hood on the back of a woman's parka in which she may carry an infant. Related is amoutik, a light "summer" parka.

ASSEAN

Assean is the Englishing of an Algonkian term for breechclout, a foot-wide strip of leather or cloth about 5 feet long. It is slung over the genitals between the legs and secured by a belt around the waist so that the excess length hangs down in front and back. Voyageurs adopted it for canoe travel because of its comfort.

ASSOMPTION BELT

The Assomption belt came to be the sole piece of finery that a voyageur put on to get decked out in what our grandfathers might have called their Sunday-go-to-meetin' clothes. The town of Assomption, Québec, produced the best quality of these predominantly red worsted sashes in a design known as arrow sash. It was a brightly coloured waistband wrapped twice around the midriff, about 5 inches wide, and 8 to 10 feet long. The big fur companies used it all across the country as a trading item. Voyageurs also dubbed it *ceinture à flammes* or *ceinture fléchée* depending on whether the design had flames or arrows. Other names: Red River belt, scarf belt, voyageur sash.

ATIGI

The atigi is an inner shirt or jacket of skins with the hair turned toward the body, from the Inuktitut *attike* 'covering.' Over the atigi fitted the kuletuk or outer jacket with the hair outside. A woman's atigi might have a fur hood, called an amaut, to hold a baby.

BABICHE

Babiche is originally Acadian French for the Mi'-Kmaq word *apapish* 'thread, cord, lacing.' Babiches were strips of raw moose or caribou hide used for netting, meshes, and thongs. An English synonym was iron-of-the-country. A rawhide whip to spur on horses was also called babiche and made from dehaired moose skin.

BEAVER: DRY & GREASY

In the history of the fur trade, there were two kinds of beaver pelt—dry beaver and greasy beaver—usually known by their French names, *castor sec* and *castor gras*. Dry beaver or parchment beaver was pelt that had been stretched and dried. British hatmakers much preferred greasy beaver (also called coat beaver) skins from which the guard hairs had been removed. Then five to eight skins were stitched together to make a

beaver coat that was worn by the aboriginals and some voyageurs with the fur next to the body for a year. The fur became drenched with human body oils and made superb beaver felt from which the famous British beaver hats were manufactured. The formula for the felt was three greasy beaver pelts to one dry pelt.

A footnote about the origin of the animal's name may be in order, for I have seen one etymology in a bargain-basement American dictionary written by an anonymous lexicographer who makes up word origins when he doesn't know them! This letterless sage posits an imaginary verb, *to beave*, meaning 'to work hard,' from which our workaholic aquatic rodent was named beaver. In truth, beaver is an animal name widespread in Indo-European languages:

- *beofor* (Old English)
- *biber* (Modern German)
- *bebrus* (Lithuanian)
- *bebru-* (Old Slavic)
- *fiber* (Latin)
- *babhrus* (Sanskrit 'brown')

The Indo-European (IE) stem idea was probably a reduplication of the IE root for brown, **bhru*, a form like **bhebhrus* whose basic semantic weight is brown-brown. Reduplication is used in many languages to intensify the root meaning. A brown-brown animal would have been a beast whose brown colouring was particularly vivid, memorable, or useful.

BREECHCLOUT

Breechclout was the English term for the leather loincloth of most North American first peoples. Canadian French coined its own term, *brayet*. The English word *breech* has cognates in all the German languages. Its oldest Teutonic sense is 'cloth for the loins.' But, as breech acquired new senses in the Germanic languages, meanings like 'rump' or 'bum' developed (hence a breech birth in which the baby is born bum-first). The original sense was displaced and had to be reinforced in English by adding another word for 'piece of cloth,' namely the Old English *clut*.

CANADIAN GRAY

Canadian gray was woollen homespun worn by farmers in French Canada, *les habitants*, i.e., those who had or held land from a *seigneur*, a rich colonist to whom the French king granted land under feudal tenure. The earliest habitants [no italics since the word was borrowed in English, too] were indeed little more than tenured serfs, and their gray woollen clothing was copied by those heading west to homestead on the prairies.

CANADIAN SHOE

The Canadian shoe was a high moccasin with thick, oiled leather uppers reaching sometimes to just below the knee, but always well above the ankle, and, if laced, called larrigans. But there were many synonyms: beef-skin moccasin, *botte sauvage*, Indian boot, shoe-pack. If you bought them a size too large, you could wear three or four pairs of yarn socks.

CANOTS

Canots 'canoes' is current Québécois slang for common black toe rubbers.

CLAMON

The Tillamook, a Salish people of the Pacific coast, had an excellent war garment called a clamon. Made of worked, half-inch elk skin or tanned, urine-dressed moosehide, the clamon covered nearly the whole body and was actually an arrowproof body armour. An opening on the right side of the clamon permitted free arm movement during battle.

DUFFLE SOCKS

Duffle socks or duffles were an invention of northern Canadians based on white trappers observing native peoples making a thick boot lining out of Hudson Bay blanket material cut in strips. The fabric is not Canadian. Duffle is a tightly woven wool cloth with a thick nap, first produced early in the seventeenth century by Belgian weavers in the town of Duffel near Antwerp. The duffle sock may be ankle-length or higher, depending on the height of the boot it lines. The sock is often made long enough so that a few inches of the material can be folded down over the top of the boot for insulation and to help keep snow out. Duffles are customarily worn over regular inner socks. In the north, duffles also referred to leggings made of blanket cloth.

FOUR-POINT BLANKETS

Point blankets were made of wool as trading items for the Hudson's Bay Company. The prototypes were produced by Thomas Empson of Witney in Oxfordshire in 1780. The points were markings about 1 inch long in blue and then red wool woven into the blanket, at first representing the trading value of the item. For example, a four-point blanket would be given by the company in exchange for four beaver pelts. After 1850, the point referred only to the size of the blanket. A four-point blanket is now 72 inches wide by 90 inches long. Smaller suppliers of homemade blankets usually put an identifying mark on their product, and these too were called points.

ICE CREEPERS

Ice creepers, often just termed *creepers*, were invented in the Canadian north to improve rubber wading boots that had the unpleasant habit of skidding on slippery bare ice. An ice creeper was an X-shaped metal plate armed with spikes that could be fastened to overshoes or boots to provide a grip. Creepers then became common in Victorian times in Canadian cities like Montréal and Toronto in the days before sidewalks were kept clear of snow and ice.

MACKINAW

Mackinaw, a felted wool cloth with a thick nap, usually made in red and black plaid patterns, is an English version of the French-Canadian word *Mackinac*, itself a shortened form of the name of an island in the channel between Lake Michigan and Lake Huron, the Straits of Mackinac. Its Ojibwa name *mitchi-makinak* 'big turtle' refers to a low central hill on Mackinac Island, which roughly resembles a turtle's shell. Mackinaw cloth was used to make blankets and lumbermen's jackets. The Hudson's Bay Company official periodical, *The Beaver*, states that the first mackinaw coats were made of Hudson's Bay Company point blankets during the war of 1812. British soldiers campaigning on both sides of the Straits of Mackinac were freezing their limey butts off, and their leader, Captain Charles Roberts, could get no provisions of regular army greatcoats through the battle lines, so he merely appropriated a local warehouse of point blankets and had coats made of them for his shivering men. Although this anecdote is faintly odorous with a whiff of "folk story," its repetition no doubt contributed to the spread of the term, for *point-blanket jacket* disappears in the citations of the day and is replaced by *Mackinaw coat*.

MOCCASIN

White explorers found first peoples who spoke the languages of the huge Algonkian family, from Kentucky north to the lands of the Inuit, wearing these leather shoes with flat soles—moccasins. For example in Ojibwa, the form is *makisin* 'container for feet.' Their soft leather form was infinitely more comfortable on beaten forest trails than the heavy miners' boots brought to the New World by early explorers. In the north, sled dogs who had to pull weight across rough ice in the spring were fitted with leather bags for each paw called dog moccasins. A popular form of gambling, the moccasin game, involved tossing buttons and spent bullet shells into a moccasin, and shaking the shoe before each player tried to guess the number of objects inside.

MUKLUK

Mukluks are waterproof kneeboots originally made from the skins of the bearded seal, which is called in the Inuktitut of the western arctic, *muklok* 'large seal.' The warm boots may also be made of reindeer skin with moosehide soles, and many have leather-thonged drawstrings at the top. Mukluked Canadian soldiers tromping on winter manoeuvres are no strange sight either; their boots roughly resemble these Inuit originals except that they are made of rubber, nylon, Gortex™, and other synthetic materials, though the inner linings may be of wool and deep-napped felt. For several years in Alberta the city of Edmonton tried to out-stampede Calgary with a celebration called Mukluk Mardi Gras. But it went the way of all flash.

STANFIELDS

Stanfields are long johns or long-handled underwear made by a manufacturer of knitwear in Truro, Nova Scotia—Stanfield's Limited. A scion of the family, Robert L. Stanfield, was a success in provincial politics as premier of Nova Scotia. But from September of 1967 to February of 1976, Stanfield had less allure as the national leader of the Progressive Conservative Party. He was hesitant as a talker, to put it mildly. He spoke like a hiccup trying to decide if it was a pause. Stanfield combined that with a dawdling, aristocratic vagueness that might have suited a wealthy Regency squire but was disastrous seen close-up on television.

STROUD

Stroud was a heavy British woollen cloth manufactured originally in the village of Stroud in Gloucestershire for the Hudson's Bay Company, and it was used in the Canadian north for three hundred years to make warm blankets, leggings, greatcoats, and parkas.

TOGGY

A toggy was a beaverskin coat, calf-length, popular among trappers and fur traders in the pioneer north. The design and the name was copied from a native garment called by the Cree people *miskotaki* 'coat.' After a year's wearing, the beaver toggies' leather was supple and greasy with human body oils, and this made what was called coat beaver, the greasy beaver skins preferred by British hatmakers.

TUQUE

Over the centuries many preposterous hats have been offered as solutions to the problem of keeping Canadian noggins cozy in winter. None suits this Canuck better than the tuque, a knitted wool cap invented by anonymous European sailors who pulled large socks over their foreheads to keep warm at sea.

The lowly tuque has survived being tasselled, plastered with logos of NHL hockey teams, and tarted up in fluorescent glow-in-the-dark colours. Buck-toothed yokels don tuques. So do moguls buffaloing down Bay Street through blizzards.

The word is Québécois French, a slight variant of *toque*, which in France meant a cap that knocked (*toquer*) against the back of the neck or shoulders because it had a long, droopy end. The French word was imported from Spain in the fifteenth century (Spanish *toca*) to describe a pageboy haircut actually worn by pages. *Tocar* in Spanish means 'to touch.' Pageboy hair hung down and touched the shoulders, like the end of the sock cap that came along a little later.

La Tuque, P.Q., received its name from a riverbank cliff that looks just like the early fur trapper's headgear.

WONDERBRA

Wonderbra™! A Canadian word for our very own contribution to mammary density. Instead of elevating and separating the breasts, the Wonderbra pushes them up and squeezes them together. This brassiere was invented in 1964 by Canadian designer Louise Poirier, for Canadelle, a Canadian lingerie company. Playtex bought Canadelle; now Playtex is owned by Sara Lee, the folks who make frozen cheesecake.

Putting the puck in the net, wordwise

A ssyrians did it. Ancient Egyptians did it. Aztec warriors, Greek shepherds, Romans at the baths did it. Noisy games with a ball moved by players with sticks echo and ricochet off the walls of every great civilization in history. Northern Europeans moved such games to the ice in winter. Since Canadians invented the game of modern hockey and most of the words specific to it, this chapter highlights the sports jargon of our national game.

Northern British versions of two games, bandy and shinty, were infrequently played on ice "*over 'ome.*" When British soldiers shipped across the Atlantic to garrison forts at Halifax and Kingston in the 1840s, they brought Dutch skates with them, and, observing some of the winter games played on ice by the aboriginal peoples, games like snowsnakes, they began playing shinty on ice. It was a slapstick pandemonium of slap shots at first, with fifteen or twenty players per team and a spherical rubber ball impossible to control with a thin hooked stick.

Dutch immigrants to New York played rough and tumble ice games in colonial times, too. But they never systematized play or codified rules. Canadians did all that, and much more, as some of our hockey words attest.

BLUE LINE

There were no blue lines in hockey until well after 1911 when the Patrick family formed the Pacific Coast Hockey Association and built two covered arenas in Victoria and Vancouver, both with artificial ice. The Patrick League, as it is sometimes called, introduced many innovations to pep up play and make the game more interesting to spectators. The Patricks were the first to put numbers on the players' backs so fans could identify individual players easily, and so owners could pack more people into each game by building higher ranks of seats. The same league improved the offside rule in hockey. Originally if a player was ahead of the man who had control of the puck, he was offside. The Patricks divided the ice surface into three parts by painting two blue lines. In the centre zone between the blue lines, forward passing was permitted. This revved up play and eventually produced a good synonym for defenceman—blueliner or bluelinesman. The defencemen collectively could also be called the blueline corps. The Patrick League also permitted a goalie to leap, jump, or dive to stop the puck. And they later introduced the assist.

CHICOUTIMI CUCUMBER

The *Chicoutimi cucumber* was the nickname for one of the National Hockey League's best goalies, Georges Vézina, who stopped puck for the Montréal Canadiens from 1910 to 1925. His stoic expertise and general mien between the posts earned Georges the cool-as-a-cucumber nickname based on his hometown in Québec. Now the Vézina trophy is awarded each year to the best NHL goalie.

DEKE

Here's a verb that caroms back into my memory from shrieking public school recess yards of childhood. "Pretend you fell off the teeter-totter, Casselman. Yell a lot. That'll really deke out the teacher. The yard monitor today is Miss Shaw, the nervous one. She'll run over to see what's up. Then we can sneak out of the yard across the street to the candy store and be back before the bell rings. Well, you gonna do it, eh?" But I was a priggish young whelp. Teacher's pet. No, I wasn't going to deke out the teacher. Besides, my father was the principal of the school. To deke came to our schoolyards from Canadian hockey slang where it's short for decoy. If you pretend to take a shot at goal, if you feint a move and draw an enemy defence-man out of position, if you do anything to decoy the opposition, you've pulled the big deke. Noun, verb, adjective—deke bounces off the boards wherever pucks sing on ice.

GONDOLA

Il lance! Il coupe! On March 22, 1923, sportscaster Foster Hewitt broadcast his first radio play-by-play of a Canadian hockey game. His trademark shout, "He shoots! He scores!" was later translated directly into French for broadcasts of Montréal Canadiens games. Mr. Hewitt also named the peculiar broadcasting box high above the ice at Maple Leaf Gardens in Toronto, by referring to it one night as "the gondola." Its oblong shape suggested the Venetian boat metaphor to the broadcaster.

HOCKEY

Just how old is the word *hockey*? I saw one claim in a printed history of Canadian sport that the term was coined in Halifax, Nova Scotia, in the 1860s! Hockey as a word meaning a game of field hockey with two teams, sticks, and a ball is more than 450 years old. The earliest citation in print? The archives of the town of Galway in western Ireland have this passage from 1527 A.D.: "the horlinge of the litill balle with hockie stickes or staves." A citation of 1530 concerns a bent stick used in croquet called a hock, which is a vowel-shortened form of hook. But the word that might be the source of hockey is much older. As early as 1314 A.D. French had *hoquet* for a slap, a sudden blow, or even a hiccup. From a different root but identical in form is *hoquet* for a shepherd's crooked staff or stick.

HOSER

A hoser is the all-Canadian, beer-swilling, tuque-headed yokel, as popularized by Bob & Doug McKenzie, TV characters created by SCTV stars Rick Moranis and Dave Thomas.

A hoser is one who hoses. As a colloquial verb, for some thirty years, to hose has meant to clobber the opposing team in a hockey game, also to screw someone up, to mess up another's plans.

KITTY-BAR-THE-DOOR

Kitty-bar-the-door is 1960s Canadian sports slang for tough, defensive hockey. The expression was coined by Art Ross of the Ottawa Senators team. When your team is leading, the defence puts the pressure on, to keep that enemy puck out of your net.

PUCK-OFF

PUCK

Puck-off. No, it's not a lisped obscenity. Puck-off was the original and now obsolete term for a face-off in hockey, that high-adrenalin moment when the referee drops the puck into play. The name had to be changed because of frequent alteration of the first letter. As for puck itself, it's another Canadian invention. The first record of a puck used in a hockey game instead of the then standard India-rubber ball belongs to Kingston Harbour, Ontario, in 1860. Puck's origin is mysterious, but may involve a British dialectical variation of poke. Puck began as a verb: "He pucked the ball with his hockey stick."

RINK

Ice hockey borrowed the term *rink* from a Scots dialect curling term referring to the area on the ice marked off for a game of curling. After decades of being played on frozen ponds and rivers, ice hockey games finally moved indoors, probably at McGill University in the 1880s. Wooden boards 1- or 2-feet high helped define the playing surface and protect spectators. But rink as a noun takes us back to medieval jousts. In Old French, *renc* meant 'rank or row' and was the ground marked off for a joust or knightly combat. By 1375 A.D. it's in English as renk.

ROLLER HOCKEY

In 1992 the first professional league was formed for teams who play hockey on in-line roller skates. Among Canadian teams are the Vancouver VooDoo, the Edmonton Sled Dogs, and the Montreal Roadrunners. There are, of course, some variations in the rules that make roller hockey different from ice hockey. For one thing, the game is played on the cement floor of hockey arenas.

SNOWSNAKES

Snowsnakes is a widespread game of Canadian native peoples in which each player slides a long, polished wooden rod over a smoothed or iced field of snow. The head of the rod is often carved to represent a snake's head. There are many variations across our land, but usually the player whose snowsnake traverses the course most quickly wins. In some places, the winner gets to keep the other contestants' snowsnakes.

Virtually the entire technical vocabulary of ice hockey is the invention of Canadian players and coaches, e.g., blueline, game misconduct, penalty box, doing stops-and-starts during practice, spearing, boarding. What of the machine that re-ices the rink between periods? Was Mr. Zamboni a Canadian of Italian extraction? Even if he were not, his last name makes a doubly appropriate term for his invention. *Zampone* is Italian for 'big foot or big paw.'

ZAMBONI

Watch that one. He's as sly as a lynx!

"**S**ly as a lynx" is a popular phrase in Québec folk speech, *malin comme un pichou*. Pichou comes from the Cree word *peshewah*, the Canada lynx, the wildcat with the tufted ears. *Lynx* is the Latin name for the northern European cousin of our North American cat. Related words appear in Greek, *lugx*, and German, *Luchs*. It's no surprise that a habitant farmer watching a patient lynx stalk sheep might have thought the animal sly. Humans, of course, have been projecting their own fears and emotions onto animals since Aesop first spun a beast fable. When Europeans came to Canadian shores, they needed new names for the strange critters they encountered, and so borrowed most unique Canadian animal names from aboriginal languages.

Deaf as a haddock
Dirty as a duck's puddle
Rough as a dogfish's back
Far as ever a puffin flew

Newfoundland folk sayings

CANDLE FISH

The oolichan, a very greasy little Pacific smelt, was an important source of oil for natives and settlers of our west coast. Oolichan oil had medicinal properties, contained vitamins A and D, and was more pleasant to the palate than cod-liver oil. A writer named Molyneux St. John offered one explanation of the common English name, in a book entitled *The Sea of Mountains: An Account of Lord Dufferin's Tour Through British Columbia in 1876*: "candle fish; so full of oil that it can be lighted at one end and used as a candle."

CARIBOU

This species of North American reindeer gets its French and English name from an Algonkian language. In Mi'-Kmaq, for one, *halibu* means 'one that paws or stratches,' from the caribou's habit of pawing through snowcover to find moss. The word has spawned dozens of Canadian words, including the locale of the famous 1860 gold rush in British Columbia, the Cariboo. There is an arctic lichen called caribou moss, *Cladonia rangiferina*, that is a staple of the animal's diet. The Inuktitut word for caribou is *tuktu*, seen in the arctic place name, Tuktoyaktuk, which means 'resembling caribou' and refers to a kind of reindeer. In Québec *le caribou* is a headbanger of a drink made by adding alcohol to cheap red wine.

ATUK = CARIBOU

Atuk is another Inuktitut form of the word for 'caribou,' and the name of the title character in Mordecai Richler's zesty satire of 1950s Toronto literary life, *The Incomparable Atuk.*

DOLLY VARDEN TROUT

The Dolly Varden trout is a fish of our Pacific and western rivers and lakes. Not a trout, it's actually a char with gaudy orange speckles on a greenish skin. Dolly Varden is a character in Charles Dickens' novel *Barnaby Rudge*. The 1841 historical romance centres on the anti-Catholic riots in London in 1780. Dolly Varden is a buxom flirt, the daughter of a locksmith, who knows how, within her means, to dress flamboyantly enough to attract men and earn the approving comments of women. Dolly is a charming little coquette, and his prose makes it clear that Charles Dickens approved most heartily of her. So did his Victorian readers. During the book's first printing Dolly Varden bonnets became all the rage in London. Thus it was quite natural, a century later, for some literary angler to name a vividly speckled fish after Dolly.

DUCK FACTORY

The duck factory is a phrase coined by Canadian wildlife managers to praise the sloughs and marshy areas of Canada's southern prairies. There breed many of North America's waterfowl, especially ducks that are hunted for sport.

From the turn of the century to the early 1930s silver fox fur was fashionable as coats, muffs, and collars. Prince Edward Island was a centre of fox breeding and many Islanders made fortunes in the fur business. As T.K. Pratt, editor of the superb *Dictionary of Prince Edward Island English* (1988) makes plain, this good fortune contributed some new terms to the language of the island. "To fox a horse" was to have an old nag slaughtered and its meat chopped up for fox food. Prices for a good pair of breeding silver foxes were remarkable. In 1913 one pair brought $30,000. Some fox farmers became millionaires and built ornate mansions at various locales on the island. Often these stately homes are all that remain of the fox-breeding industry, lonely Edwardian sentinels dotting the countryside as reminders of how fleeting even a cool million can be. "A fox house" is still a descriptive for these large homes built by "fox money."

TO FOX A HORSE

Heard in the valedictory greeting of the Canadian arctic, "See ya when the ice worms nest again." Doggerel-versifier Robert W. Service invented the jest in his little opus "The Ice Worm Cocktail." He claimed the joke began during the Klondike gold rush days. Its contents varied, but usually it was a shot of rye with one or two pieces of overcooked spaghetti lolling at the bottom of the glass. But, wouldn't the pasta called vermicelli be more apt? Vermicelli means little worms in Italian. Recently a zoologist has found certain worms that live in glaciers and called them ice worms. Spoilsport!

ICE WORM

The succulent viscera of this noble mollusk from Malpeque Bay on Prince Edward Island has caused grown gourmets to swoon. Malpeque is also the official name of a federal electoral riding on the island. The name is a Canadian French rendering of the original Mi'-Kmaq place name *makpahk*, which means 'big bay.'

MALPEQUE OYSTER

Is Northern Dancer the most famous named animal in Canadian history? At Windfields Farms near Toronto, Canadian zillionaire E.P. Taylor indulged his favourite hobby of breeding thoroughbred racehorses. And on May 2, 1964, one of his most agile steeds finally won the Kentucky Derby, the first Canadian-bred racer ever to do so.

NORTHERN DANCER

The French language seems to find great metaphorical clout in the image of the cow. Some bovine figures of speech do moo

QUÉBEC COWS

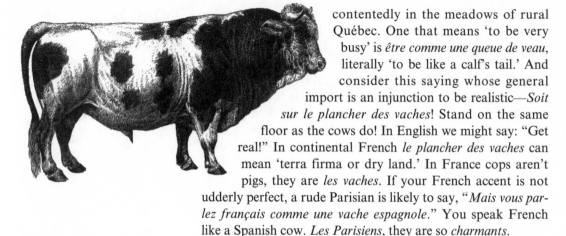

contentedly in the meadows of rural Québec. One that means 'to be very busy' is *être comme une queue de veau*, literally 'to be like a calf's tail.' And consider this saying whose general import is an injunction to be realistic—*Soit sur le plancher des vaches*! Stand on the same floor as the cows do! In English we might say: "Get real!" In continental French *le plancher des vaches* can mean 'terra firma or dry land.' In France cops aren't pigs, they are *les vaches*. If your French accent is not udderly perfect, a rude Parisian is likely to say, "*Mais vous parlez français comme une vache espagnole*." You speak French like a Spanish cow. *Les Parisiens*, they are so *charmants*.

SALMON WORDS

British Columbia joined Confederation on July 20 in 1871. Among the gifts it brought to the Dominion were colourful place names based on the most prized fish of west coast waters. Salmon Arm and Salmo (the zoological genus of the fish and the Latin word for 'salmon') are obvious. Less so is Coquitlam, from a Salish tribe who call themselves Kawayquitlam after their totem animal, which was the sockeye. The name means small, red salmon. Qualicum Beach, Vancouver Island, means place of dog salmon. Whonnock, B.C., means humpback salmon place, while the Similkameen means salmon river. One authority does say Similkameen means swimming river. Finally, in considering important fish, we must not forget that prize catch, former B.C. Premier William Vander Zalm, whose surname means 'of the salmon' in Dutch. The name Vander Zalm recalls, to those who know the language of the Netherlands, a familar Dutch figure of speech, *het neusje van de zalm* 'the snout of the salmon,' considered a delicacy in Holland. The phrase means the pick of the lot, the choicest piece. Some of us who remember Vander Zalm's time in office might find the connection quite, quite fanciful.

SLINK

It's illegal to catch or possess a slink in Nova Scotia. So, should Maritime politicians be on guard? Atlantic salmon spawn in rivers and then return to the sea. After they spawn, they're thin and weak, and called slinks on Cape Breton Island and in some other areas of Nova Scotia. In certain Elizabethan English dialects, slink meant lean or [the meat or hide] of an inferior animal. In Newfoundland, a slink is a young cod.

SNOWBIRD

As early as 1749, our pioneers were calling the snow bunting, snowbird. It's a plump, tasty arctic sparrow, often roasted just as people of Mediterranean lands roast the ortolan—on a spit. Of course, roasting songbirds is not as politically correct as it used to be. So perhaps we ought only to think of snowbirds as Canadians who head south in the winter. Yes, they escape the harshness of the Canadian climate, but not always that of Floridian thugs. Oh, let's just put on that CD of Anne Murray singing "Snowbird" and forget all about murdered vacationers and innocent birdies turning on spits and basted in their own delicious juices to a palate-tempting crispness.

SPLAKE

In the mid-fifties ichthyologists at the research labs of the Ontario Department of Lands and Forests hybridized the **SP**eckled trout and the **LAKE** trout, looking for a cross that would feed voraciously on lamprey eels who had invaded the Great Lakes. The splake has been a modest success, although the eels beset us still. Fishermen report that it's a feisty catch for the rod and reel brigade. Less prolific was the drably named muspike, a hybrid of the **MUS**kellunge and the **PIKE**. So unfeisty was the poor muspike that it failed to reproduce well in natural waters.

3P. BEAVER

The three-penny beaver is a critter of renown in the annals of Canadian philately, where it is considered Canada's first postage stamp. Issued in 1851, it was the first stamp in the world that did not depict a ruling monarch.

TULLIBEE & OTONABEE

"Tullibee" is how English trappers mangled the Cree word for the mongrel whitefish. The voyageurs did not do too bad a mangling job either. It's *toulibi* in Canadian French. In Cree it is *otonabi*. But to our ichthyologists it resounds with the splendid zoological species name of *Leucichthys tullibee*. That might be an apt name for a miser in a Harlequin romance.

The Cree word, incidentally, got better treatment further south in Ontario where flows the perky Otonabee River, past the hamlet of Lakefield. Lakefield has two main claims to fame. It is home to the Peterborough Canoe Company that for more than one hundred years has made a successful canoe of wood—based on the birch bark model—and called the Peterborough canoe. And author Margaret Laurence lived for many years in a house near the banks of the Otonabee River whose curious current is described in the opening passage of one of Canada's greatest novels, *The Diviners*. Major portions of *The Diviners* were written at her little cottage on the Otonabee, a few miles outside of Lakefield on the way to Peterborough.

WHISKEY-JACK

The whiskey-jack or Canada jay, or grey jay, *Perisoreus canadensis*, of our northern forests has many nicknames: moosebird, camp robber, lumberjack. Native trappers eat the bird, roasted on a spit. But whiskey-jack or whiskey-john is how early English trappers heard the Cree name *weskuchanis*. It means 'little blacksmith,' named because of the sooty grey coloration of the bird. The ornithological name is interesting, too. *Peri* means 'around' in Greek. *Soreus* is from the verb *soreuein* 'to pile things in a heap.' The whiskey-jack loves to steal objects from camp and pile them up near its nest.

Fressing* dulse and slurping gooeyducks

F ood is one of the blunt, stark Saxon words that strike like monosyllabic hammers on the metal of an English sentence. It was *foda* in Old English or Anglo-Saxon, akin to the verb *fedan*. Food for animals, fodder, comes from the same root. So, too, does foster, a frequentative form whose prime and sensuous meaning is to feed frequently, hence to nourish, to rear. It finally gives us words like foster child. By the way, the Indo-European root *pa that shows up in Germanic languages as food and *Futter* is the same that gives the Latin *pabulum* for 'animal fodder,' akin to the Latin word for 'bread' *panis*, and to other English words borrowed from Latin like pastor, pasture, and repast, which have nourishment

*To fress is to devour greedily. See page 113.

as their basic idea. Remember that Latin *p* gives Germanic *f* or *v*; compare pater with father or Vater.

Food words of specific Canadian origin set the gastric juices flowing, if you are fond of hearty fare like bangbelly, fricko, and pemmican. Some foods that are prepared chiefly from Canadian plants and wild herbs will be found in Chapter 5. Words like the Gaelic dulse and the Ukrainian kutia are not Canadian in origin, but acquired a meaning peculiar to our shores. But enough of this little menu. The feast awaits.

BAKEAPPLE

The bakeapple is a Maritime fruit, also called baked-apple berry, that thrives in soggy bogs on Cape Breton Island, and in Nova Scotia and Newfoundland. Its raspberrylike fruit is amber when ripe, hence the common name. The botanical name is *Rubus chamaemorus*. It's also called cloudberry. In Gordon Pinsent's 1974 Newfoundland novel, *John & the Missus*, a couple enjoy tea-buns and bakeapple jam.

BANGBELLY

Bangbelly is a pudding or pancake of Newfoundland, baked, or more usually fried over an outdoor fire. It's made with flour, baking soda, molasses, and pork fat—fishermen used to substitute seal fat. Sometimes it was cut in strips and floated on top of thick pea soup. A belly-bang was low Elizabethan slang for a fart. Perhaps this noble provender takes its name from a mere reversal of the elements in belly-bang? Or, is it so heavy that it bangs the belly when eaten?

CANOLA

In 1994–95 canola surpassed wheat as the largest cash crop in Canada. It used to be called rape, from *rapum*, the Latin word for 'turnip.' But rapeseed as a term, even in the 1940s, was tainted by the fact that it is spelled and pronounced exactly

like sexual rape (from an entirely different Latin word *rapire* 'to seize and carry off'). Canadian farmers first grew the yellow-flowering crop during World War II when rapeseed oil proved to be an effective lubricant for ship engines. After the war, Canadian scientists led by R.K. Downey hybridized rape to produce an oil high in monounsaturated fats and low in cholesterol. The euphemism *canola* was formed by compounding *Can* (Canadian) + *ola* (Latin, *oleum* 'oil'). Canola oil is used extensively in food processing, in margarines and salad dressings, as well as in soap manufacture, in synthetic rubber, and as a fuel and lubricant.

DIGBY CHICKEN

Digby chicken is a tiny herring that is smoked and salted. Maritimers call fillets of the little fish Digby chips. Both are named after the Nova Scotia fishing port that commemorates Admiral Robert Digby, commander of H.M.S. Atlanta, one of the ships that conveyed the Loyalist founders of the town to the shores of Nova Scotia in 1783.

DULSE

Dulse, the treasure of Black's Harbour, New Brunswick, is an edible seaweed, purply pink, and versatile, *Rhodymenia palmata*. Its dark, iodine-rich fronds add salty zest to soups and stews. Dulse is dried and eaten raw, or it can be toasted. The name was brought to Canada by speakers of Gaelic where *duileask* means something like 'sea bits.'

DUTCHMESS

Dutchmess may be the pride of Lunenburg, Nova Scotia's local cooking. Dutch is *Deutsch*, 'German.' And mess is not a mess meaning an untidy jumble. It's mess meaning a serving of food. Lunenburg Dutchmess is salted cod and potatoes dressed with bacon bits and onions. By the way, all meanings of mess stem from Old French *mes* 'a portion of food put in front of the eater' from the verb *mettre* 'put' or 'place.' Latin had *missus* to mean 'one of several courses during a meal.'

FRICKO

Fricko or frickle on Prince Edward Island is the jaunty Englishing of a French word, *fricot* 'stew.' In some parts of the island it's an Acadian chicken stew with dumplings. In another Acadian variation fricko is chicken fried in batter with pork, onions, and chopped potatoes.

FUNGY

Fungy or fungee (pronounced fun-jee) is deep-dish blueberry pie in Nova Scotia, also called blueberry grunt. Grunt is the plorping sound made as baking drives pockets of heated air out of the gelatinous mass of the cooking blueberries.

GOOEYDUCK

Gooeyduck is the wonderfully slurpy slang word for a tasty clam of Canada's west coast waters. It was not named because the glistening innards reminded someone of a duck pressed into a goo. One may dine on that in Paris. Another spelling is geoduck. The word is from Nisqually, from which it was taken into Chinook Jargon, the old trading language of southern British Columbia. The gooeyduck is the largest burrowing bivalve in the world, and that habit caused the Nisqually tribe to call it *go-duk* or 'dig-deep.' Its very deep burrows make it a tricky clam to harvest.

GROCETERIA

Groceteria appears to be a Canadian coinage, first printed in 1925 within an advertisement in the *Canadian Labor Advocate* for Kirkham's Grocerteria. Later they dropped the second r. This word for a self-service grocery store blends *groce*(ry) + the earlier (cafe)*teria*.

HOT ARSE

In Newfoundland, a hot arse, in the realm of high-class cookery that we are here traversing, is a tin kettle with a broad bottom, useful for bringing water to the boil fast—especially useful for a quick cup of tea. People also call such a utensil a flat-arsed kettle.

KUTIA

Kutia is a traditional Ukrainian treat served on Christmas Eve or during the winter holiday time. It's made of wheat, nuts, honey, and poppy seeds. It might be served with a loaf of braided bread called *paska*, or with *kalach*, a ring bread. And the pious would include a *maslo*, a cross formed of clove-studded butter.

LATEER

Lateer is a term from the Canadian sugarbush. When the maple sugar has been boiled down to its proper stage, all gooey and ambrosial, you take a ladle and sling hot maple syrup across a snowbank. As it cools, it solidifies and turns into maple taffy or lateer, from Canadian French *la tire* 'toffee,' from the verb *tirer* 'to pull, to draw.'

NANAIMO BAR

Nanaimo bars are a baked treat popular all across Canada, often as little cut squares of biscuit topped with a sweet cream filling and covered with chocolate. They may have been concocted in Nanaimo on Vancouver Island. A number of local native bands amalgamated in the mid-nineteenth century, calling their union *sne-ny-mo*, or 'big, strong tribe.'

PABLUM

Pablum! To think that a food so bland was invented by Canadians! Gosh, it's just not like us. Doctors Drake, Brown, and Tisdall, searching for a simple, nutritious breakfast for infants, spent many hours at Toronto's Hospital for Sick

Children stirring vile gruels and loathsome porridges. Did they, like Macbeth's three witches, utter little rhymes as they whipped up their alimentary goo? In any case, Pablum first went on sale in 1930. Insipid it may be, but so wholesome! It contains wheat germ, alfalfa, oatmeal, cornmeal, wheatmeal, and other treats. When they came to christen their new product, the doctors or someone at the food company that was manufacturing the product did display a sense of humour. They found their name for the new cereal in Latin, where *pabulum* is the word for 'horse feed,' or 'animal fodder.'

PEMMICAN

Pemmican is a Cree word compounded of *pimii* 'fat' + *kan* 'prepared.' Buffalo meat was beaten with a pemmican pounder, mixed with fat and cranberries, and then sewn as a hard ball into a pemmican bag made of skin. Pemmican had a shelf life that would make any modern food-packaging company green with envy. It lasted forever and supplied iron and protein on the longest, remotest trips through the wilderness. Canada's fur trade, and hence the opening up of the country itself, were absolutely dependent on pemmican. There were, of course, variations in the ingredients, hence names like deer or moose pemmican. Tight in its bag, pemmican would keep even if dumped overboard from a canoe.

ROBIN RUN

The robin run in a Canadian sugarbush is the first flowing of maple sap, which is rich in sugar. After a robin run, sap flow often diminishes or stops. Then follows the frog run, the secondary flowing of sap, not as sugary as the first, hence inferior for making maple syrup. Sugaring-off in the sugar bush in a sugar shanty has many terms not often met with elsewhere. One I use in the game of Scrabble ® is spile. In a sugar bush the spile is the metal spout pounded into a maple tree to draw the sap. The word was brought to Canadian maple syrup production from Scottish dialects where a spile was a wooden peg, plug, or spigot. Spile found its way to England from German dialects where *Speil* means 'a pin, a skewer, a splinter.' Spile stems from the same root as the verb *spill*.

SOAPOLALLIE ICE CREAM

Soapolallie ice cream is a foamy British Columbia treat made from ripe soapberries that have been macerated with sugar. Then take a broad wooden spoon and whip them briskly until they foam and froth into what is also called Indian ice cream. *Soapolallie* is Chinook Jargon. *Soap* means 'soap,' because they froth up so. *Olallie* is Chinook for 'berry.' The root shows up in the word for a potent homebrew of our west coast called olalliechuk, which is a berry wine. *Chuk* is Chinook Jargon for 'water.' Tribes of the southern Pacific coast also made a berry bread called olallie sapolel.

A mari usque ad mare, Dude!

Early allegorical engraving of North America

T his is the first of two word-flights across the country to check curious origins of Canadian place names. Scarborough in Ontario means 'Harelip's fort.' Etobicoke is an English version of *adoopekog* 'alder trees near the river,' a name in the Ojibwa language of the Mississauga or Anishnabeg people. The same folks named the Credit River in Ontario *missinihe* 'trusting water' because early whites traded at the river's mouth with local first peoples and sometimes gave them credit for goods obtained against the next season's furs.

Scholars say there are 300,000 places and features of Canada already named, and two million still to be named—a daunting vista for the official government body that adjudicates our toponyms. Don't let its own fuddy-duddy moniker

Balzac
Carvel
Durward
Fedorah
Innisfree
Lochinvar
Mazeppa
Meander
Philomena
Phoenix
Uncas
Vulcan
&
Westward Ho

Names of towns and former towns in Alberta that have literary origins

BRITISH COLUMBIA

fool you. The Canadian Permanent Committee on Geographical Names is a colloquium of questing spirits who also try to solve disputes that arise about place names.

Once-proud names sometimes sink into the muskeg of political uncorrectness. Mount Stalin in high British Columbia and Stalin Township near Sudbury seemed ugly remembrances of the Russian mass murderer. In 1986 Stalin Township became Hansen Township, in honour of Rick Hansen's Man in Motion wheelchair tour for worthy charities. Mount Stalin became Mt. Peck, after a local hero and outdoorsman.

Infrequently, names become an embarrassment. Paska Township near Thunder Bay was simply the Cree word for 'shallow' taken from Paska Lake, which is shallow. But as some Finnish Canadians pointed out to the government in 1959, paska is also the Finnish word for shit. Oops! The place is now named after the Finnish family who protested, Suni Township.

And this chapter concludes with a tale of how we might have been Mesopelagians, instead of Canadians.

LOTUSLAND

Long-time *Maclean's* magazine columnist Allan Fotheringham claims to have first applied this classical tag to British Columbia. Although Foth's intimate knowledge of Homeric minutiae **is** bruited about on every lip, skeptics point out that many east-coast American writers had been applying the term to California for decades before Fotheringham's dubbing. The Greek poet Homer, in his *Odyssey*, wrote of those original druggies, the *lotophagoi*, Lotus-eaters who gobbled down far too much extract of the lotus tree, forgot their family, friends, and homes, and wanted to do nothing but fritter their lives away. Lotusland is not an apt tag for B.C.'s bustle and economic drive.

Skookum means 'big and mighty' in Chinook Jargon, a lingua franca—a trading language—based on the speech of the Chinook Indians, with words from French, English, Salish, Nootka, and other local tongues thrown in as needed. Chinook Jargon was used for over a hundred years until the turn of the century by aboriginal peoples and the white traders who plied the Pacific coast. A town in southeastern British Columbia where Skookumchuck Creek empties into the Kootenay River, is named Skookumchuck, that is, mighty water. It's also Chinook for 'white water rapids.' The adjective produced nicknames like Skookum Jim, one of seven men who discovered gold at Bonanza Creek on August 17, 1896, at the start of the Klondike Gold Rush.

A synonym for a jail on the Pacific coast was skookum-house 'strong house' or skookum box. Skookum tumtum meant a strong, brave heart. Tumtum was the sound of the heart beating, not a reference to the English nursery word for stomach. Heehee tumtum was a merry heart; sick tumtum meant one was sad. The word *skookum* came into Chinook Jargon from the Chehalis language where *skukm* meant 'powerful, brave, or large.'

Aklavik means 'grizzly bear place' in Inuktitut. Inuvik means 'place of men.' Innu is Inuktitut for 'human beings.' The caribou played a pivotal role in Inuit food and culture, and many of the arctic place names reflect this. Pangnirtung means 'bull caribou place.' Tuktoyaktuk means 'caribou lookalike,' that is, reindeer that resembles a caribou. Akpatok Island in Ungava Bay is Inuktituk for 'bird place.' Auyuittuq National Park on Baffin Island means 'ice that does not melt.'

The Beaufort Sea is named after Rear-Admiral Sir Francis Beaufort (1774–1857), the British hydrographer who devised

SKOOKUM

—➤●◄—

CHINOOK JARGON

Because we have so many west-coast words from Chinook Jargon, let's look at a common grace offered at meals:

Tyee papa, mahsie klashe mucka-muck 'Chief father, thanks for the good food.'

Tayi comes from the Nootka language and means 'older brother.' *Tyee* in Chinook Jargon came to mean 'big boss.' Thus, God is here called Big Boss Papa. Mahsie is French 'merci.' Klashe is Nootka 'good.' And muckamuck is a Salish word for 'food.'

—➤●◄—

THE NORTH

BEAUFORT

the Beaufort scale to measure wind velocity from force 0, dead calm, to force 12, which is a fierce hurricane.

KEEWATIN

Keewatin is the name of a district in our Northwest Territories. It is Cree for 'the north wind.' There is little poetic force to the word in Cree where it betokens the face-freezing, blood-congealing blast that kills humans if they take no heed of its danger. Keewatin was one of the names tossed out by those who chose Manitoba to name the province. It also has limited use as a first name for Canadian boys and girls—for example, Keewatin ("Kee") Dewdney, brother of Canadian poet, Christopher Dewdney.

WHITEHORSE

Whitehorse, capital of the Yukon, possibly takes its name from some poetic prospectors who were descending the Yukon River around 1880. They thought the white-water rapids with their long, purling caps resembled the manes of white horses flying in the wind.

YELLOWKNIFE

Since 1967 Yellowknife on the north shore of Great Slave Lake has been the capital of the Northwest Territories. Its name is a translation of the name of an indigenous Dene tribe who made implements from yellow copper.

ALBERTA

Amisk, a hamlet near Wainwright, Alberta, is the Cree word for 'beaver.' The province also has my personal favourite Canadian place name: Bluesky, Alberta. Near Drumheller is Dalum, named by Jen Hvaar, an early settler, after a district in his native Denmark. Falun, Alberta, was settled by miners around 1900 who came from a Swedish town of the same name.

HAIRY HILL

Hairy Hill, Alberta, is a hamlet whose name recalls a buffalo scratching place. When herds roamed the prairies, buffalo stopped at this hill to rub ticks and fleas off their coats by scratching themselves on the many thorn bushes in the vicinity.

HARMATTAN

Drylanders roughing it in the dust-bowl days of drought had one among them who knew a bit of Twi, an Akan dialect spoken in Ghana, and so named a town in Alberta, Harmattan. Winds to be feared have names in parched places, and the harmattan is such a gale. It blows north up towards the Sahara in the African winter, raising clouds of red dust high in the air.

HOBBEMA

Hobbema, Alberta, was settled by immigrants from the Netherlands, who chose to remember Meyndert Hobbema, a famous landscape painter of seventeenth-century Holland who specialized in placid scenes of the countryside near Amsterdam where he was born.

MYRNAM

The name of Myrnam, Alberta, is of purest Ukrainian origin. It is a pious and humble prayer in the language of the founding settlers of this little place, мир нам, *myr nam* 'peace to us.'

THORSBY

North of Pigeon Lake, Alberta, is the resonant Viking-sounding place name of Thorsby. Norwegians homesteaded here in Thor's town or "by," which means settlement in Old Norse, and shows up all over Britain and North America in names like Whitby 'white stone-town' and Derby 'deer-town.'

SASKATCH-EWAN

The province takes its name from the river. The Cree people called it *ki-siskat-chewani-sipi*, which means 'quick flowing river.' In the Cree phrase, one can hear the sonorous onomatopoeia that is a feature of most languages, including English, where we form some words to imitate sounds—for example, buzz, pop, moo. *Ki-siskat* is a quick word. *Chewani* flows. And *sipi* we recognize from many aboriginal river names, particularly the Mississippi, which means 'big water.' Another English translation of the word Saskatchewan gives a name to the city of Swift Current.

SASKATOON

Unique among Canadian cities, the pert metropolis of Saskatoon was founded as the proposed capital of an alcohol-free country. The teetotalers in question began in Ontario in 1882, and aptly chartered themselves as The Temperance Colonization Society. That same year they bought 100,000 acres of land from the Dominion Government in what is now the province of Saskatchewan. By 1883 a party of settlers was eager to flee the gin-soaked inferno of Ontario. They went west by train to Moose Jaw, then trekked overland to a place the Cree Indians had named because there were many saskatoon berry trees in the vicinity. The Cree word for these succulent purple berries is *mi-sakwato-min* 'berries from the tree of many branches.'

Like the other prairie provinces, Saskatchewan boasts a polyglot quilt of place names that mark patterns of ethnic settlement. Kalyna is the Ukrainian word for cranberry. The town of Hory is Czech for mountains. Orcadia is New Latin based on *Orcades*, the Roman name for the Orkney Islands north of Scotland. La Ronge is a reference to trees felled by beavers *par la ronge* 'by their gnawing.' Sod-busters and stubble-jumpers might have been their nicknames in the east, but prairie pioneers were tough and in naming their places, honest.

MANITOBA

In many Algonkian languages of North America, *manitou* is the word for the chief deity or the supernatural spirit to whom reverence is due. The province of Manitoba takes its name from Lake Manitoba. It's from Cree *manito-wapow*, or 'spirit narrows,' a site-specific toponym that refers to a particular beach of pebbles on Manitoba Island in Lake Manitoba. Lake water cresting on these pebbles made a peculiar rushing sound that indigenous peoples said was the true voice of the manitou. In Ontario, similar holy places are Manitoulin Island and Manitouwadge. In *Place Names of Manitoba*, Robert Douglas offers another origin, from the language of the Assiniboine tribe, *mini-tobow* 'water of the prairie,' again referring to Lake Manitoba. The *mini* root is all over the map of western North America, in place names like Minnesota, and in Longfellow's poem, "Hiawatha," where we meet the native princess, *Minnehaha* 'Laughing Water.'

MANITOU

There are manitous of earth, air, water, and fire. Some are beneficient, some malicious. One very poetic interpretation of the northern lights sees the aurora borealis as the flickering spirits of the dead dancing in homage before the great arctic throne of the high manitou. Gitchi manitou in many Algonkian tongues means 'good spirit.' Matchi manitou is 'bad spirit'—a lesser, wicked deity who in some prairie cosmologies presides over an underground hell, aswarm with serpents, where evildoers go after death to suffer the very torments of Laocoön.

A manitou stone was lucky for any prairie tribe who possessed one. It could act as a powerful medicine stone, since it fell from the sky according to legend. For, indeed, a manitou stone was a meteorite that had fallen from the sky within tribal memory. Even to touch such a rock could bring good fortune or improve ill health.

ONTARIO
PETAWAWA

About 12 miles northwest of Pembroke, Ontario, lies the large military establishment of Camp Petawawa, named in 1905, the year it was set up, after the Petawawa River, a tributary of the Ottawa. *Pitaweewee* in one of the Algonkian languages means 'hear many waters' in reference to the pleasant babble this shallow river makes as it purls over smoothed stones.

SCARBOROUGH

Scarborough means 'harelip's fort,' a fact no doubt unknown to Elizabeth Simcoe when she named the village because the local bluffs reminded her of cliffs near the town of Scarborough in Yorkshire. The wife of Upper Canada's first Governor General, John Graves Simcoe, needed only to add a knowledge of Old Norse to her many accomplishments. Scarborough in England was a Viking settlement originally. We know because it was recorded in a Viking saga that one Thorgils Skarthi founded the North Yorkshire settlement around 965 A.D. Now, Viking warriors liked frightening and sometimes repellant nicknames. Skarthi meant 'harelip' in Old Norse. In Old English the settlement became Skaresborg, Harelip's Fort. One further example of Viking naming habits is found in the origin of Nottingham. It was first named Snottingsheim, or in Old Norse, farmstead of a Viking named Snot.

Fishing nets on Lake Ontario

TIMMINS

The mining community in northern Ontario was named after Noah Anthony Timmins (1867–1936) who staked a claim on the site in 1909. He became president of Hollinger Consolidated Gold Mine Ltd. and promoted the giant Noranda-Hollinger copper mining project in Québec. Near Timmins in 1903 a prospector named Fred LaRose attempted to scare off a wild animal by tossing a hammer at it. Instead, his hammer struck the largest vein of silver ever uncovered in history. It was Noah Timmins who developed the LaRose silver mine for commercial purposes.

QUÉBEC
BALCONVILLE

Balconville is Québécois joking slang for the ordinary guy's holiday destination. Where are you going on your vacation this summer? is the question. The answer? Balconville! This implies that one is too poor to go anywhere, and will spend the holidays on the balcony of one's apartment. Montreal writer David Fennario wrote a play set in this milieu entitled *Balconville*.

GASPÉ

Gaspé names a peninsula or cape, a bay, a basin, a town, and a county in Québec, whose fields and coves spread from the south shore of the St. Lawrence to the Baie de Chaleur. La Gaspésie boasts many putative origins, but it's likely Mi'-Kmaq *gespeg* '(northern) end (of our territory).' Some onomastic researchers favour derivation from the name of Gaspar Corte-Real, a Portuguese navigator who may have touched land around 1500 near the village of Gaspé.

LACHINE

Sarcasm in Canadian place names is rare, but here's one gem. When René-Robert Cavelier, sieur de La Salle first came to Montréal in 1667 he was constantly babbling, like so many explorers of the day, about finding a route to China across some unknown western sea. Brothers of the Sulpician order who held Montréal as a seigniory granted La Salle some land on the island, which they laughingly called La Chine, the French word for China. One of the most famous people born in Lachine was American novelist Saul Bellow, who won the Nobel Prize for Literature in 1976.

THE ROC

This term gained prominence during the eighties, chiefly among American academic economists writing and speaking about Québec. ROC or R.O.C. refers to the **R**est **o**f **C**anada. A frequent spoken phrase is "Québec and the ROC," with ROC pronounced to rhyme with rock. This breezy, impudent acronym has now found its way into Canadian academic speech as well.

NEW BRUNSWICK COCAGNE

The village and harbour of Cocagne in New Brunswick was named for Cockaigne, a mythical paradise in medieval French literature where "houses were made of barley sugar cakes and streets were paved with pastry." It was named by Nicolas Denys (1598–1688), the great recruiter of settlers for Acadia, after he camped at the harbour mouth for a week. Denys is the author of an important early book on Acadia, *Description géographique et historique des costes de l'Amérique septentrionale* (1672). This pastry heaven was a popular medieval concept in almost all languages of Europe, for example, in Spanish, *cucaña*; in Portuguese, *cucanha*; in Italian, *cuccagna*; all deriving from medieval Low German *kokenje* 'a sweet little cake,' being the diminutive of *koke* 'cake.' That word is cognate with Latin *coquere* 'to cook.'

SKEDADDLE RIDGE

Skedaddle Ridge reminds us that there were American draft dodgers hightailing it to the north woods of Canada to evade service long before the Vietnam War. During the time of the American Civil War, this hill in southern New Brunswick was a favourite spot of American southerners living and working in New England who were in sympathy with the Confederacy and who therefore did not wish to fight for the North in the Civil War. Rather than engage in time-consuming argument with Northern Army recruiting officers, they skedaddled off into the piney fastnesses of New Brunswick.

XMAS

In central New Brunswick flows North Pole Stream, hard by North Pole Mountain. Adjacent peaklets are named Mount Dasher, Mount Dancer, Mount Vixen, Mount Prancer, Mount Comet, Mount Blitzen, Mount Donder, and Mount Cupid. All are taken from Clement Moore's "A Visit from St. Nicholas," more familiar in its opening line, " 'Twas the night before Christmas. . . ."

NOVA SCOTIA
ACADIA

Nova Scotia means 'New Scotland' in Latin. So stated the royal grant of land issued to Sir William Alexander in 1621. Until 1713, the area was officially called Acadia, which at the time included parts of Québec and New England. Now Acadia is generally used to mean the area of original French settlement in our Maritime provinces. The Italian navigator Giovanni da Verrazano first named it *Archadia* in 1524, while he explored the east coast of America as commander of a French expedition. He also discovered what became New York Bay, and the Verrazano Bridge to New York City is named after him. He misspelled the Latin word *Arcadia*—possibly because of its pronunciation in his particular Italian dialect. The Romans borrowed the word from the ancient Greeks who used it to denote a geographic area of mountainous forest in the centre of the Peloponnese. For the Greek pastoral poets like Theocritus, Arcadia (Greek Ἀρκαδία) was a symbol of rural simplicity linked with the joys of the shepherd's life, tending flocks and making music with flute and pipes all the day long. It is probably the source of one of the oldest jokes in the European tradition. What do you call an Arcadian with forty mistresses? A shepherd. The god Pan haunted the caves and streams of Arcady. Sportive nymphs bounded happily through upland pastures, and centaurs frisked in the clover. Arcadia was such an evocative token of pastoral ease that it passed into all the later languages of Europe. Although the precise origin of the word is lost, a study of classical Greek makes clear the reverberations that Arcadia set off in the Greek mind. Ancient Greeks heard similarities in its sound to *arkys* (ἄρκυς) 'a hunter's snare or net.' Arcadia was the stomping grounds of the goddess Artemis, the virgin huntress known to the Romans

---

MI'-KMAQ ORIGIN OF ACADIA

Some researchers who study toponyms state that Acadia is Mi'Kmaq (sometimes Mi'kmaq) or Micmac in origin. They say early explorers heard the Micmac word for 'place where you find things' and it was enough like Arcadia in sound to suggest that name to the explorers. The Micmac word is *akaadik* and shows up in place names like Shubenacadie River 'place where you find ground nuts' and at the end also of names like Passamaquoddy Bay 'place where there are plenty of pollocks.' The pollock is a marine food fish found in the bay. The root also appears in Tracadie Bay, P.E.I.

as Diana. It reminded them also of the Greek verb *arkein* 'to be strong, to endure, to be sufficient,' and it's very common impersonal form, *arkei moi* (αρκεῖ μοι) meaning 'it's enough for me; I'm happy, content.'

PRINCE EDWARD ISLAND MINEGOO & ABEGWEIT

Minegoo. First, Mi'-Kmaq hunters came to the island in the winter time by canoe to fish and take wild fowl, and after drying their catch along the shores of Bedeque Bay, they would return to permanent winter camp on the nearby mainland. Minegoo means 'island' in Mi'-Kmaq. It was one of the ways Mi'-Kmaq people referred to Prince Edward Island. The other was the very poetic Abegweit, which means 'cradled on the waves' in Mi'-Kmaq. Some authorities say the Mi'-Kmaq root is *abahquit* with the more prosaic meaning of 'lying parallel with the waves,' or *epegweit* 'lying in the water.' In any case, most people who have called it home have been more than fond of its fields and shores. Here is Lucy Maud Montgomery, author of *Anne of Green Gables*, writing in 1939 in *Prince Edward Island*: "You never know what peace is until you walk on the shores or in the fields or along the winding red roads of Abegweit on a summer twilight when the dew is falling and the old, old stars are peeping out and the sea keeps its nightly tryst with the little land it loves."

A CNR car ferry that used to ply the waters of the Northumberland Strait between New Brunswick and P.E.I.

was christened M.V. Abegweit. In 1962, the body of water it crossed was officially named Abegweit Passage.

Samuel de Champlain in the journal of his exploratory voyages called it *Ile de Saint Jean* in 1604. The British possession of the island in 1759 caused a simple translation to St. John's Island. Then in 1798 the British garrison at Halifax was being commanded by Prince Edward, Duke of Kent, and some local royal sycophant, some cringing lickspittle toady, thought it might be nice to name yet another piece of real estate after yet another imperial poobah. That Prince Edward was the father of Queen Victoria. Prince Edward Island joined Confederation as a province in 1873.

LABRADOR

No one knows the precise origin of this name. After days of perusing ancient sources in five languages, I'm going to write a new blues song, "Nobody Knows the Etymology I've Seen." The canny British etymologist Eric Partridge in his *Origins* likes the tale of the explorer Gaspar Corte-Real who touched shore in 1500 on a voyage of piscatorial quest and sailed back to Portugal carrying a shipload of Inuit slaves! Historical proof of this particular atrocity is scant. In sixteenth-century Portuguese, the euphemism for "slaves" was spelled *labradores*. Modern Portuguese is *lavradores*, but the word now means 'farm-workers.' One of the names for Newfoundland on early Italian maps is *Terra del Laboratore* 'land of the worker.' Then into the lexical fray enter scholars who say another Portuguese, one João Fernandes, a rich *lavrador* (but the sixteenth-century spelling?) or landowner in the Azores came north through the Atlantic in his own ships looking for the fabled cod fishery. A cod-fearing man, he took his codpiece, and perhaps several whole fishes, and sailed off, leaving the name of his former trade as a toponym to bedevil future etymologists. Some historians give Fernandes credit for discovery of the coast of Greenland and some of the coast of North America.

An interesting folk alteration of the very word *Labrador* occurs among early Acadians in Nova Scotia who heard Labrador as *la bras d'or* 'the arm of gold.' And so they gave the name to Bras d'Or Lake.

Labrador. Quite a fuss spins around the spelling. Is Labrador sturdy Spanish orthography? Yes. Could it be Portuguese or Italian, mangled by an early monoglot cartographer? Yes. My picayune contribution shall consist in the observation that no affectionate adjective for the continental part of Newfoundland has yet appeared. I therefore suggest: *labradorable*.

NEWFOUNDLAND CRIBBIES

The Cribbies was a slum section of St. John's, Newfoundland. Cribbeys in eighteenth-century British slang were blind alleyways. St. John's has many vividly named parts of town, such as Maggotty Cove and Dogstown. Nowadays one might call a resident of the town a cribby, although it's a bit of a put-down. Any low-class way of speaking in St. John's may be dismissed as cribby talk.

HARBOUR GRACE

Harbour Grace in Newfoundland is a translation of the original name of the northern French port, Le Havre. It was founded in 1517 as *Havre-de-Grâce*, little harbour of grace, of thankfulness. Perhaps grateful Norman sailors made port one night after a harrowing storm on *La Manche*, the English Channel. Both the French and the English word *grace* stem from the Latin *gratia* 'gratefulness.' *Havre* is medieval French borrowed through Middle Low German *havene*, which is ultimately from or cognate with a Viking word for harbour, *höfn*, brought down the European coast by the Norsemen, who gave their name to Normandy. English has *haven*, and compare the German word for harbour, *Hafen*, and the German port of Bremerhaven. And, that no further roots shall be here adduced, be thankful!

PRIMA VISTA

Prima Vista was John Cabot's first name for Newfoundland when he spotted land on June 24, 1494. Another was translated as "new founde isle." It became "New founde launde" in British documents by 1502 along with the French *Terre Neuve*. Early editors of Cabot's journals like Hakluyt said the name *Prima Vista* was Latin, and quoted Cabot's description as "*terra primum vista*" 'the land seen first.' They may have forgotten Cabot's real name was Giovanni Caboto from Genoa, and may not have known that *vista* is **not** a Latin word. Land first seen in Latin would be *terra primum visa*. *Prima vista* is Italian for 'first sight (of land).' Navigator Giovanni da Verrazano called it *Terra Nova* on his 1529 map. Newfoundland stuck.

CANADA

And let us pause to celebrate the defeat of those pillars of colonial Albion who were quashed in their bid to christen us British North America. Finally in 1867, after a very modest flurry of parliamentary gobbledy-squabble, our elected betters picked the old and the familiar, Canada. It first appeared in the writings of Jacques Cartier in 1534. As Cartier excitedly pointed at the native village of Stadacona and kept asking through interpreters what it was called, the guide kept saying, "It's a village, dummy." In many Iroquoian languages, *kanata* means 'village or community.'

Over the years aspirants have offered many preposterous etymologies that attempt in a folksy way to explain the origin of the word *Canada*, like the rumour that Spaniards visited our bleak shores earlier than Cartier, found no gold, and wrote on their maps *aquì nada*, 'there is nothing here.' In an early Spanish dialect, it could have been *aca nada*. The early explorer Hennepin (no relation to Henny Penny) said Spaniards, loathing the country, called it *Capa di Nada* 'Cape Nothing.'

But even now, in what may be the autumn of our national life, the word can stir our senses. Remember a man who was first to cross the country and reach Pacific waves. He wrote: "We mixed up some vermillion in melted grease, and inscribed . . . *Alexander Mackenzie, from Canada, by land, July 22, 1793*."

EFISGA URSALIA COLONIA VESPERIA TUPONIA CABOTIA

O Efisga, our home and native land! Mesopelagia, the true north strong and free! Mesopelagia is Greek for 'the land between the seas.' Frighteningly, Canada was not the only name our forebears considered when in 1865 they began thinking about a name for the dominion that they wanted to make of the provinces of Canada, Nova Scotia, and New Brunswick. We should be glad they chose Canada, and not—

- Ursalia (land of bears)
- Borealia (northern place)
- Cabotia (after explorer John Cabot)
- Tuponia (acronym for **T**he **U**nited **P**rovinces **o**f **N**orth **A**merica)
- Colonia (phooey!)

The hideous tongue-twister Albionora was given a serious chance. Get it? Albion (England) of the Nor-th.

One dewey-eyed poetess wanted the land to be called Vesperia, land of the evening star. Then, as the lady explained, not being too conversant with common English pronunciation or sense—this is true—she cooed, why, the name of the country would rhyme with diphtheria!

What about Efisga? A revolting acronym based on the first letters of **E**ngland, **F**rance, **I**reland, **S**cotland, **G**ermany, and **A**boriginal lands.

Canadians in slangy parlance are Canucks. Some dictionaries, including the compendious *Oxford English Dictionary* itself, give a lexical shrug, a long pouty sigh, and opine that this nickname for a Canadian is merely a shortening of the English adjective. Well, that simply will not do, chaps. Canadian etymologists point to the Iroquoian noun *kanuchsa*, one who lives in a *kanata*, a village.

CANUCK

Janey Canuck was the pen name of an early Canadian feminist writer, Emily Gowan Murphy (1868–1933), who wrote newspaper pieces and, in 1901, her first of four books, *The Impressions of Janey Canuck Abroad.* She took part in many campaigns to secure women the right to vote, and in Edmonton in 1916 she became the first female police magistrate in the British Empire.

JANEY CANUCK

Rudyard Kipling, novelist, poetaster, and tireless tub-thumper for British Imperialism, visited *the colonies* frequently, and was much loved by the Anglo elite of Victorian Canada. In 1897 he published a bit of doggerel in *The London Times* with the title "Our Lady of the Snows." Two lines were much quoted early in this century as descriptive of how Canadians ought to regard Britain:

OUR LADY OF THE SNOWS

> *Daughter am I in my mother's house,*
> *But mistress in my own . . .*

The natty poet-pipsqueak with the florid mustache feminizes Canada. And note the proprietary smugness of the possessive *our* in the phrase "Our Lady of the Snows." The phrase was much used in the decade that followed by British newspapers. McGill University gave Kipling an honorary degree in 1907. In 1908 he won the Nobel Prize for Literature.

But the "land God gave to Cain" remark about Canada makes Kipling's tag seem positively benevolent. Charting the bleak Labrador coast in 1534, explorer Jacques Cartier used this biblical phrase to describe his impression of the country. It harks back to Genesis 4:16: "And Cain went out from the presence of the Lord, and dwelt in the land of Nod, on the east of Eden." Nod is a Hebrew word for 'exile.' Cute line, Jacques, *vraiment* cute.

THE LAND GOD GAVE TO CAIN

FAKE AS CANADIAN DIAMONDS

But, pleasantly, fate and avarice caught up with Cartier. And greed made a spring fool of Jacques when he returned to France in 1542 after a third voyage to the New World. He sailed home with barrels of rocks that he thought contained diamonds and gold. Cap Diamant commemorates one area where Cartier found these deceiving minerals. For he was merely the first of many Europeans to be fooled by those twinkling tricksters of geology, quartz and iron pyrite (fool's gold). Continental French still has the expression, *aussi faux que les diamants Canadiens* 'fake as Canadian diamonds.'

Vulgar words, but in a well-mannered Canadian presentation that would not embarrass an Anglican vicar...

I f that Anglican vicar were into grain leather restraining devices, rubber underwear, and had printed at the bottom of his calling card, "Don't stop, even if I tell you to."

But seriously, folks, we have here to deal with bodily functions and matters best spoken of when the adults have left the room. I well recall my utter shock in the mid-seventies when I was working at CKVU-TV in Vancouver. One sunny day I popped out of the studio to eat lunch on a park bench nearby. Carved into the wooden back of the bench was a phone number and, in the same jackknife hand, the letters *B&D*. I was puzzled.

Though I had had a cloistered upbringing that would not have disconcerted the Singing Nun, I was nevertheless acquainted with the meaning, if not the practice of, for example, S&M. The actual practice of sado-masochism I was to engage in later, while trying to deal with middle management at CBC television in Toronto. Still I could **not** guess what B&D might mean. A kindly co-worker explained that one dialled the telephone number and received an invitation to bondage & dinner! A Canadian perversity, if ever there were one.

The ingredients of this chapter are much milder and concerned with human nature. Perhaps, as we read it, we may recall the Roman playwright Terence on the subject: *humani nihil a me alienum puto* 'I consider nothing human to be truly alien to me.'

BURPS

In our culture, to eruct is rude. Yet there are places in the world where a volley of postprandial eructation is the zenith of a guest's good manners. To eruct is to burp. Down east they say, *It's better to belch it than squelch it.* And suffer the pain. A writer in Burnaby, B.C., offers this after someone burps out loud—*Bring it up again, and we'll vote on it.*

EXCREMENT

Great writers have considered the topic, so why shouldn't we? Horace, that august and Augustan Roman poet spoke of another, smuttier writer's *cacata carta*, his shitty sheets—a rare instance of alliteration being translatable. The British novelist and essayist Anthony Burgess once seriously proposed that English should have a specific word for canine excrement, and he suggested the phrase: dog merd. Even that white-bearded sage of Canadian literati, Robertson Davies, discusses the products of defecation in his University of Toronto novel, *The Rebel Angels.*

Like every other word, the blunt word *shit* has an etymology. In Old English around 1000 A.D. the verb is *scitan*, cognate with the Germanic verb *scheiden* 'to separate, to be apart.' It is that which has split off from us, is apart from us. It is akin to the modern German *scheissen* with its vulgar compounds like *Scheisskopf* 'shithead.' On several documented occasions Hitler had the perspicacity to refer to himself as a *Scheisskerl*, an Austrian version of shithead. The Indo-European root is *skei* 'to split, to cut.' Even the fancy Latin euphemism that we use in English, excrement, has the same semantic weight. *Ex* means out of, and -*crementum* is the same root as the verb *cernere* 'to separate.' Excremental words in most European languages share the same idea. The vulgar English word *turd*, for example, is *tord* in Old English whose ultimate Indo-European stem is **der* 'to split, to separate.'

The common folk speech of Canada, as one might imagine, has made frequent use of the excremental reference.

It's damper than duck dung. (of Vancouver weather)

Sure as there's cold shit in a dead dog.

He couldn't say shit, if his mouth was full of it!

That's as easy as stuffing soft shit up a wild cat's ass with the narrow end of a toothpick.

If bull shit were a whistle, he'd be a brass band.

It's a cake of lies with bullshit icing. (on hearing an exaggeration)

Crazy as a shithouse rat.

Also heard in the tamer version—***crazy as an outhouse mouse***—though in my perusal of the zoological literature I can find no evidence of the mental disequilibrium of jakes-haunting rodents.

Just remember, you can't get manure from a rocking horse.

In 1964, writer Merle Miller published *Lyndon: An Oral Biography* of former American President Lyndon Johnson. In it a young Lyndon gets to meet then President Harry S. Truman. As they chat, the Texas political neophyte asks Truman for his philosophy of life. Harry scratches his head and replies, "Never kick a fresh turd on a hot day." Just one Missouri farmboy talking to one Texan farmboy. Now I do know this is not a Canadian anecdote, however it is illustrative of the thematic strands being so deftly braided through this chapter.

One Americanism prevalent in Canada is the expression ***up shit creek without a paddle***. But entirely Canadian is our common euphemism: ***up the well-known stream without the necessary means of conveyance***.

FLATULENCE

Breaking wind is the subject of many Canadian folk expressions. In 1982, a Winnipeg correspondent, Dr. Hartley Smith, wrote me that "after breaking wind, my grandfather used to say—*An empty house is better than a bad tenant.*" Barbara Makortoff of Castlegar, B.C. remembers *He was all over the place, like a fart in a glove.* A. Strohhofer of Saskatoon added this folk description of a hot prairie day—*It's drier than a popcorn fart.* And Rod Frost of Mindemoya, Ontario, heard this rhyming farm advice:

> *The fartin' horse will never tire;*
> *The fartin' man's the one to hire.*

To any person overly fond of inquiring just who had recently broken wind, some Canadians of Scottish ancestry were wont to answer, *The fox smells his own hole.* From Pierceland, Saskatchewan, W. Robertson sent this stark description: *He could outfart the Old Fart himself.* Now let us make this topic disappear *faster than a fart in a dance hall.*

Le pèter, flatulence, as in most languages of the world, is a common subject of folksy figures of speech in Québécois French. When everything has been done correctly, one might say there is *pas un pet de travers* 'not a fart out of place.' A slangy way to die is *pèter au fret* 'to fart in the cold,' 'to kick the bucket.' Scram! may be translated as *va pèter dans le trèfle!* 'Go fart in the clover.' To be bursting with pride about something is *se pèter les bretelles* 'to fart off your suspenders.' And *pèter le feu* 'to fart fire' is to be very angry.

AVOIR LE TROU DE CUL JOYEUX

means 'to break wind in public,' literally 'to have a happy asshole.'

MERDE

If you say *merde alors*! in Paris, you might be admiring something. The word is often pronounced *marde* in Québec, as in these sayings:

Mange d'la marde.
Eat shit! Go to hell!

Maudite marde!
Shit!

Rare comme d'la marde de pape.
Quite rare, literally 'rare as the pope's excrement.'

Vous vous faites aller la marde de tête.
You are concentrating really hard, literally 'you are going to pass a "brain" turd.'

A Canadian folk saying, widespread after World War I, indicated lack of intelligence—"He couldn't pour piss out of a boot, if the instructions were printed on the heel." This expression originated in 1915 when Canadian soldiers were issued new army boots made of stiff leather. Oddly enough, a legitimate method of softening the leather was to urinate in the boots and leave it in overnight. Of course, it helped if one did empty and wash the footwear in the morning, before attending to one's military duties.

Another phrase expressing military dubeity might be heard after the boast, "We're going to win this one." Sure, if pee was port wine.

And consider this tidbit of British Columbian recreational boaters' slang: *Water's flatter 'n a plate of puppy pee.*

URINATION

If ye have tongues, prepare to wag them now

This chapter celebrates the power of Babel. The Canadian word-stock would be watery soup indeed without steamy verbs and clattering nouns and tangy place names tossed in from many of the world's tongues. In this chapter you'll meet languages you never heard of, and be surprised you are using household words or place names that come from a tongue unknown to you. You'll learn Canadian words new to you. As you wolf down the linguistic bouill-abaisse of Canadian English, you'll find it afroth and zesty with international spices. Here's hoping the occasional lexical fish-head will bob up to amaze you. By far the greatest number of uniquely Canadian terms are borrowed from the aboriginal languages of North America, and so they predominate here.

ABNAKI
TAMARACK

The Abenaki people live in Québec and Maine. They speak an Algonkian language in which their name is *Wabanakiyak* 'people of the dawn' or 'men of the east.' English has borrowed tamarack and tump from Abnaki. Tamarack, our common larch, stems from the fact that aboriginal peoples often named trees after the use made of their wood. Larch wood could be soaked in warm water and bent into gentle curves. So in the language of the Abenaki, *akemantak* means 'wood for snowshoes.' We mangled the word into pioneer English as both hackmatack and tamarack. And snowshoes can still be made of the beautiful tamarack whose autumn leaves stand out yellow against the green conifers they grow beside.

TUMP

Tump is related to the Abnaki word *madumbi* 'pack strap.' The tump strap or tumpline or headstrap is a leather thong that passes around the forehead and is firmly attached to a backpack. Voyageurs portaging a canoe could use it to carry smaller loads slung low on their backs, while their shoulders supported the canoe. Modern adventurers who use the canoe also make use of the tump.

ACADIAN
FRENCH

Acadien, Acadian French, is spoken along our east coast in Québec, New Brunswick, Nova Scotia, Prince Edward Island, Cape Breton Island, and it is also heard in some communities on the north shore of the St. Lawrence and the islands in the Gulf of St. Lawrence. Acadian settlers came chiefly from the French provinces of Aunis, Poitou, and Saintonge, and this historical fact accounts for the wonderful, burly clout of *Acadien*, for the stock of old French vocabulary items and bits of ancient syntax preserved in the amber of this robust dialect. Standard French for wheelbarrow may be *brancard*, but in *L'Acadie* it's *boyart*. The mail man might be a *facteur* in France, a *postier* in most of Québec, but in purest *Acadien* the name of his occupation recalls the days of coach and four, because he's a *postillon*. English borrowed this to get postillion, one who rides a post-horse or one who rides the near horse of a team when there is no coachman. Another Acadianism is *bec* for any high ground, instead of the Standard French *élévation*. Fence in SF is *clôture*, but in Acadian French it's a mouthful, *bouchure*.

BARACHOIS

Barachois is an Acadian French word that is used in English on Cape Breton Island, and in Nova Scotia, New Brunswick, and sixty-six times in Newfoundland place names. *Barachoix* was Norman French for 'sandbar.' Early Basque fishermen used it too, referring to a sandbar or gravel bar in front of a saltwater pond, where they could haul up their boats. In Canada's Atlantic provinces it means a saline pond near a larger body of water that is cut off from it by a sandbar or narrow strip of land. Sometimes one sees it Englished as barrisway or barrasway. Newfoundland has Barasway de Cerf (a pond where you might see a deer), and the delightful mouthful L'Anse au Loup Barasway (Wolf Bay Pond). Also on the Rock the diligent toponymist finds Rocky Barachois Bight. Barachois is a very frequent element in Maritime place names. Almost at the tip of the Gaspé peninsula is the Québec village of Barachois-de-Malbaie. Near Shediac in New Brunswick is another big B. Newfoundland's south coast claims Barachois Bay and Barachois Point.

MACLEAN

In Nova Scotia there's MacLean Barachois, pleasantly combining the memories of two of the province's founding linguistic forces: Gaelic and *Acadien*. MacLean as a Gaelic surname combines Mac + Gillie + Ian to mean 'son of the servant of John.' All that remains of the gillie root is the ell. Gillie could also mean devotee, one devoted to a saint. So it is probable that the originating ancestor was the son of an early Christian who held pious regard for St. John the Baptist. Ian or Eoin or Iain are Gaelic variants for John.

ALGONKIAN

Note that Algonkian is not spelled the same as Algonquin Park in Ontario. Algonkian (or Algonkin) is the technical name in linguistics for a vast family of North American Indian tongues, whose peoples lived and live from northern Québec across Ontario through our prairie provinces and down into the United States. Among the related languages that comprise Algonkian are Cree, Ojibwa, Mi'-Kmaq, Blackfoot, Cheyenne, and Arapaho.

ABITIBI

Abitibi originally was *abitah-nipi* or 'halfway water.' An Algonkian-speaking people lived near present-day Lake Abitibi, and French trappers originally met them to trade fur at a place called "halfway water" because it was halfway between the trading settlements on the Ottawa River and Hudson's Bay. The Algonkian *nipi* meaning 'water' also shows up in the Ontario lake and district name Nipissing. From *nipi-*

sisinan or 'little water,' because Lake Nipissing was large but smaller than any of the great lakes. In 1882, the CPR chose a level portion of shoreline along the north bay of Lake Nipissing for railway yards. This is the origin of the name of the city of North Bay, Ontario.

OTTAWA

Of the many Algonkian-based words in modern Canadian English, one of the important ones is Ottawa. It was originally the name of a tribe of trading people who dwelt in southern Ontario. Canadian French called them Outouan or Outaouais. Compare the Cree word for trader, *ataweu*, and the widely used Algonkian verb *adawe* 'to trade.' The tribal name was first used in English to refer to the Ottawa River. Until 1855 the settlement that became Canada's capital was Bytown, named after Colonel John By of the Royal Engineers, the man who supervised the building of the Rideau Canal. The Ottawa tribe controlled the traffic along the Ottawa River. But aboriginal peoples fought among themselves, just as white tribes do. And it so happened that *oda-wa* in the Huron or Wendat tongue meant 'bark-eaters.' So the Wendat often called the Ottawa people, bark-eaters. This insult implied that the Ottawa were very poor and didn't plan well. Aborginal tribes only ate bark in the dead of a severe winter, when summer stores of food had run out and game was scarce.

ARABIC
BUG

Before flashlights, a bug was a candle set in a tin can. A hole cut in one side of the tin can let light through. Fraidycats of yore used it to go to the outhouse in the middle of a dark night. Or it might light the way to the barn at night, for a farmer checking on a sick cow. Bug was a contracted form of

French *bougie* 'candle, lantern.' Bougie entered French from Arabic. When Algeria was a colony of France, the Algerian town of Bijiyah shipped candle wax for export to Marseilles.

BASQUE

Basque as an element in Canadian place names is common in the Atlantic provinces because Basque fishermen came early from their homeland in the Pyrenees to fish the cod and hunt the whale. Chauffaud-aux-Basques in Québec takes us back to the days when Basque fishermen built drying racks for their cod catch at the mouth of the mighty Saguenay River. Note the English word *scaffold* and the French *chauffaud* and the Italian-based *catafalque* all stem from a Greek word that meant a platform over a trough. Port aux Basques in Newfoundland is clearly descriptive. Isles-aux-Basques are islets where early Basque whalers put ashore to render blubber into oil for shipment back to Spain.

Basque is the great mystery among European languages. Linguists have never found any other tongue on earth that is related to *Euskara*, which is what Basques call their mother tongue. They have searched in Africa, in the Middle East, in the remotest mountains of Asia. No relatives.

There sits Basque, spoken astride both slopes of the western Pyrenees by the Bay of Biscay, with some speakers in three French provinces, and the majority in four Spanish provinces. Basque was spoken before Romans conquered Spain, before the Celts. It may, ventured one scholar, be the language spoken by the cave painters who daubed their magic bison on the subterranean walls at Altamira. A study of Basque words shows that they arose in a paleolithic culture. All the terms for cutting and striking tools, like pick, axe, and knife stem from the root *aitz* 'stone.' One of their oddest words is *Jinkoa* 'God.' No one else on this planet has a word for deity that even faintly resembles this term. But it may be the origin of our English expression, By Jingo! and of jingoism.

The Latin word for a Basque person was *vasco*, plural *vascones*. It became *basco* in early Spanish. The root gives rise to many European place names, like the former French province of Gascony, and a learned English word for boastfulness borrowed from French, gasconade. From *vasco* stems the Spanish province of Vizcaya, which in French becomes Biscaye, which in turn gives its name to the Bay of Biscay. Was the Portuguese navigator Vasco da Gama a Basque? Certainly Ignatius of Loyola, founder of the Order of Jesuits, was Basque.

L'ORIGNAL

L'Orignal is Québécois for 'moose,' from French *orignac*, which derives from the Basque word for 'deer or stag,' *orenac*. L'Orignal is also the name of a hamlet on the Ontario-Québec border, which takes its name from a nearby moose-crossing on the Ottawa River. The wee burg of L'Orignal is quite well-known for the number of traffic tickets issued there by local members of the constabulary (known in the vernacular as the OPP). Be careful when driving through pretty little L'Orignal. I speak only from very personal experience. I have driven through the place twice, and received two of the ten traffic tickets I've had in my life. Although I myself no longer drive through L'Orignal, if necessity bids you travel thither, consider this as you pass through. There is a French-Canadian verb phrase, *devenir orignal* 'to get horny' or literally 'to become the moose, i.e., have a big horn.' Perhaps that's what happens when cops in L'Orignal think about the wallets of all those potential visitors motoring through their town?

BLACKFOOT
SIKSIKA
KAINAH
PIEGAN

Blackfoot is the whiteman's name for a group of Algonkian-speaking tribes who call themselves the Siksika, the Kainah, and the Piegan. Now they live on reservations in Alberta and Montana, but once these were nomadic hunters who migrated with the great buffalo herds across the wide Canadian prairies that now bloom with many Blackfoot names. Legend says they were Blackfoot because their moccasins were black with the ashes from many prairie grass fires. *Siksika* means 'black foot.'

Okotoks, Alberta, takes its name from the Blackfoot word *okatoksituktai* 'plenty of stones,' referring to a pebbly

crossing-place on Sheep Creek along the Calgary-Fort Macleod Trail. Pakowki Lake was named as a practical warning in Blackfoot. It means 'bad water.' Peigan, north of Pincher Creek, Alberta, remembers one of the Blackfoot tribes, the Piegans, who used to live near Lethbridge. And south of High River, Alberta, lies Pekisko, Blackfoot for 'foothills.' The town of Ponoka means 'deer or elk' in Blackfoot. Another town, Etzikom, is Blackfoot for 'coulee.' The Siksika people were not above the common practice of giving insulting names to tribes who did not speak their language. For a time, a Na-dené-speaking people were their allies in the Blackfoot Confederacy. When they split up, the Blackfoot called them Sarcee, the 'no good' ones. The Sarcee still have a reserve west of Calgary.

SARCEE

L'Arche is French for 'the ark,' that is, a refuge like Noah's ark. Canadian Dr. Jean Vanier has founded hundreds of *L'Arche* houses for the mentally handicapped all over the world. His first *L'Arche* was opened in France in 1964. The word has entered many European languages.

CANADIAN FRENCH
L'ARCHE

Le Château St. Louis in Québec City is the ornate former residence of the Governors of Québec. The building gave its name to a French and English tag to describe the post-1791 gang who ran Lower Canada. The *Château Clique* was a pack of English lawyers and officials who, along with French seigneurs and businessmen, controlled and exploited the province, much like Upper Canada's Family Compact, in fact much like Mulroney's "Ritz Clique" two hundred years later.

CHÂTEAU CLIQUE

Consider this prairie turn of phrase: *What ever happened to Fred? Dunno. Went for a dump and the gophers got him.* Québec French gave us the name *gopher* for this pesky ground squirrel. *Gaufre gris* or the grey honeycomb was the Québécois name for this North American varmit. *Gaufre* is French for 'honeycomb,' referring to the series of interlocking tunnels in a gopher's burrow.

GOPHER

"Mush! Mush! On, you huskies!" cried Sergeant Preston of The Yukon to 1940s radio listeners, thus introducing a whole generation of Canucks to the word once widely used in the arctic to spur on sled dogs. Although it might sound like a word from Inuktitut, early French trappers first used it, borrowing the term from the Canadian French command to a horse to go: *marche! marche!* Yes, it's Québécois for giddyap.

MUSH!

POUTINE

And verbal borrowing over the neighbour's linguistic fence works both ways. For example, *poutine* is plain fare from *la cuisine Québécoise*. You'll find it on the menu throughout most of Ontario, too, and in New England, even New York City. Recipes vary, but generally poutine is french fries with gravy, corn, and melted cheese. The word itself is an early Canadian French borrowing of the English word *pudding*.

SHIVAREE

This entry for shivaree is long because I have found the ultimate root of the word, a Greek root missed by the *Oxford English Dictionary* and by all dictionaries of French. Shivaree is an Englishing of *charivari*. There's no dispute about that, and it's been in dictionaries for a century. The *Oxford English Dictionary* (1933 edition) quotes the famous French etymologist Emile Littré who in his *Dictionnaire de la Langue Française* (1863–1877) attests a fourteenth-century French term *charivari*, the mocking serenade of an unpopular person.

But among North American pioneer settlers, a shivaree was the mock celebration of a wedding. The purpose of the shivaree in most of rural Canada was to catch the newlyweds in bed on their wedding night, then stand outside their house, and beat pots and pans, causing a general uproar, all to introduce a note of humour into what might have been an evening fraught with virginal tension. A shivaree takes place in Robertson Davies' novel, *Fifth Business*. And there's one in the Rogers & Hammerstein musical, *Oklahoma*. For years the subtitle of the British humour magazine, *Punch*, was *The London Charivari*, a subtitle that was borrowed from the title of a much earlier Parisian satirical magazine.

The *New Shorter Oxford English Dictionary* states, with a snotty abruptness that does not at all become so encompassing a tome, that charivari is "Fr., of unkn. origin." Now the OED puts the puck in the net etymologically so frequently that the constant reader is always saddened to observe its general reluctance to accept the discoveries of non-British philology. But really, chaps, there is nothing unknown about the origin of charivari. Medieval French medical texts written in Latin positively bristle with a little item of pathology termed *caribaria* or *charivarium*. When it first entered medical Latin and early French, it meant headache or hangover, and a secondary meaning easily arose, in which *charivarium* came to be applied to that which caused the hangover, namely the roistering hubbub of the night before. By the time it had become acclimatized in old French and had dropped its Latin ending, *charivari* meant, as well as the wedding prank, a hullabaloo in the streets caused by a crew of boozers on their way home from the tavern.

Both the *Oxford English Dictionary* and the many French dictionaries that followed Littré then say that *charivarium* is of unknown origin. Well, I found it. Medical Latin borrowed *caribaria* directly from classical Greek where καρηβαρία means a hangover, or being heavy in the head with drowsiness or with drink. Why, by the entwined snakes of Aesculapius' caduceus, the great man, Aristotle himself, uses the word, in his charming little treatise on sleep and wakefulness, known under its Latin title of *De Somno et Vigilia*.

The components of karebaria are a Doric word for 'head' κάρηνον + βαρύς 'heavy.' Or the first element may be κάρος, a noun that means 'heavy sleep.' Κάρηνον is an obscure relative of the much more familiar classical Greek word for the 'skull,' κρανίον, which the Romans borrowed as *cranium*, giving rise to English *cranial*, etc. It also helps make up the word *craniotomy*, the drilling of a hole in the head, a surgical gesture we might recommend to the person who wrote that entry in the *New Shorter Oxford English Dictionary*, in the interests of letting out some of that British lexical sang-froid!

SNYE

In the dialect of the Ottawa Valley, and many other parts of Canada, a snye is a side-water channel that rejoins a larger river, creating an island, and sometimes conveniently providing canoeists passage around turbulent rapids or a waterfall. The word is an Englishing of the Québécois French *chenail* 'channel.'

VOLTIGEUR

Voltigeur was a continental French word that first meant 'one who leaps up' (*voltiger* 'to leap'). Then in France it developed the meaning of 'sharp-shooter or horseman.' But in French Canada a *voltigeur* was a militiaman with special training in what we would today call guerrilla warfare tactics. In 1812 they might have said *voltigeurs* were good bush fighters. It usually meant they had had experience hunting with native peoples or hunting native peoples. The term was not confined to Lower Canada or to Québec. About 1850 on Vancouver Island we find the Victoria Voltigeurs, a company of armed militia formed to protect the colony from attack "by Indians."

CHINESE
GUM SAN

During the nineteenth-century era of gold rushes in Canada's northwest, Chinese immigrants, mostly from San Francisco, came north as prospectors. Their general expression for our west coast area was *gum san* 'gold mountain.'

CHINOOK
JARGON

Chinook Jargon is a lingua franca based on the speech of the Chinook Indians, with words from French, English, Salish, Nootka, and other local tongues. Chinook Jargon was used for over a hundred years until the turn of the century by aboriginal peoples and white traders on the Pacific coast.

CHICAMIN

One hundred years ago, chicamin was a very common term for money, all over the northwest and west of Canada; and you still hear it now and then today, though usually from an old-timer. In Chinook Jargon *chikamin* meant anything made of metal. It entered the trading language from Vancouver Island Nootka where *tsikimin* was the word for 'iron.' In a similar manner, British English used brass to refer to coins or money.

CHINOOK
WIND

The Chinook wind is a warm, dry easterly that blows down from the Rockies across southern Alberta and Saskatchewan. A Chinook can take a brutally cold February winter morning in Lethbridge and make it feel like June by noon. One hears it as a verb, too: *Chinooked last night. Threw all my blankets off. Sweating like a stuck pig.* The Chinook arch is a great vaulted strip of blue sky seen high up over the Rockies above the western horizon that foretells the arrival of Chinook winds. The old Chinook sky that betokens balmy days ahead may see the peculiar Chinook clouds that lead the weather system in over the Rockies. Chinook clouds seem to be spinning or rolling because of the rising and falling air currents produced as they swoosh over the stone ridges of the mountains. In the jargon of meteorologists such clouds are sometimes said to come in lenticular waves. Calgary newcomers who get that vernal itch during a mild day of winter are said to be suffering from Chinook fever.

The wind takes its name from a people who lived along the north shore of the Columbia river at its mouth until well after whites took over the area. Their language is often called Chinookan. Its name comes from Chehalis, a Salish tongue of western Washington state, where *tsinúk* is the word for village, or perhaps the particular name of a former village now abandoned and its site lost to history.

In the 1970s, when I was a producer at CBC Radio's *This Country in the Morning*, Peter Gzowski tried to introduce and promote a new Canadian national holiday to fall on a date between New Year's and Easter. We ran a contest in which our radio listeners sent in suggested names for this midwinter feast. The winning entry was Chinook Day. Alas, it never came to pass. But a Chinook wind still does, late in the prairie winter to preview spring.

HIGH MUCKAMUCK

High muckamuck is a term I remember my father using as a way to describe any arrogant S.O.B. of an official. As he was a school principal, it sprang up often when he spoke of school boards. The term, common in Canadian and American English, is a borrowing, with a touch of folk etymology, from Chinook Jargon. *Hyiu* meant 'much' and came into the catch-all trading language from the Nootka tongue of Vancouver Island where *ih* means 'big.' *Muckamuck* was food in Coast Salish. In the days when food gathering took much time and skill, anyone who had lots of food was an important and successful person.

HYAK

Hyak was a potent word-of-all-trades in the old Chinook Jargon. As an imperative verb, it meant 'hurry up' or 'get a move on.' As an adjective and adverb it was perhaps the most widely known Chinook Jargon word on our west coast. *Hyak! Quick!* In a variant spelling of *hyack*, it came to have the specialized local meaning in British Columbia of volunteer fire-fighters, because they tried to get to fires quickly. That usage shows up even today in the proud name of the Honourable Hyack Battery of New Westminster, B.C.

Finally, a few terms in Chinook wawa (talk) whose origins you can guess: *tik-tik* was a watch or a telegraph office, *la puss* was a cat, *tumtum* was heart or soul, and *chik-chik* a wagon or wheel.

SIWASH

Siwash began its verbal life as an insulting voyageurs' term for a native person, and it is still an insult. It is a slurry jumbling up in Chinook Jargon of *sauvage*, the voyageurs' French term for any member of an aboriginal people, equivalent to savage or wild one.

Although siwash is vile and derogatory, or perhaps just because of its swinish bigotry, it gained wide use. Siwash tongue was a synonym for Chinook Jargon. To siwash once meant to travel quickly, deftly, and lightly, making use of natural shelters on the trail, or sleeping in the open as a First Nations person might do. Siwash wind is a Pacific Coast localism for any fresh gale that blows up briskly. A Siwash blanket is low cloud cover that portends weather warmer than if the ceiling were higher. In his book, *Many Trails*, R.D. Symons says that "most ranchers in the interior (of B.C.) loosely refer to all Indians as Siwashes." A synonym for a beach-comber is a Siwash logger.

Antkiti Siwashes were legendary native giants of Chilko Lake, well southeast of Redstone, in British Columbia. R.D. Symons, who writes splendidly about our western country, states that sometimes an Antkiti Siwash may return to track and haunt those living in the interior of the province who have sinned against the spirit of the land.

COAST SALISH SOCKEYE SALMON

Once upon a time I was camping near Pacific Rim National Park on Vancouver Island. One morning as I hunched over a tidal rockpool to observe a starfish lazily munching on a hapless mollusc, an elderly gentleman (whom I seem to encounter in every natural setting) approached. Let's just call him the World's Foremost Living Expert—on pretty well every topic known to human conversation. We exchanged a bit of amiable lip-flap, and in the course of his jawin', the grizzled old salt asked me if I knew that the sockeye salmon received its name when hearty fishermen of olden days waded into the water and took the fish by belting it in the face. "It's an urge that could overtake any of us," I said, adding that I didn't see how the SPCA could permit such enormities.

Then, humbly and with a deep contrition that would have made Mother Teresa envious, I suggested there might be another explanation, having to do with a local aboriginal language; but by then the World's Foremost Living Expert was a hundred feet up the beach where I perceived that he had waylaid another innocent and was busily explaining The Origin of the Universe As Revealed to One Preston Manning. Something about the fundament. Or was it the firmament?

Sockeye salmon makes one of the best eating fishes in the world, but it is often served quite hideously tarted up by an intrusive chef who has applied scales made of paste. Why not put a dead raven in the jaws as well? The Salish are a people who live, among other places, on the southern part of Vancouver Island and some surrounding islets. Sockeye is the English version of the Coast Salish *suk-kegh* 'red fish.' An apt name for this frisky Pacific salmon.

CREE

The Cree people live in Québec, Ontario, and preponderantly in Manitoba and Saskatchewan. Their Algonkian language has left its firm mark on every prairie map, with place names like Watino and Winagami in Alberta meaning 'valley' and 'dirty water lake.' *Keewatin* is the north wind in Cree. Another common Cree word borrowed by English is muskeg, from *muskak* 'swamp.' The root is in many Algonkian languages; compare the Chipewyan word for 'a grassy bog,' *muskig*.

MUSKEG

Cree, however, is not the original name of this people. In 1744 a band living south of James Bay was dubbed by early French-Canadian missionaries, *Les Cris*, and this was short for the Ojibwa word *kiristino*, itself borrowed from a nonstandard French form for Christians, *Christinaux*, which suggests the Cree converted early in the Jesuit missionary efforts to promote their European religion and destroy aboriginal ones.

HUSKY

Husky is a Cree word from the same root as the term *Eskimo*. Husky came into English through a Cree version *askimeo* or 'snowshoe people.' But this entered English as huskemaw, a name for a breed of Inuit dog, the husky. English use was influenced also by the previously existing and unrelated adjective, husky, which means robust.

~~ESKIMO~~

A note follows about the politically incorrect label, Eskimo. Eskimo is **not** an Inuit word, and is not liked or used by Inuit people except in jokes and ironical statements. French fur traders picked up the term *Eskimo* from the Montagnais natives of eastern Canada. In the Montagnais' Algonkian language, *aiachkimeo* were 'those who lace up snowshoes.' French and British explorers heard it as something like "Eskimo." The people call themselves Innu or Inuit. Inuit is the plural of *inuk*, a person. It means 'the people.' And their language is Inuktitut, which encompasses meanings like 'the way of the people' or 'the Inuit way.'

CZECH
BATAWA

Batawa, Ontario, near Trenton is a town named after a shoe company—one of the largest manufacturers and retailers of footwear in the world. Thomas J. Bata brought a long family history of shoemaking from his native Czechoslovakia when he emigrated to Canada in 1939. Naming the town, he added the *-wa* suffix to make it appear more like a Canadian place name of aboriginal origin, on the analogy of names like Ottawa, Mattawa, or Petawawa.

DANISH
SNOOSE

Snoose is a Canadian borrowing from Danish where *snustobak* is a moist, chopped snuff, the kind chewed; it is also called Copenhagen schnoose. In W.O. Mitchell's novel *The Vanishing Point* about Alberta whites and native peoples, one reads, "chewing snoose . . . that morning."

I believe I was present during one of the longest public discussions about snuff in the history of Canadian discourse. And now—oh, oh—here comes another CBC anecdote. In the 1970s when I was one of the producers of *This Country in the Morning*, a frequent guest was Bill (W.O.) Mitchell, Canada's most prominent literary sternutophile (lover of snuff). It was sometimes my job to issue forth from the old CBC radio building on Jarvis Street to collect Bill Mitchell at his hotel room and ensure that he arrived in the studio on time for our show. We would often pause in the CBC cafeteria in the damp basement of the radio building so that W.O. could snort a pinch or two. That's the same cafeteria Don Harron described as "the place old flies go to die." One day Peter got W.O. talking about snuff on the radio, and partaking of it live too, and despite very frantic signals from the radio control room, their snuffy conversation lasted for more than forty-five minutes. All inmates of that old pile on Jarvis Street had little sayings about the building. Mine was "the CBC radio building is the only place in Toronto where fire doors lead to fires."

DELTA INUKTITUT
PINGO

Delta Inuktitut is the dialect of the Inuit tongue spoken in the delta area of the Mackenzie River. A pingo is a strange upsurging of ice into a giant mound that may rise 150 feet or more. It is covered with soil and debris, the ice swell being formed by pressure as ice in the subsoil expands. The core is solid blue ice. Pingoes are often seen in semidried lakebeds of the arctic. Pingo derives from Mackenzie Delta Inuktitut *pinguq* 'hill'; and in the late 1940s was first used as a geographic term by arctic botanist Dr. E.A. Porsild.

DUTCH
BACK STOOP

Back stoop comes from Dutch *stoep*, a little porch with benches, but ultimately from the same Germanic root as step. Back stoop, the little veranda at the back door of a house, is a Canadian coinage, and is a fine place to plunk yourself for a quiet read on a Sunday summer afternoon.

BOKKEPOOTJES

Bokkepootjes 'goats' footsies,' are usually purchased in a Dutch bakery in Canada, lovingly ovened for Canadians of Dutch descent. *Bokkepootjes* are delicious Dutch pastries, shaped like little hooves and dipped in chocolate. Medieval iconography associates the billy-goat with the devil. And *bokkepootjes* are devilishly tasty. In the Dutch term, you can see *bokke*, from the same root as the English word *buck*, 'male goat.' *Pootjes* 'little feet (of an animal),' has the familiar and widespread Indo-European root for foot **ped* that appears as *pied* and *patte* in French, and in many Latin and Greek derivatives like pedal and podiatrist. Even English *foot* and Germanic *Fuss* are related—all one, big, wide, happy, foot family.

There are some Canadian place names that come from Dutch like Barnegat, Alberta, from Dutch *barende gat* 'breakers inlet.' This may be taken from Barnegat Bay in New Jersey, named by Henry Hudson in his seventeenth-century local explorations.

FRANGLAIS
UNE BUNCHE DE BOMMES

Franglais began its sniffish life as a continental French pejorative describing French with plenty of *anglais* words tossed in—too many for most French academics and for most literary and separatist Quebecers too. I first heard *une bunche de bommes* at a hockey game in Montréal. The bunch of bums was the opposing team, getting clobbered by *Les Canadiens*. Sure, it's franglais, but our franglais: Québécois French with Canadian English. *L'affaire est ketchup!* means 'it's a sure thing; we got it made, guys!' Or consider *avoir de la molsonne* 'to have big arms.' To have biceps big as beer bottles? In Paris, that paranoid watchdog of the French language, *l'Académie française*, still meets in stern conclave to suppress abominations like *le parking* and *le sweater*. They fail. But now in Québec intellectual separatists are studiously purging their speech of *le maudit anglais*. Perhaps in a few years this spritely franglais will be fit only for the language museum of some thick book?

GAELIC
SKIR DHU

In its Canadian form, Gaelic came to Cape Breton Island and what would be called Nova Scotia first. Scots Gaelic is still spoken in pockets of the Maritimes and Gaelic place names in Nova Scotia survive, some pure in their dour thorniness like Skir Dhu, Gaelic for 'black rock,' or Ben Eoin 'John's mountain.' Cape Breton has a *Mod* every year, a Gaelic assembly that includes Scottish food and games. A more modest party is called a *ceilidh* (pronounced KAY-ly) in most of Canada. Although they are not strictly Canadianisms, many Gaelic roots lurk in older English borrowings like the word *whiskey*, which is ultimately from Gaelic *uisge beatha* 'the water of life,' itself a loan translation into Gaelic from medieval Latin *acqua vitae*, which also gives the Scandinavian *akvavit* and the French *eau de vie*. The town of Pibroch, Alberta, takes its name from one who knew the art of bagpipe playing. Gaelic *piobaireachd* means 'piping,' but refers to bagpipe variations on a march tune or on a dirge.

GERMAN
BRÜDERHEIM

Bruderheim, Alberta, was settled by adherents to the Moravian Church, sometimes called The Brethren's Church. *Brüderheim* is German for 'brethren's home.' Twenty families of Moravians from Volynia in Russia homesteaded in Alberta in 1893 and gave this name to their new colony.

Moravian missionaries set up trading posts in Labrador as early as the eighteenth century. And there was the Moravian Grant of 1792, in which the Brethren were given 25,000 acres of land on the Thames River near Lake St. Clair, land on which they settled a band of peaceful Delaware and Muncee peoples whom they helped to migrate north after some of these native peoples had been attacked in Ohio in 1791.

COBALT

Silver ore found near the town of Cobalt, Ontario, in 1904 was loaded with compounds of the metallic element cobalt. The element was named after mythical Germanic sprites, kobolds.

They dwelt in the earth and were trickster-elves, whose life purpose was fooling humans. Cobalt ores are silvery and magnetic, so that miners first encountering cobalt-rich ore can be tricked into thinking they have discovered a big silver lode. Cobalt occurs naturally in compounds. In German mines it is often found in combination with arsenic and sulphur. So it seemed during the fourteenth century to German miners (dare we call them rootin' Teutons?) both worthless and toxic, much like the dastardly kobolds. These sprites are among the first-named elves in Indo-European languages. The father of Greek farce, Aristophanes, took notice of κόβαλοι, *kobaloi*, mischievous goblins summoned to help thieves in his Old Comedy romp, *The Knights*. Aristophanes used the word and its derivatives in two more of his eleven extant comedies, *The Frogs* and *Wealth*. What a merry time-trip the word has had, from Athens in fifth century B.C. to dank medieval mines in the Harz mountains of Germany, then across the Atlantic to northern Ontario at the start of the twentieth century.

FETSCHPATZ

Fetschpatz is a German-Canadian food treat you may find while grazing at the Kitchener Market in the heart of Ontario's Mennonite country. In his book *Our Own Voice*, R.E. McConnell states that fetschpatz means 'fat sparrow.' Not quite. *Fetschpätzen* (local spelling) are dumplings fried in fat and served hot slathered with maple syrup. Rather than an adjective + noun—*fett* 'fat' + *Spatz* 'sparrow'—the term is more likely to be two nouns in apposition, a common way in German to form long nounal descriptives, namely, by the agglutinative piling-up of nouns. *Fett* as a noun means 'lard.' This little dumpling, from its physical shape, is a lard-sparrow, *ein Fett-spatz*. The grease in which it was fried would have been originally lard.

FRESS

To eat like an animal is to fress, a verb common in the area around Lunenburg, Nova Scotia. German immigrants introduced this word, from the German *fressen* 'to devour, to be gluttonous.' Originally the verb was an intensive form of *essen* 'to eat,' *ver-essen*. And compare the German and Yiddish noun *fresser* 'glutton.'

GREEK

Although Greek words account for more than 50 percent of the roots used to make new scientific and technical terms in English, the tongue of ancient Athens does not seem to have

much to do with present-day Canada. But that's only until
we delve deeper into language, and see the synaptic flurry of
connections among world languages, which any bit of linguistic study can make clear. Indeed, I hope this little volume
demonstrates that interconnectedness. Still, as we've seen,
Greek does show up as the origin of even folksy words like
shivaree.

BRONTE

On the other hand, although Greek place names are scarce on
the map of Canada, one toponym can be traced back to Greek,
that of Bronte, Ontario, now part of Oakville. Founders
wished to honour British naval hero, Lord Horatio Nelson,
one of whose titles was Duke of Bronte. Bronte is a little village on the slopes of Mount Etna in Sicily, an island that was
Greek long before the Roman empire. Bronte is the Greek
word for 'thunder,' and refers to the rumbling of the volcanic
Etna. The root shows up in one of our words for a dinosaur,
the thunder-lizard or brontosaurus.

CRYPTOGLAUX

As for the use of Greek word-forming elements in making up
scientific names, let's use just one example from Canadian zool-
ogy. It bears the longish binomial appellation of *Cryptoglaux
acadica acadica*. What a mouthful to label the Acadian owl, a
little brown subspecies of the saw-whet owl, the only subspecies
found in the Maritimes, which accounts for its adjectives *acadica acadica*, scientific Latin for 'Acadian.' The Greek part is the
genus name, *Cryptoglaux*. Κρυπτός, *kryptos*, means 'hidden.'
And γλαῦξ is Attic Greek for 'owl.' The owl was sacred to the
goddess Athena, who gave her name to Athens, which is why
many ancient Athenian coins have an owl on them. To indicate
too much of a good thing, English has expressions like *carrying
coals to Newcastle*. Classical Greek used to say *bringing owls to
Athens*.

HEBREW

Echoes of biblical Hebrew resonate from hundreds of Canadian
place names taken from Holy Writ. Although it is not the subject matter of this book, Hebrew also forms the roots of thousands of our common first names like John, Mary, Janet, Jean,
Juan, Michael, etc.

GARDEN OF EDEN

I guess you knew Garden of Eden is in Nova Scotia? There is
also a Garden of Eden near Renfrew, Ontario. The biblical
Hebrew may be transliterated *gan eden* 'garden of delight.'

Some delight! A cranky Jehovah, a duplicitous reptile, and the problem, utterly unsolved in Genesis, of how to engender the human race and not fall victim to the genetic dangers of inbreeding, because according to the account in Genesis we are all inbred descendants of the same family and should have five or seven ears, little pink eyes, and think Rush Limbaugh is clever. Holy Writ never explains where Mrs. Cain originated. The first and only reference to this mysterious lady is "And Cain knew his wife." Always a comfort. But whence cometh Mrs. Cain, she who introduced chromosomal diversity, thus sparing humanity an eternity as albino cretins? Well, sparing most of us. Where the heck did Mrs. Cain hail from? American lawyer Clarence Darrow first asked the question during the Scopes Monkey Trial. Was Jehovah holding a second genesis over in the next county and not telling anyone?

In Canada, Nazareth is near Rimouski; Mizpah is in Alberta; and Hebron is in Labrador. One very piquant toponym of biblical provenance is Baraca, Alberta, formerly a post office near Brooks. Mrs. E.E. Boggess, a Lutheran minister, suggested the name, from Hebrew *berachah* 'a blessing.' The similar *baraka* means 'blessing' in Arabic, a Semitic language related to Hebrew. Poet Robert Graves introduced it into English as baraka to mean a vital sense in works of art.

HUNGARIAN

Kaposvar in Saskatchewan is the site of the first significant Hungarian colony of immigrants to Canada. It dates from 1886, and is named after a source hamlet near Budapest. Other Hungarian place names of our prairies, some now deserted, are Bekevar, Saskatchewan, which means 'fortress of peace'; Sokhalom 'many hills'; and Mätyásföld 'Matthias' land.' Esterhazy, Saskatchewan, recalls Count Paul Esterhazy, a Hungarian-American of 1880s New York City who learned of the very wretched conditions in which Hungarian miners were working in Pennsylvania. Esterhazy took care of resettling many of them in the potash-rich area of Saskatchewan.

HURON*
NIAGARA

Niagara, a Huron or Wendat word meaning 'thunder water' aptly describes the falls on the Niagara River. But Mohawk people called it *Oh-nya-ka-ra* 'at the neck' referring to their geographical metaphor of Lake Erie as the head joined by the neck of the Niagara peninsula to the body of Lake Ontario.

*For Huron as an insult, see page 173.

Oscar Wilde toured Canada and visited the famous cataracts in 1882, one year after the town of Clifton (town on a cliff) officially became Niagara Falls. It was already a popular honeymoon destination. Later on the same trip, when Wilde gave a press conference in New York City, one of the reporters asked him what he thought of the honeymoon capital. Wilde said, "Niagara Falls must be the second major disappointment of American married life."

ONTARIO

The Huron (or Wyandot or Wendat as they called themselves) named Lake Ontario from which the province takes its name. In Wendat it means 'large lake,' but other Iroquoian languages like Mohawk have possible root words also, like *onitariio* 'beautiful lake' and *kanadario* 'shining water.'

ICELANDIC
GIMLI

The first Icelanders came to Canada in 1873 after several natural disasters on the island of Iceland, including the eruption of the Hecla volcano. Their main permanent settlement on Lake Winnipeg began in 1875. But Gimli is not the home of the Norse gods, as W.B. Hamilton states in the *Macmillan Book of Canadian Place Names*. The chief Norse deity, Odin, dwelt in Asgard, where he very kindly set aside certain large mead-halls for selected humans. These banquet chambers included Valhalla, hall of the slain, where warriors who fell in battle could feast and fight again for all eternity. Among the nearby buildings was a great hall with a golden roof called Gimli, and here, after their earthly journey was complete, Odin welcomed men who had been particularly righteous during their lives.

We have mentioned Gimli. Among other Icelandic place names in Manitoba are Grund 'a grassy field' and Arborg 'town on a river.' In Saskatchewan there is the hamlet of Thingvilla, Icelandic for 'town where the *thing* or council meets.' Then come obvious names like the Icelandic River, and the more obscure Icelandic toponyms like Lundar in Manitoba. Another locality first settled by Icelanders is Elfros, Saskatchewan, near Foam Lake. They named it for wild roses growing in profusion near the original encampment. In Icelandic, Elfros means 'valley of the roses.'

INUKTITUT

Inuktitut is the language of the Inuit. There are about fourteen dialects, including seven spoken by Canadian Inuit. For exam-

ple, we have already mentioned Mackenzie Delta Inuktitut. We could add Netsilik, Copper, Iglulik, Caribou, Baffinland, and Labrador. There is a welcome move to change the English denotative labels to Inuktitut words. Only a few dozen words of Inuktitut have made their way into English. Among them are kayak, mukluk, and anorak.

One of the earliest and most common words is igloo, from the eastern Inuktitut *iglu*, which means 'home or dwelling' though not necessarily one of ice. The Innu may build a shelter from sod, as seen in the name of a place in Labrador, Igluksoatulligarsuk Island, which means 'houses-made-of-sod, a great many of them.' Iglulik or Igloolik in the Northwest Territories means 'place of many igloos.'

IGLOO

Inuktitut borrowed words from other languages quite early after encountering western explorers—words like *pautigee*, which means 'brown-coloured person,' and comes from the English adjective *Portuguese*. Inuit people have petitioned to have many of the English names of arctic places changed back to their Inuktitut originals. This is slowly taking place. In 1987, the town of Frobisher Bay on Baffin Island became Iqaluit 'place of fish.' The body of water named Frobisher Bay was left in English. Similarly, Notre-Dame-de-Koartac became Quaqtaq.

IQALUIT

In Inuktitut *ukpik* means 'snowy owl.' Ookpik™ is a registered trademark for a happy little owl doll made of sealskin, which became a symbol of Canada when adopted by the federal Department of Trade and Commerce in the 1960s. Jeannie Snowball, an Inuit woman of Fort Chimo in northern Québec, invented the wee thing, but was not responsible for its transformation into kitsch. Fort Chimo is now officially called by its old Inuktitut name, Kuujjuaq.

OOKPIK

From the Inuktitut word *pibloktoq* comes a new technical term in psychiatry, piblokto, referring to a dark-of-winter craziness

PIBLOKTO

among some Inuit people, whose chief symptom is an acute attack of screaming, crying, and running through the snow madly. Many of us further south in Canada experience similar lunacy, only we call it cabin fever.

IRISH GAELIC
SHANTY

Shanty meaning a crude hut in the woods used originally by lumberjacks has two root words as its origin. One is *chantier*, a logger's cabin in Québec, the word brought over from continental French where it referred to a timber yard, dock, or workplace. But Irish Gaelic also claims the origin, from *sean tig* 'old hut,' because many Irish immigrants to Upper Canada were lumberjacks, as well. It is not a question of one origin or the other. The two separate lexical items just blended to ensure widespread use of shanty.

ITALIAN

Italian place names dot the map of Canada. Terra Cotta, Ontario, means 'baked earth' in Italian, and was named because good clay for pottery work was found nearby. Gondola Point in New Brunswick recalls small ferry boats called gondolas used on some local rivers. Como-Est in Québec reminded early settlers of the beautiful surroundings of Lago di Como in the northern Italian lakes district. In British Columbia looms Mount Garibaldi in honour of Giuseppe Garibaldi, hero of the Italian *Risorgimento*. Next door in Yukon Territory is Mount Malaspina, after Alessandro Malaspina, the Italian navigator who explored the northwest coast of North America in 1791 while working for Spain. And Bassano in Alberta near the site of Horseshoe Bend Dam commemorates an Italian noble, the Marquis of Bassano, who owned a hefty chunk of CPR stock in 1884. Verona, Ontario, simply repeats the name of a favourite Italian city.

JAPANESE
GOW

Gow is a Canadian export—worth more than $1 million a year—that you may not know. Gow is a delicacy in the cuisine of Japan—it is herring roe (fish eggs) spawned on a small piece of seaweed. Some B.C. fisheries actually plant severed fronds of algal seaweed within schools of spawning herring, and harvest the result for immediate air freighting across the Pacific. The delicacy was known to B.C. native peoples, whose ancestors may have brought the discovery with them eons ago when they first crossed the Bering Strait to enter North America. Gow is a rough Englishing of a Japanese word that signifies 'little eggs.'

SANSEI

Sansei is a Japanese term that applies to many Japanese-Canadians. They use the following terms among themselves, and all of them appear from time to time in public print:
- *Nikkei* (a person born in Japan who lives abroad)
- *Issei* (a person of the first generation born outside Japan)
- *Nisei* (a person of the second generation born outside Japan)
- *Sansei* (a person of the third generation born outside Japan)

JOUAL

This put-down term for popular forms of Québec French was popularized in a notorious editorial in the Montréal newspaper *Le Devoir* in 1959 by André Laurendeau, an elitist moaner about how Québécois used to speak better French in the past. Joual is a pronunciation of *cheval* 'horse.' The word as slang for *cheval* has been around for almost one hundred years, e.g., in W.H. Drummond's nineteenth-century poem, "Mon Choual 'Castor.'" Monsieur Laurendeau was able to promote his pompous claptrap a few years later as co-chairman of the Royal Commission on Bilingualism and Biculturalism (1963). But, as Montréal dramatist Michel Tremblay showed later, joual adds zest and colour to Québec French. Like the patois of any language, it is a fertile seed-bed of new words, and it is a sign of linguistic health, not corruption. Many spunky upstarts of Québécois neology get dismissed as joual—words like *niaiser* 'to bug somebody' and *écrases-marde* 'rubber boots' but literally shit-stompers, a fitting name, as anyone who's ever worn them dunging out a stable, will tell you.

KAWAY-QUITLAM SALISH

Coquitlam, B.C., takes its name from a Salish tribe who call themselves Kawayquitlam after their totem animal, which was the sockeye. The name means small, red salmon. And Salish is their word for people.

KUTCHIN
KLONDIKE

Kutchin is one of the members of a once large group of languages now called Na-dené. This Dene tongue is spoken in the Yukon and Alaska. In 1981 linguists estimated that about eight hundred people can still speak Kutchin. The Kutchin word for river gives us two geographical names familiar to most Canadians, Klondike and Yukon. Klondike derives from the name of a local river in the Kutchin language where *thron dyuk* means 'hammer river.' The Kutchin people hammered stakes into the river shallows to trap salmon. And, of course, we know the creeks and streams of this tributary of the Yukon River, particularly Bonanza Creek, carried gold that was discovered on August 17, 1896, thus setting off the Klondike Gold Rush. The popular poems of Robert W. Service helped make the word Klondike famous wherever English was read.

YUKON

Established on June 13, 1898, Canada's Yukon Territory also takes it name from a local river, a mighty river. We know a Kutchin word for 'river,' *dyuk*. To that, one simply adds a short Kutchin augmentative ending *-on* and obtains *dyuk-on* or 'Yukon or big river.'

LAPPISH
TUNDRA

Tundra is one of the three Canadian arctic terms we borrowed from Russian. The others are taiga and sastrugi. But the Russians borrowed tundra, too, from Lappish, the correct English label for the language spoken by Laplanders. Lappish is related to Finnish and Hungarian and to a few other languages of Europe. Tundra is in its original form a Lapp word *tundar* 'hill,' related to Finnish *tunturi*. Laplanders applied it to the sandy plains that border the Arctic Ocean. Then Russians used it to name the barrens of Siberia. When the first Russian explorers reached Alaska they applied the term to the flat, almost treeless barren lands at the top of North America. Finally English and French explorers began to use the word. Outcrops of rock give the tundra a rolling, stubby-hilled aspect.

LATIN

Latin place names crop up here and there like little Roman bumps on the Precambrian Shield. Aurora, Ontario, is named for that hard-working early riser, the Roman goddess of the dawn, who peeped forth each day, shook her dewy locks, and rode in a chariot across the sky, presumably towards noon. Marmora, Ontario, was founded near a marble quarry, and its name is the plural of the Latin word for marble 'marmor.' One also finds made-up Latin names, like the little town of Rusylvia in Alberta that is compounded of Latin *rus* + *silva* 'countryside' + 'forest.' Arva, Ontario, means 'ploughed fields' in Latin, while Terra Nova is 'new land,' also found in Ontario.

MALECITE

Maleseet or Malecite is an Algonkian language of our Maritimes, especially New Brunswick and Nova Scotia. The common term *bogan* for a little creek or backwater stream that branches off a larger body of water is sometimes seen in its longer form *pokelogan*. Both stem from the Malecite term *pekelaygan* 'place to stop.' Some New Brunswick place names originate in Malecite, too, like Nackawic and Nackawic Stream from *nelgwaweegek* 'straight water.'

MICMAC OR MI'-KMAQ

Le mic-mac is a racist noun in Québec that first appeared in Acadian French. But it is still heard frequently in joual and slangy speech. It means something tricky, a small intrigue, a mess. *Il y a du micmac là-bas* means that 'something fishy's going on down there,' or, 'it's all messed up down there.' The word is derived from the name of the indigenous Maritime people. Literally thousands of Micmac words appear as place names in our Atlantic provinces. This derogatory use of Micmac is one of the reasons for the growing use of a spelling form that more closely approximates the sound of the name in their language, *Mi'-Kmaq* (or Mi'kmaq), seen in French and English academic writing, and among the people themselves, possibly from *ni'-kmaq* 'my kinfolk,' a common greeting.

NOOTKA

Klee Wyck means 'laughing one' in the Pacific coast language of Vancouver Island's Nootka. Canadian painter and writer Emily Carr (1871–1945) received the nickname from the Nootka whom she met on painting field trips; and she used it as the title for her 1941 book, which contains sketches of the life and stories of some west coast peoples.

Nootka place names of B.C. include Nootka Sound and Nootka Island from *nootk-sitl* 'going around' or 'those who make a circuit of the island.' The village of Ucluelet, on the west coast of Vancouver Island, near Pacific Rim National Park, is Nootka *yu-clutl-ahts* for a tribe who had 'a safe landing place.'

Nootka is not the correct name for the twelve tribes of related people who live mostly along the west coast of Vancouver Island. They call themselves: *Nuu-chah-nulth* 'those who live all along the mountains.' Nootka is part of the larger Wakashan language group, and the Nootka have lived on the island for 4,000 years.

KLATAWA

Nootka gave many words to Chinook Jargon including *klatawa* 'to go, to travel, a journey'—all meanings that derive from the Nootka word *tlatw'a* 'a paddling.' You can still hear the phrase "go klatawa" or go visiting.

KLOOTCH

Kloochman or klootchman or the more common klootch, all terms for an aboriginal woman, were much used in Chinook Jargon to replace the insulting "squaw." Kloochman derives from the Nootka *lhutsma* 'wife or female.'

SQUAW

Squaw started its verbal life as the quite acceptable Cree word for 'woman,' *iskwao*. But it soon became an insult in the mouths of whites. And to aboriginal peoples who do not speak Cree or other Algonkian tongues, squaw is merely an English insult to their women, and is totally unacceptable.

But—wouldn't you know it?—prejudice is ever persistent, and now in the north klootch has come to be used in the same sneering way that squaw has. Klootch sometimes is also the insult label for a white man who marries an aboriginal woman.

NORWEGIAN

On his first voyage of discovery, Norwegian explorer Roald Amundsen navigated the Northwest Passage and fixed the exact location of the magnetic north pole. He passed his first winter of 1903–4 in Canada's high arctic in a little harbour he found for his ship, the Gjöa. He named the snuggery Gjöa Haven. Norwegian immigrants to Canada have also left scattered place names on our map, such as Bodo, Alberta, after Bodo Fjord in Norway.

OJIBWA

Ojibwa is the Algonkian language of the Ojibway or Ojibwa people whose ancestral home is the environs of Lake Superior from which they spread westward.

CHIPMUNK

Chipmunk is a Canadian term, from the Ojibwa *atchitamon*, which means 'head first,' descriptive of the way the little rodent comes down a tree trunk. The word was first used to name the red squirrel. In 1946 deHavilland flight-tested its first Canadian-designed-and-built commercial aircraft, the DHC-1 Chipmunk.

MIMICO & OMEEMEE

Wild pigeons or rock doves gave their onomatopoeic names to two Ontario communities. Mimico, part of Etobicoke since 1967, is from the Ojibwa for wild pigeon. Omeemee is Cree for the same bird. Both words imitate one of the bird's calls.

OLD NORSE

Helluland is an early name for part of Canada, and means boulder-land in Old Norse, the language of the eleventh-century sagas, which tell of voyages to North America by Norsemen who divided what they found into three named areas. Helluland was probably their most northerly landfall, Baffin Island. Markland ("wood" land) may have been what are now Canada's Atlantic provinces. And Vinland ("vine" land?), most scholars now agree, was located somewhere on the coast of one of the present-day New England states.

POLISH

Polish immigrants have contributed greatly to Canada but their language has left only a few place names to remind us of the beautiful Polish language. These include Sir Casimir Gzowski Park on Toronto's lakeshore and a hamlet in Alberta named Krakow after the ancient capital city of Poland. This was the suggestion of the town's first post-mistress, Anna Humutka. Stubno in Alberta was named by its first postmaster, Mr. Stepanick, after his natal town in Poland. Is there a doctoral thesis here on pioneer postmasters of the Polish persuasion?

PORTUGUESE
BACALHAO

The most influential Portuguese word in all of Canadian history is *bacalhao* 'codfish.' Cod and a possible western sea route to China are the magnets that first drew large numbers of Europeans to North America. Baccalaos was an early name (1555) for our entire Maritime region. Variants abound, such as Baccaro, Nova Scotia, and Baccalieu Island, Newfoundland, which are respectively Spanish and French versions of the word. And, just for authentic measure, it is sometimes called Bacalhao Island. The Baccalao bird is a local name for murres that nest on Baccalieu Island.

MOTHER CAREY'S CHICKENS

Certain sea birds must never be harmed intentionally by a sailor. We all know the calamitous luck that befell Coleridge's Ancient Mariner when he killed the albatross. Similar strong superstitious awe of the petrel or storm petrel or sea swallow exists today among many sailors and fishermen. Maritime fishermen call petrels "Mother Carey's chickens." One of the honorific titles of the Virgin Mary as patron of sailors is the beautiful Latin phrase *stella maris* 'star of the sea.' But even more common in the Romance languages is *Mater Cara* 'dear mother.' In Portuguese it's *Matara Cara*. Such is the likely origin of the phrase "Mother Carey's chickens."

PANJABI
KIRPAN

Kirpan is a word in Panjabi, an Indo-Aryan language of India's Punjab. Also a word in Hindi, the kirpan is one of the five K's of Sikhism that concern what pious Sikhs must wear. The kirpan is the sword of knowledge, a ceremonial dagger, symbolizing "cutting" one's ego, as well as self-respect. The five Ks are:

- *Kirpan* (a dagger symbolizing self-respect)
- *Kesh* (uncut hair as a symbol of simple purity)
- *Kanga* (a wooden comb to keep uncut hair presentable)
- *Kara* (a steel bracelet that reminds the pious Sikh not to commit sin with his hands)
- *Kachh* (short white breeches worn as underwear to symbolize morality and marital fidelity)

More than 200,000 hard-working and law-abiding Sikhs contribute their industry to Canada. But because they have kept their distinctive religious dress, they are easy subjects for bigots who stupidly seem not to realize that groups can be different and equal. The turbanlike headdress worn by Sikh men is a centuries-old way to keep long hair neat.

RUSSIAN
SASTRUGI

The early Russian explorers of the west coast of North America have left their word for 'snow ridge,' *sastruga*. Sastrugi are ribbed furrows of snow sculpted by the wind, often in rows parallel to the wind direction. To Russians these snowbanks seemed to have been smoothed like wood by a planing tool; the metaphor buried in the word *zastruga* is from Russian woodworking, where струг, *strug* is a plane.

KERENSKY
SOBOR
WOSTOK

There are a few Russian place names sprinkled by settlers across our map, including several of interest in the prairie provinces. Kerensky in Alberta is named after Alexandr Feodorovich Kerensky, the Russian statesman and orator who served as minister of justice and prime minister after the February Revolution in 1917. Just to stay in Alberta, other Slavic place names include the little community of Sobor, which in Russian is собор, *sobor* 'religious council' or 'synod.' Wostok, Alberta, is the Slavic word for 'east,' восток, which might seem more familiar as the part of the name of the Russian city of Vladivostok, literally 'place that rules the east.'

DOUKHOBOR

A special analphabetical place is here set aside for the Russian word *dukhovorets*. About 7,000 Doukhobors, members of a pacifist Christian sect, came to Canada in 1899, after they were attacked in their native Russia for refusing to serve in the Russian army. A radical anarchist sect of the Doukhobors call themselves The Sons of Freedom. Canadians may remember their arson, bombings, and nude protest marches in British Columbia. Doukhobor as a name began in Russia as an insult. *Dukh* is Russian for 'spirit,' either the Holy Spirit or a goblin. *Vorets* means 'wrestler.' Thus *dukhovorets* 'spirit-wrestler,' is the equivalent of holy roller. But after being called this in Russia, the group decided to adopt the name as suggestive of those who contend about spiritual questions.

SAMOYED
PARKA

Parka is one of the few words that has made its way into Canadian English from the Samoyed languages spoken by Mongoloid peoples who live on the arctic coasts of Siberia. Samoyed is the Russian word for these peoples and their group of languages. It had entered Russian as a word by the sixteenth century, and is certainly never used by these peoples themselves, because Samoyed means 'self-eater or cannibal' in Russian. When the Russians first encountered the Samoyed, they were struck by their clothes, in particular by the deerskin garment with a hood worn by men and women. The Samoyed word for this outer windbreaker was *parki*. In Russian *parka* also denoted the deerskin or pelts from which the garment was made. In the 1740s Peter the Great of Russia sent explorer Vitus Bering to map and reconnoiter Alyeska, the land across the arctic strait. Bering and those Russian fur trappers who came after him for the next hundred years saw Aleutian Inuit people wearing a similar garment, and called it a parka. Inuit borrowed the word as *purka* to mean 'a skin or outer coat.' And then English borrowed it again as parka.

SANSKRIT

Sanskrit is an ancient language of India, directly related to most of the languages of Europe as a member of the huge Indo-European linguistic family. Sanskrit is the source of many modern languages of the area including Bengali, Hindi and Urdu, Nepalese, Panjabi, and Sinhalese.

INDUS

Indus, Alberta, is named after the great river of northern India, from which the country takes its name. River names all over the world are among the oldest and most persistent place names. Many predate the invention of writing, and a great number mean quite simply 'river'—among these are English river names like Avon, Wye, and Thames. Indus, too, derives ultimately from the Sanskrit word *sindhu*, which means 'river.' It is also the origin of the word Hindu.

SWASTIKA

The town of Swastika, Ontario, now part of Kirkland Lake, fought against a name change during World War II. Residents pointed out that the swastika existed as a good luck charm for four thousand years before it was fouled by the Nazis. Hitler liked the symbol because of its German name, too— *Hakenkreuz* 'hooked or chopped cross,' a seeming rebuke to Christianity. Swastika in Sanskrit is *svastika* 'well-being symbol' from *svasti* 'well-being' and hence 'good luck,' being compounded of *su* + *asti*. *Su* 'good' is cognate with Greek *eu* in English words like euphonious 'good-sounding' and euphemism 'good-speaking.' *Asti* 'being' is related to the Latin and Greek verbs of being with forms like *est* and ἐστί, *esti*.

SCOTS GAELIC BANNOCK

Bannock is also called trail biscuit, bush bread, river cake, and galette. The word is Scots Gaelic, *bannach*, for a thin oatmeal cake. As to its taste, it is perhaps best to recall Dr. Samuel Johnson's definition in his famous dictionary (1755): "Oats, *n.* a grain which in England is fed to horses, but in Scotland supports the people." To Canadian settlers bannock was flour, lard, baking powder, salt and water, done over an outdoor fire in a frying pan if one was on the trail, and at home pan-fried or baked in an oven. This rough bread, not for milady's dainty palate, is remembered in the little town of Bannock, Saskatchewan.

SPROGS

Sprogs shows up in phrases like "Get your sprogs off my clean rug, you lummox!" In Irish and Scottish Gaelic, *spaug* or *spag* is a big foot or boot. On Prince Edward Island, sprogs are indeed boots or big feet.

SPANISH

Spanish place names in Canada abound on the west coast, with a few others dotting the interior. Orillia, Ontario, is the Spanish word for 'riverbank or shore.' The place was named by Sir Peregrine Maitland, Lieutenant-Governor of Upper Canada (1818–1828) who had done military duty in Spain. Quadra Island and the electoral district Vancouver-Quadra are both named for Juan Francisco de la Bodega y Quadra, of the Spanish navy, who sailed on two exploratory voyages up the B.C. coast in 1755 and 1779. Port Alberni commemorates Don Pedro de Alberni, founder of a failed Spanish colony at

Nootka, B.C. Juan de Fuca Strait was probably not first seen by Juan de Fuca, a Spanish-Greek sailor whose real name was Apostolos Valeranos. The Spanish River in Ontario recalls a pioneering Spaniard who married a native woman and homesteaded on the river's banks. Nearby Espanola is an Englishing of l'Espagnol, the way local French speakers referred to the same pioneer.

SWEDISH
OMBUDSMAN

This office of a political representative for citizens who feel abused by a government originated in Sweden in 1809. *Ombud* is a Swedish word for 'agent.' The first ombudsman in Canada or North America was G.B. McClellan, a former RCMP commissioner who was appointed in 1967 as ombudsman of Alberta.

There are also a few Swedish place names, such as Stockholm, Saskatchewan.

TLINGIT
HOOTCH

Tlingit is a member of the Na-dené family of languages. It is spoken by a people inhabiting southern Alaska and some offshore islands. In 1981 approximately 1500 people still spoke the language. *Tlingit* in Tlingit means 'the people.' Hootch, a word for homebrew, first popularized in the Yukon during the days of the Klondike gold rush, has spread across Canada. Hootch is short for hootchinoo, which is the mangled English form of a word in the Tlingit language, *khutsnuwu*, or Grizzly Bear Fort, the name of a people and their village on Admiralty Island, where hootch was first brewed from molasses, yeast, local berries, and other ingredients best left veiled from mortal knowledge. Place names of Tlingit origin include the Stikine River—following the worldwide habit of naming rivers with the local word for river. *Stikine* means 'great river' in Tlingit.

TSIMSHIAN

Tsimshian is a Penutian language of a people living on the north Pacific coast. The name means 'of the Skeena River.' A little place near Prince Rupert, B.C., is Kitwanga, which is Tsimshian for 'many-rabbits-people.' Canadian English also has the Tsimshian word *huldowokit* for a sorcerer who can send evil thoughts by telepathy to injure another person. The word may also refer to the evil spirit so sent.

TUNGUS
PIKA

Pika is one of the few words that entered Canadian English from Tungus, a language of eastern Siberia. This engaging little varmit—the Tungus call it *piika*—also lives in our western mountains. The little mammal is sometimes called the rock rabbit or the whistling hare, because it signals danger with a high-pitched call. The pika burrows in grassy hills where it hoards dried hay stashes for winter munching.

TURKISH
TAIGA

Taiga is the correct geographical label for the subarctic zone of coniferous forests. Cold and dry, taiga shrubs and low trees provide browse for caribou. It is a Russian word originally applied to the vast conifer stands that swathe their subarctic. The word, though, comes from Turkish, where *dag* means 'mountain.' It entered Russian through Turkestan where it once meant 'wooded hill country.'

UKRAINIAN
BANDURIA

The banduria is the Ukrainian national folk music instrument, frequently seen in Canada wherever Ukrainian folk dance troupes perform. It is a large, lutelike instrument with a big sounding board and a long neck where its strings are plucked. The word came into Ukrainian from Spanish, in which a similar instrument is the *bandurría*. The earliest form known is the Greek πανδοῦρα, *pandoura*.

PYSANKY (THOSE EASTER EGGS!)

Pysanky are the well-known Ukrainian Easter eggs (sing. *pysanka*), decorated with traditional Ukrainian designs and folk motifs. There are also *krashanky* (sing. *krashanka*), which are dipped in dye of one solid colour. *Krashanky* are hard-boiled and can be eaten, unlike *pysanky*. The special pen used to decorate *pysanky* is called a *kistka*.

There are many Ukrainian place names in our prairie provinces. Alberta has Ispas 'Saviour'; Mazeppa, after a Ukrainian folk hero; and Stry, Slawa, and Sniatyn.

TSYMBALY

The *tsymbaly* is a Ukrainian dulcimer brought to Canada by immigrants from Western Ukraine. The instrument's strings, stretched across a wooden sounding board, are struck by a pair of small hammers. The word entered Ukrainian from Russian, цымбáлы, *tsyembalye*, which means 'cymbals.' But its form is influenced by *czimbalom*, the Hungarian dulcimer. All the Slavic and Hungarian words, as well as French *cymbalon*, originate in the ancient Greek term κύμβαλον, *kumbalon*, which was a small cup-shaped cymbal. The root is pervasive in all Indo-European languages, since the cymbal was one of the earliest musical instruments.

WELSH
BANGOR

Bangor in Saskatchewan was named by a very interesting group of immigrants who came to the prairie province from Patagonia in southern Argentina. Upon arrival, they spoke only Welsh and Spanish. Bangor is a town in north Wales that was the site of a very early Christian monastery. A bangor in Welsh was a place for monks built of wattle and daub.

MADOC

Madoc in central Ontario, a few miles above Belleville, is one of Canada's few place names from Welsh, worthwhile recalling so that St. David, patron saint of Wales, will smile upon us. In Welsh mythology, Madoc was a mighty explorer and prince who sailed from Wales and discovered North America around 1170 A.D.

PENGUIN

Penguin as a bird name probably originated in Newfoundland, among early Breton fishermen. It referred not to the present penguin, a bird never found in northern waters, but to the extinct great auk. There is a printed reference in 1578 to Newfoundland's Penguin Island. But the birds described are auks.

Breton is a living language of northern France closely linked, in the Brythonic language family, with Cornish, Manx, and Welsh tongues of the British Isles. For example, penguin as the name of an island breaks up nicely into two Breton roots: *pen* 'headland of an island' + *gwyn* 'white.' Now it so happens that Penguin Island did have a headland of whitish rocks, as reported by early explorers. We know the Celtic colour word *gwyn* from its frequent appearance in personal female names like Gwendolyn, King Arthur's Guinevere, and Gwyneth, as well as Gwyn used as a male first name in Welsh and English. The general sense in the personal name words is 'fair-skinned one or fair-haired one.'

WOODS
CREE
SHAGANAPPY

Shaganappy is a Canadian prairie adjective frequently and fondly used in W.O. Mitchell's collection of tales about *Jake and the Kid*. Its general import is run-down, inferior, cheap. The word began life in Woods Cree as a noun, *pishagan-abii*, literally 'frayed cord,' which was their term for a rawhide thong. Because the shaggy, dumpy ponies that pulled carts and wagons in the early west were often hitched up with rough rawhide harnesses, it came to be applied to the poor beasts of burden as well. Mitchell likes the word so much that he also uses it in his novel *The Kite*.

Hirsch in southern Saskatchewan is the site of a colony founded in 1892 by a Jewish Colonization Association begun by Baron de Hirsch. Forty-seven families settled here, each with a $500 loan if they homesteaded on colony land.

As Jewish migrants during the Diaspora spread up the Rhine Valley in medieval Germany, they often adopted Germanic names, and their dialect, begun here, became known as Yiddish. After settling, some Jewish merchants took last names based on the signs on their shops. Hirsch is such a surname. It's German for 'deer.' The founder of the name may have had the painting of a deer above the door of his shop. Such a sign meant that his true first name in Hebrew was Naphtali. Certain biblical names like Naphtali had symbols associated with them. This symbol was called a kinnui. For example, in the Bible, Jacob blesses Naphtali and calls him "a swift-footed deer." Thus deer becomes the kinnui of the male personal name Naphtali. So it may be used to represent any Naphtali who operates a business, by having a deer sign at the front door of his shop.

All the following Jewish surnames arise from the Naphtali-kinnui-Hirsch nexus: Herschenhorn and Hirschhorn (deer[s'] antler), Herschel, Herz, Herzog, Hirschfeld, the French Cerf, and the Slavic Jellinek, Jellin, and Yellin. Among the most famous Jewish surnames to originate in this manner is that of the banking family, Rothschild. Rot + Schild meant the founding ancestor could be found "at the sign of the *red shield*."

Edenbridge in Saskatchewan began as another Jewish colony with the name Yiddenbridge. Although "yid" has become a racist insult in English, it is certainly nothing of the kind in Yiddish, where it is simply the word for a Jewish person. The plural might be spelled Yidden in English. *Yid*, like many words in Yiddish, comes from Hebrew where *yehudi* means a Jew or literally 'of Judah's tribe.'

YIDDISH
HIRSCH

EDENBRIDGE

CHAPTER 13   THE FOUR SEASONS

Spring, summer, fall, & winter words

A season in Old French, *seson*, was a time of sowing, from the Latin noun *satio, sationis* 'seed-time.' The labels of our seasons are among the oldest words in English, except for autumn.

Autumn we borrowed from Latin *autumnus* 'the harvest time of plenty.' The ancient Romans deemed autumn related to the verb *augere* 'to increase,' because the crops increase and give their yield at harvest time. Modern etymologists at first dismissed this explanation as a quaint folk etymology. Many now think it might just be correct. Others say the Romans originally named the fall season *vertumnus* from *vertere* 'to turn,' since it is the season when the weather turns from warm to cold. But they kept getting their seasonal name *vertumnus* mixed up with an Etruscan god of the seasons named *Vertumnus* (similar in form but stemming from quite different Etruscan roots—we think). So the Romans altered the first syllable and made the word *autumnus*. Such a crafty transformation would be unique to Roman word formation. Unique events in linguistic history ought to be treated with caution. It is perhaps best to settle for etymologist Eric Partridge's shrug of a label "o.o.o."—of obscure origin.

Spring springs from the springing up of new green plants. Summer comes from Proto-Germanic where the root **sem* seems to mean simply that, summer. Fall, now chiefly North American for the season when leaves fall, did begin in England as a synonym for autumn in the middle of the sixteenth century.

Winter's root is wet, literally. The same Germanic root that gives water and wet makes the first vowel nasal and so adds an "n," thus **ued* → **wet* → **went* → **wint* → *winter*. Or winter may stretch all the way back to a root form in prehistoric Indo-European **ueid* that gives Celtic words for 'white'; compare for example Old Irish *find* 'white,' and many other Celtic cognates like Welsh *gwyn* 'white' and perhaps even the Druids 'people of the white oak' from **dru-ueid* or oak-white. **Ueid* could also make the Druids the 'oak-knowers' from their veneration of the tree and its mistletoe.

Now toss all that etymological nitpicking to one side. English supplies verbs to describe what the critters do seasonally. To hibernate is to pass the winter in a state of torpor. To estivate is to the pass the summer so. But we need a verb to describe what many of us do all the year round. With all due humility, I suggest **totannate** from Latin, *totum* 'all' + *annum* 'year' meaning to pass the whole year in a state of torpor.

Real Canucks, of course, are not torpid navel-gazers, and it is no surprise that we have coined more new winter words than spring, summer, or autumn words. We may lollygag through the other seasons, but the lethal Canadian winter must be wrestled, tricked, subdued, and flung to the temporal mat.

SPRING
SARAH BINKS

When spring arrives, what songstress is more fitting to welcome March 21, the day of the vernal equinox, than Sarah Binks. Manitoban humourist Paul Hiebert created the amateur prairie poet in his 1947 spoof of homey versifiers. Sarah wrote in her "Song to the Four Seasons":

Spring is here, the breezes blowing,
Four inches of top-soil going, going;
Farm ducks rolling across the prairie;
Spring is here—how nice and airy!

BLINDMAN'S SNOW

On Prince Edward Island, blindman's snow was a late snowfall in the spring that local folk medicine said was good for the eyes. The melted snow had reputed power to cure other bodily ills. Sore feet were soaked in the melt-water. A snow in late April or May might also be called poor man's fertilizer.

MAI

Mai was a term used by French Canadians, especially voyageurs, to name a tree used as a landmark. A pine or a spruce on a promontory had its lower limbs cut off so it would stand out clearly and be visible from an approaching canoe. *Un mai* could be used to indicate a place of portage or a change of direction. Canadian English borrowed the idea but translated it as maypole, which is not what *mai* meant in old French. *L'arbre de mai* 'the maytree' was a custom in the French countryside that consisted of planting a spring sapling each year in honour of or in memory of someone held dear.

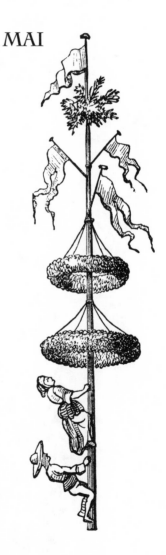

When early French immigrants reached North America they were interested to discover native peoples of the north had the custom of the lobstick. The Cree called it *piskootenusk*. A prominent pine or spruce was trimmed of its lower branches to commemorate a friend, or—much more ancient—the man who cut the tree made it a living, botanical embodiment of his spirit. The lobstick was a mysterious talisman whose health as a plant reflected the health of the human's spirit. But the lobstick would fall when the human died.

The veneration of trees, the sacred ground of groves, and the tree as symbol of the male warrior spirit are all ancient and widespread among northern peoples around the world. Dancing about the maypole, selecting a May Queen, and lighting bonfires are remnants of spring fertility ceremonies. With bark peeled, glistening resinously in the spring sun, the maypole was indeed a giant phallus. Men and women circled it with joy and song, paying honour to the fecundating principle of nature. But now, in this penis-hating end of the century, let us convene all apostles of misandry to ensure that such frolic is banned.

ROBIN STORM

You've opened the cottage, primed the pump, set the summer chairs on the new cedar deck, shared a christening goblet of Chateau Qui Sait, and, just as you settle into the hammock to imbibe the piney brio of it all, a thick snow squall blows in across the lake to welcome the start of June. It's a late-in-the-season storm familiar to most Canadians, and some call it a robin storm, in a cheerful attempt to lessen its chill.

SPRING-BURN

Spring-burn brings back pioneer land clearing methods. One chopped down trees in the fall and winter. The first dry spell gave opportunity to burn off all the trees not used as fuel or lumber. This might also be done to collect potash used in homemade soap. Excessive or too vast a spring-burn eventually resulted in eroded, worthless soils. The land was indeed clear, forever.

SUMMER
GELATO

Gelato is a splendid summer gift to Canada by immigrants from Italy. The adjective means 'frozen' or 'icy.' The noun means the unique, deep-flavoured ice cream whose tastiest specimens I have lapped up in Toronto's Little Italy. Home-made in small batches, it is vivid on the tongue with natural flavourings that access one's taste buds quickly and efficiently since *gelato* is not glopped up with excess milk solids and fats as are most North American ice creams. Did Marco Polo bring the idea of ice cream back from China? Legend says the Chinese iced cream as early as 3000 B.C. Italy has been pre-dominant in its manufacture since medieval times. The ice

cream cone dates only from 1909. *Gelato da passeggio*, ice cream on a stick, is also an Italian invention. And let's be italophilic. One knows *gelato alla fragola* is going to taste better than strawberry ice cream, particularly when made with small, wild strawberries grown juicy ripe in the crevice of some Muskoka boulder.

AUTUMN
THE FALL OF THE LEAF

The fall of the leaf is the full phrase, as old as Shakespeare, that gives us our common word for autumn. North American immigrants gave it wider currency here than it has today in England. On the day of the autumn equinox it ought to be pleasant to note the Elizabethan phrase may still be heard now and then in Newfoundland English. An elderly man or woman reflecting on his or her years may say, "I be in the fall of the leaf."

Nosey weather on Prince Edward Island means it's time to don wool sweaters and warm caps, and that it's cold and windy enough to give anyone working outdoors the sniffles.

GETTING THE STRAP

On any first fall day of school for any young scholar, it will be morally and politically quite incorrect to recall the bad old days of corporal punishment in Canadian schools. Many of us have at least heard of the now-illegal rubber strap applied to hands and behind. But, back in the 1820s and 1830s when unregulated one-room school houses began to spring up across what would become Canada, the errant pupil could be switched with a willow rod or a tawse, a nasty Scottish leather strap cut into narrow strips at the end. If a pupil was found out as a liar, hot mustard might be applied to his tongue. If one chatted excessively during instruction, one might have a thick wooden stick placed in one's mouth with the injunction, "Keep it there until recess!" Thank goodness, student behaviour has improved so greatly over the years that such excesses are no longer required.

QUICK CHALK

Homemade chalk? School days of yore, in remote classrooms in the Canadian wilderness, often dictated make-do solutions to supply shortages. Here's one such recipe, quoted in Jean Cochrane's *The One-Room School in Canada*. For homemade chalk: "Five pounds of plaster of Paris and one pound of wheat flower; mix with water and knead. Roll it on a pin board 3 feet × 9 inches. Roll mass into a ball. Cut slices from it and then cut in strips. Then roll smooth and round. Dry them for at least 12 hours."

SCHOOL CAR

Fall signals the tolling of school bells, or perhaps nowadays it is an electronic jolt applied directly to the student spinal cord. Far more innocent and beneficent was the school car, an Ontario innovation, a travelling schoolroom lodged in a converted railway car, invented in 1926 by Ontario public school teacher, Fred Sloman. By the late 1940s northern Ontario had seven such vehicles. They stopped on a remote siding for several days and children came out of the bush for classes and to get homework to do, then the school car moved down the track to the next isolated siding.

TEACHERAGE

Teacherage was used in the last century and early in this one, on the prairies and in Ontario, to denote a little house that a teacher lived in, often one very cheaply built by the local school board. It is a formation based on previous words like parsonage and vicarage.

WINTER BIVVER

Bivver is a wintry Newfoundland verb, meaning 'to shiver and shake,' especially with cold. *I'se all a-bivverrrrr this morning* = I'm shaking with the cold. A trilled r like brrrrr! is often added facetiously to the end of the word. As a noun, bivver means a trembling of the lips, or just a shaking. The exact origin of this onomatopoeic verb is lost. Could it be a nursery word for shiver? In any case, succinct aptness merits its wider dispersal. Snowmobilers ought to bivver as they juggernaut smelly, whining engines over pristine snow mounds and perhaps rare plants underneath.

TO BLOW THE XMAS PUDDING

To blow the Christmas pudding is not to commit culinary error. Picture instead a warm noon kitchen on a Christmas Day in Newfoundland. Wreathed in rummy steam, the cook proudly bears the pudding from the stove and prepares to sprinkle final splashings of the amber distillate on its thick-fruited and stout-nutted goodness. At the kitchen door a rifle shot rings clear across the cold air to honour deft cookery and add a festive sound. Blowing

the Christmas pudding is a memory of more ancient noble feasts where hot puddings were piped to high table, or even saluted with cornet and drum as they were borne in upon high-held silver plates.

BOBSKATES

My father, Alfred M. Casselman, remembered learning to skate on a farm pond near the town of Williamsburg, Ontario, in the winter of 1912, on a pair of hand-me-down bobskates. A bob was one of the wooden runners on a bobsleigh or bobsled. Bobskates had two wooden runners with the blade end of blunt steel, and a pair of leather straps so one could quickly attach the bobskates even to an old pair of work boots. The very word *bobskates* summoned for him long-ago Saturday afternoons when winter chores were done, and he and his brothers and a couple of cousins were numerous enough to field an entire hockey team of Casselmans.

C'EST L'HIVER

In 1965 *chansonnier* Gilles Vigneault penned what has become an unofficial anthem of Québec, "Mon Pays," a song whose opening lyric speaks to all Canadians who are not Florida-nesting snowbirds: *Mon pays, ce n'est pas un pays, c'est l'hiver,* 'My country, it's not a country, it's winter.' Although a sentimental favourite, the lyrics of the song are actually a bleak howl of despair. Everywhere the singer looks to find identity and warmth, he instead encounters an obliterating and cold nature. A garden is not a garden, but a bare plain. A road is not a road, it's a ghastly blank of snow. Indifferent, monstrous nature—greenly or whitely waiting to devour the puny human pioneer—is a constant through much Canadian literature, as Margaret Atwood pointed out in *Survival*, her critical appraisal of this theme.

GUIGNOLÉE

La Guignolée is a New Year's Eve tradition in towns and villages along the St. Lawrence, in which groups of young men, *les guignoleux*, clad in bright winter garb, go from house to house singing Christmas carols and knocking on each door with a stick in time to the rhythm of the song. When the door is opened, they beg money for the poor.

This Québécois coinage derives from the name *Guignol*, a puppet figure much like the English Mr. Punch in Punch and Judy puppet shows. Guignol was a hand-operated marionette featured in puppet stories filled with blood and gore, hence the English borrowing to describe gruesome theatrical films or performances: Grand Guignol. There was a popular theatre in Paris with this name where such marionette performances were given. Secondary meanings of *Guignol* developed in French such as fool, policeman, and any farcical tomfoolery. It is from the later sense that early Quebecers coined *Guignolée* to describe their boisterous but kind-hearted shenanigans in the snow.

ICE-BLINK

In arctic or subarctic waters an experienced mariner can often predict massive sea ice long before it is visible, by looking up. Ice-blink is a strange whitish glow near the horizon or on distant clouds caused by light reflected off the ice onto clouds or onto moisture in the atmosphere. But to a visiting landlubber at sea in the arctic for a first voyage, the blink of the ice is as spooky as the shrieks and banshee noises ice makes in its mindless sundering, grinding, and bullying.

MAL DE RAQUETTE

Mal de raquette? A disorder, eh? Could it mean sick of visiting the Windsor Casino? No. It's snowshoe lameness, a malady whose pain and indigenousness are incontrovertible. Joints swell and taut muscles stretch to the snapping point after too many miles of the peculiar stride that is necessary in walking on snowshoes. Strained tendons may also cause vivid currents of pain to shoot up and down the nerves of the leg. But as one lies recuperating, shins slathered with some emollient guck, as the pain abates, one must always remember how much more virtuous the snowshoer is than the common snowmobiler. It is this ennobling thought that will propel one once more out into the snowy barrens, cocked of eye and webbed of foot.

MON ONCLE ANTOINE

Mon Oncle Antoine are powerful winter words for me, since they comprise the title of my favourite Canadian film. Directed in 1971 by Claude Jutra, it's the story of a few lives in a general store in a small one-company village in Québec. A boy begins his journey to adulthood on a Christmas Eve not so long ago. His wonder about the adults who rule his innocent world flickers and changes into cynical knowledge over the course of the holidays one year. Jutra's bleak masterpiece is about the winter of our fate, about repression freezing the genial current of our humanity, and about the little thaws of joy that melt us together briefly.

QUELQUES ARPENTS DE NEIGE

Quelques arpents de neige is Voltaire's famous dismissal of Canada as 'a few acres of snow.' The French literary giant delivered the chop in *Candide* (1759). An *arpent* was a French land measure approximately equivalent to 1½ acres. In 1759, Major-General James Wolfe was shot to death during the Battle of the Plains of Abraham, and in that year Québec fell to the British. As a Frenchman, Voltaire detested the expense of the war in men and arms and never ceased in his belief that Canada was not worth one drop of French blood. On the eve of the battle, Wolfe recited Gray's "Elegy, Written in a Country Churchyard," which contains the following stanza:

> *The boast of heraldry, the pomp of power,*
> *And all that beauty, all that wealth e'er gave,*
> *Awaits alike the inevitable hour.*
> *The paths of glory lead but to the grave.*

According to popular historian Francis Parkman in *Montcalm and Wolfe* (1884), the general then turned to the officers with him and said, "Gentlemen, I would rather have written those lines than take Québec tomorrow."

RABBITS' CANDLES

If you have ever gazed out a winter window in postblizzard ecstasy, then you have seen rabbits' candles, sparklings of starlight or moonlight on new fallen snow. This is a folksy Prince Edward Island expression found in *Emily of the New Moon* (1923) by Lucy Maud Montgomery.

RED SNOW

Red snow is a botanical phenomenon of the arctic produced by green algae, *Protococcus nivalis*, that grows quickly on top of snow and then turns bright red. Red snow was noted in 1818 by Sir John Ross, a British adventurer who explored Baffin Island.

RÉGALE

The special Canadian use of this medieval French word for festive celebration involved the canniness of the superintendent factors of the North West Company, and then the Hudson's Bay Company. Drinking on post property was discouraged. But when trappers were setting out on a long, possibly hazardous canoe journey, probably returning to tend distant traplines, they were issued a pint of rum, with the understanding that said spirits should be drunk well away from the fort. A rum *régale* might be passed out to men coming in after a long trip, too, as long as they went off in the bush to drink it. A ration of liquor given out on New Year's Eve or near Christmas was also a *régale*.

SNOWY WORDS OF QUÉBEC

Les Québécois coined new words to describe winter below and above the St. Lawrence River, and they also extended the meanings of European French words, thus *bordée* acquires the new Canadian sense of 'a heavy snowfall' while in sixteenth-century France the word began lexical life as a term for a line of cannons ranged along one side of a ship. *La bordée* also meant firing these cannons in unison to deliver a broadside.

Ice piled up on riverbanks or shores of lakes is *bordage* or *bordillon*. Quebecers created *banc de neige* 'snow bank,' and *bouette* 'melting snow.' Wintry verbs burgeon, too. *Botter* means 'to get one's shoes or boots all gummed up with packed snow.' *Embourber* is 'to get a car stuck in the snow.' The reflexive *s'embourber* is 'to sink into the snow oneself.' *Neige* 'snow' gives the Québécoise neology *neigeailler* in which the root takes the common diminutive verbal ending *-ailler* to produce the useful impersonal form *il neigeaille* 'it's snowing a little,' 'it's just a light dusting of snow.'

If you have to make a road across a frozen lake or river you might set broken-off branches of pine or spruce into the ice to indicate where the course of the road will be even after a winter storm covers the roadway itself. Such a marker line is called *une balise* in Québec. In France it's a word for buoy, and in France *baliser* means 'to mark out a water channel with beacons' or 'to equip an airport runway with approach lights.'

A Québec word borrowed into Canadian maritime English is *frasil* or *frazil* for the slushy-chunky floes of small ice pieces that move on the surface of running water early in the spring. It might have begun as a French word for 'cinders,' *frasil*. It might stem from the verb *fraiser*, 'to shell beans' or Québec French could have borrowed it from frazzle, which can mean 'to fray, to come undone.'

On Valentine's Day we might ponder stumping, a pioneer way of announcing love. In 1845 Mrs. F. Beavan wrote *Sketches and Tales Illustrative of Life in New Brunswick, North America.* She writes that stumping was a backwoods method of publishing the banns. The engaged twosome would write their names and the announcement of their wedding on slips of paper and then stick them in the many stumps that lined the corduroy roads of Victorian New Brunswick. Passers-by who spotted the papers could unfurl them, read the latest wedding news, then carefully put them back in the holes in the stump so that the next neighbour to pass by in a buggy could catch up on the connubial bliss soon to ensue. How much more romantic was this than having the notice read from a pulpit!

Ye fine old New Brunswick courting practice of

STUMPING

That M.P.'s got a mouth on him that moves like a whip-poor-will's ass end

Feisty phrases and blunt words used to make up the Canadian political vocabulary on the grass-roots level. For example, at a political rally in Dundas county in the 1930s, Mitch Hepburn, the Liberal premier of Ontario, jumped up on a manure spreader and began his speech, "First time in my life I ever spoke from a Tory platform!" But, as one moves closer to Ottawa and the deep-piled dens of power, circumlocution and weasel words drown out plain speech. Yes, nowadays the brainless gobbledygook of sound-bite political correctness coats any clear word with a rich syrup of unction and specious caring. A one-legged janitor is a *monopodally unique, interior environmental consultant*. So, if you catch him malingering, don't you dare say, "Just mop, mope. And cut out those cheap Long John Silver imitations. And I know damn well you *sold* that leg to a Mexican dog food factory to finance your hydroponic marijuana operation in Fort Erie." No, if you seek political approval, don't ever say that. Just smile—crookedly.

BENNETT BUGGY

R.B. Bennett was prime minister of Canada (1930–35) and took the heat for the early thirties Depression and for his aloof disregard for the hardships of ordinary Canadians. He was more cordially loathed than any other prime minister in our history—until the advent of smiling Brian Mulroney. On the prairies in the 1930s, when few could afford gasoline, some farmers would remove the engine from their automobile, and hitch up a team of horses to pull the car. The resultant contraption was known all across the suffering dominion as a Bennett buggy.

BOTHERATION SCHEME

The Botheration Scheme was a popular nineteenth-century putdown among anticonfederation writers, including Nova Scotia's cantankerous journalist-turned-politician, Joseph Howe, who used it in 1865 as the title of a series of newspaper articles in the Halifax *Morning Chronicle*. Botheration was a comic lengthening of bother. "Bother it!" was a Victorian minced oath for "Bugger it!" However, it was not enough of a bother for Howe to turn down membership in John A. Macdonald's cabinet. After the fact of Confederation, Howe served in several posts including secretary of state—always a gadfly and sometimes a political embarrassment to the government.

FISHOCRACY

Fishocracy is a term from Newfoundland's long history. In the 1880s it described the wealthy merchants who controlled the export of fish, who liked things just the way they were (as the rich so often do), and who were intensely against the idea that Newfoundland should govern itself. The ending -*cracy* from the Greek κρατία for power or rule is the same that decorates such terms as bureaucracy, democracy, and plutocracy.

FUDDLE-DUDDLE

It was February 16, 1971, a day that will live forever in the annals of periphrastic namby-pambyism, a day on which Prime Minister Pierre Elliott Trudeau coined this infamous euphemism, discombobulating boobs everywhere, but, viewed from the perspective of Canadian timidity, adding a useful circumlocution to our language. He had been caught in the House of Commons silently mouthing a four-letter word. But outside the house he told the press he'd said "fuddle-duddle." As one Parliament Hill wag observed, "The prime minister wishes to be obscene and not heard."

GRITS

One axiom of Canadian politics: radicals of either extreme must move toward the centre to gain power. This is nowhere more evident than in the history of Canadian Liberalism. Liberals began as the party of those opposed to colonial vested interests, suspicious of the governor and his ruling clique. Consider the Clear Grit Party, leftist reformers who first elected candidates in Upper Canada in the 1850s. Clear grit was an adjectival phrase that meant stubborn. The Clear Grits eventually merged with the Liberal party. And Liberals today still bear their nickname, the Grits.

KING OR CHAOS

Soup kitchens were everywhere, but there was no broth at all that could warm the soul of those unemployed Canadians who had lost all hope. It was the middle of the Great Depression in 1935. Every person in the country not working hated the Conservative Prime Minister, snooty R.B. Bennett. So the Liberals ran Mackenzie King with this political slogan, and they crushed the Tories flat. King, a Machiavelli of compromise and political expediency, often discussed upcoming policy with the ghost of his dead dog, and later shared tea and scones with spectral wisps of his mommy. Newspapers of the day chose not to reveal his quick trips to Toronto to visit prostitutes.

KNIGHT OF THE RED WIG

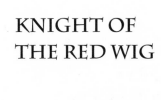

William Lyon Mackenzie (1795–1861) was a pioneering editor of his own newspaper, *The Colonial Advocate*, and leader of the reform movement that produced the abortive 1837 Rebellion in Upper Canada. Mackenzie was of short stature and had red hair, thus the supposed insult when political opponents dubbed him "Knight of the Red Wig." Another scoffing nickname of the fiery journalist was "Little Mac." Both labels only buffed his feisty image.

LAND SCRIP

Land scrip is short for land script. After the Riel Rebellion of 1870, the government of Canada issued a certificate to any Métis born before 1870. This scrip could be exchanged for 240 acres of prairie land or $240. Unscrupulous real estate speculators bought scrips from unsuspecting Métis for a few dollars or in exchange for a new rifle. These "scrip" millionaires then sold the land at very favourable mark-ups to incoming white settlers.

MAC-PAPS

Mac-Paps were Canadian volunteers of the Mackenzie-Papineau Battalion (1937–38) who fought against Franco in the Spanish Civil War. Among them was Canadian writer Hugh Garner. They were part of the International Brigades which numbered many Communists. This fact upset Prime Minister Mackenzie King who was seriously worried Canadians would think the battalion bore his name and approval. Also perturbed no end were stuffy military poobahs of Ottawa. So they whipped through Parliament the Foreign Enlistment Act of 1937, which stated that no Canucks could fight in foreign wars. The Battalion took its name from William Lyon Mackenzie and Louis-Joseph Papineau, radical leaders of the abortive 1837 Rebellion.

SOVEREIGNTY

Sovereignty ranks as one of the most duplicitous weasel words in late twentieth-century Canadian history. Sovereignty and sovereignty-association were vile euphemisms concocted by the Parti Québécois, to soft-pedal its separatism to antsy Québec voters. Anglophone journalists helped the PQ in its sly, word-shifting sleaziness by using sovereignty instead of the starker, apter nouns: independence and separation.

TORY TORONTO

Toronto was HQ for the Big Blue Machine, the Progressive Conservative power bloc and well-oiled election organization that ran Ontario from 1943 to 1985 under the premiers George Drew, Leslie Frost, John Robarts, and William Davis. But the province's reputation as a Conservative stronghold had already caused comment a century before. British novelist Charles Dickens visited Hogtown in 1842, and wrote back to his friend and later biographer John Foster, "The wild and rabid toryism of Toronto is, I speak seriously, *appalling*" [italics are Dickens].

THE WAFFLE

Jim Laxer, Mel Watkins, and nine other NDP young radical turks met on April 29, 1969, to form an extreme left-wing socialist group inside the New Democratic Party. Their manifesto identified big American companies with Canadian branch plants as a threat to our independence. The *Globe and Mail* called it the Waffle Manifesto. The NDP faction laughingly adopted it as their title. Official NDP historians, of course, would like to claim the name as their own creation, so they point to a 1969 speech by then federal MP Ed Broadbent who was chided at a political rally for waffling during an answer. Broadbent said, "I'd rather waffle to the left than waffle to the right." But that speech took place after the *Globe* editorial was printed. The Waffle alienated trade unions by intemperate criticism, and helped begin the disenchantment of the union movement with the NDP. Wafflers were purged by the NDP, and the caucus had dissipated by the mid-seventies.

In 1940 the first Canadians were conscripted for home defence in World War II. Military bigwigs, and many citizens who had volunteered to fight, looked down on conscriptees, and called them zombies, after mythical creatures of Caribbean voodoo lore; they were dead but were still walking around. The false implication was that they were cowards because they had not volunteered.

ZOMBIES

"I'd like to be an atheist, but I'm subject to chest pains."

Human beings have dreamed more heavens than the sky can hold, and conjured more hells than Jerry Falwell can assign the damned to. As architects of the hereafter, most fundamentalist religions build the shabbiest of paradises. Their teeny-weeny cubicles of eternal salvation have room only for themselves. The narrow meanness of many contemporary religions would, it seems to me, deeply offend their founders. Reading the New Testament, how can one imagine Jesus flinging shut the gates of heaven on troubled women who have had abortions, on gay people, on those who pray to gods not stamped with the right-wing Christian seal of approval? Nor are we sucked in by that current excuse for hatred: "Hate the sin, not the sinner." Oh, but they do hate—and kill. How tawdry is the devotion that congratulates and defines itself by the number of human beings it can loathe!

In this chapter a mere sampling of Canadian pioneer urges will show how eager we have been to assign place names of celestial and demonic omen to the lands and waters of home. We'll look at only one of the multitude of rich, beautiful creation myths of native peoples, and we will hear within the Blackfoot story, echoes of Eden.

BLACKFOOT CREATION STORY

Here is part of one version of the Siksika or Blackfoot myth of creation, as recorded in the *Blackfoot Lodge Tales* by George Bird Grinnell.

One day Na'pi *'old man' came out of the south to make the world. As he travelled through the void he stopped to make earth and rocks and birds and animals. Old Man determined that he would make a woman and a child; so he formed them both—the woman and the child, her son—of clay. After he had moulded the clay in human shape, he said to the clay, "You must be people," and then he covered it up and went away.*

The next morning he went to the place and took the covering off, and saw that the clay shapes had changed a little. The second morning there was still more change, and the third still more. The fourth morning he went to the place, took the covering off, looked at the images, and told them to rise and walk; and they did so. They walked to the river with their Maker . . .

As they were standing by the river, the woman said to him, "How is it? Will we always live? Will there be no end to it?" Old Man said, "I have never thought of that. We will have to decide it. I will take this buffalo chip and throw it in the river. If it floats, when people die, in four days they will become alive again; they will die only for four days. But if it sinks, there will be an end to them." He threw the chip in the river, and it floated.

But the woman turned and picked up a stone, and said, "No, I will throw this stone in the river; if it floats, we will always live, if it sinks people must die, that they may always be sorry for each other." The woman threw the stone into the water, and it sank. "There," said Old Man, "you have chosen. There will be an end to them."

COMMENTS ON THE BLACKFOOT STORY

The most striking feature in the Siksika myth is the pottery metaphor: a god formed humans from clay and left them a few days to dry under cover (i.e., in the oven), like pots made by any people who have learned to fire clay. This is a worldwide element in creation stories. Compare the Hebrew and Christian version in Genesis 2:6, 7 as translated in the King James version of 1611: "There went up a mist from the earth, and watered the whole face of the ground. And the Lord God formed man of the dust of the ground." So, even today, in brickyards of the Middle East, does the brickmaker sprinkle water on the clay before kneading it into shape. The Bible's name for the first man reflects this, too. Adam derives from Hebrew *'adamah* 'clay' or 'red earth of Israel.' The ultimately Latin word *human* also reflects this pottery myth. The prime meaning of Latin *humanus* is 'clayey' or made of *humus* 'earth, soil, clay.' The Roman word for human being or man, *homo*, as in our species *Homo sapiens*, also stems from the same root. In Old Latin it was *hemo* 'the earthen one' or 'the person of clay.' The idea must have occurred early in human history, when primitive humans first dug up an interred body to discover bones and dust. Dust thou art; to dust shalt thou return.

Another note in the Siksika creation story strikes us with its modern, casual humour. Whether humans are mortal or immortal depends on whether a dried piece of buffalo dung will float. The cosmic dice are tossed, and ya' takes yer chance, bub.

To the mythic, creational part of the story is added a mysogynist fable. Even for peoples of the American plains, it is woman who messes up paradise. The war between the sexes is waged in myth, too. Humans could have been eternal, but a woman interfered, and brought death to humanity. This was a common bit of blame-laying in fables invented by men. Again there are biblical parallels. Remember how Eve got way too friendly with the serpent and ballsed up Eden for obedient Adam. This blame-the-woman ploy of ancient myth is reflected in the very name of the first woman. Genesis · reports that, "Adam called his wife's name Eve (*Chava*), because she was the mother of all living." Well, here is our old friend, the folk etymology. The Old Testament is chockablock with

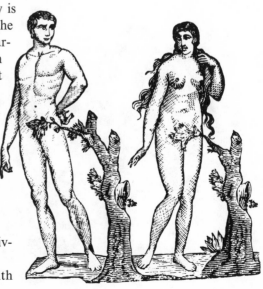

spurious derivations. In this case, the writers of Genesis thought that because the first syllable of Eve's name in Hebrew (*cha-*) sounds like the root for life הי *chai*, it was safe to imply that Eve meant 'life.' We know it in the common Jewish toast *L'chaim* להים 'To Life!'—popularized as a song in the Broadway musical *Fiddler on the Roof*. *Chai*, sometimes Englished as *he*, is also the name of a letter of the Hebrew alphabet, and one may see pendants shaped like the letter ה worn as good-luck charms on a necklace. But biblical researchers in comparative linguistics have found that Eve (*Chavva* or *Chava*) was borrowed by early Jews from their neighbours. Chavva was a Canaanite fertility mama, literally a Phoenician snake goddess, whose form was common in ancient Middle Eastern mythologies as the mother of humanity. In Aramaic and Syriac, two ancient Semitic tongues, the word for snake is *chevya*.

When we consider Eve and her shenanigans with the snake in the Garden of Eden, it is clear that here again is male myth-making seeking to control women, this time by guilt. For again the story says, *Paradise might have continued forever, but the wiles of the Eternal Feminine messed innocent males up; and so, woman, thou shouldst hide thy face in shame and guilt, for what thy sex hath so rashly wrought!* To this eternal blame of woman by man, most modern women have said, "Take a hike, wimp."

DEVILS

The foul fiend of the bottomless pit, Old Nick, has bedevilled Canadian cartographers since first they put quill to parchment on a wave-tossed ship. The roll call of the Tempter's toponyms is a sonorous one: Devil's Club Creek in the Yukon, Devils Claw Mountain in British Columbia, which also has Beelzebub Mountain.

Baalzebul was an honorific title of the pagan god of Ekron in the Old Testament, *II Kings*. It meant 'lord of the high house.' But pious Jews thought such a title belonged only to their God, and they playfully altered the Syriac with a Hebrew pun, changing the name to Beelzebub, which may be parsed in Hebrew as *ba'al zebub* 'Lord of the Flies.' He came to represent the nadir of idolatry, the falsest of false gods, and was later in Christian lore a powerful associate lord of Satan.

British novelist William Golding took the title of a novel from the translation of Beelzebub's name. *Lord of the Flies* deals with British boys marooned on a tropical island during an atomic war, most of whom succumb to evil impulses.

Devil's Bite near Calgary is a gouged-out hill. Ontario uses devil in seventy-eight place names, like Devil's Glen near Collingwood and Devil's Warehouse Island. Newfoundland boasts Devil's Knob and Devils Dancing Table. And Nova Scotia hoards Devils Cupboard and Devils Limb.

DIABLES

Lac Bat-le-Diable in Québec took its label from the nickname of a resident hunter and means 'Lake Beat-the-Devil.' Crique du Diable is 'Devil's Creek.' Newfoundland has Diable Bay and L'Anse au Diable Brook 'Devil's Cove Brook.' The Evil One seems almost ubiquitous, when one considers Pont du Diable, Rapides du Diable, Rivière du Diable, and Ruisseau du Diable. And . . . oh, to hell with it!

GODS LAKE

The Almighty gets short shrift in our place names, due more to piety than religious bashfulness, for God knows there's plenty of loud piety in Canada. Divine, indeed, is the love that dare speak its name from every smarmy-voiced, granny-squeezing religious broadcast that ever wheedled a "love donation" from

the puckered purse of a lonely widow. And viewers may rest confident that every penny of such a tele-tithe will go toward that important missionary work in Antarctica—among those heathen penguins. As far as names of the deity go, there is the village of Gods River on the Gods River emptying into Gods Lake in Manitoba, which may well mean 'straits of the Great Spirit.' Nor is the quality of the Bay of Gods Mercie strained, lying as it does at the arctic end of Hudson Bay. That's pretty well all she wrote for the G-word. Nova Scotia has Main-à-Dieu on Cape Breton Island. It looks like 'the hand of God,' but is Mi'-Kmaq as mangled by French settlers for the word *manitou* or spirit (evil in this case).

HEAVEN

As several residents will tell you, Heaven is in Ontario—in the form of Blue Heaven Lake and Little Heaven Island. A Canadian conversation about heaven that I particularly cherish occurs in *Sleeping Island: The Story of One Man's Travels in the Great Barren Lands of the Canadian North*, written by P.G. Downes and published in 1942. I happened upon this passage first while browsing through *Colombo's Canadian Quotations*. It is part of an interchange between a man of the Dogrib people and a Catholic missionary:

> *"Tell me, Father, what is the white man's Heaven?"*
>
> *"It is the most beautiful place in the world."*
>
> *"Tell me, Father, is it like the land of the little trees when the ice has left the lakes? Are the great musk oxen there? Are the hills covered with flowers? There will I see the caribou everywhere I look? Are the lakes blue with the sky of summer? Is every net full of great, fat whitefish? Is there room for me in this land, like our land, the Barrens? Can I camp anywhere and not find that someone else has camped? Can I feel the wind and be like the wind? Father, if your Heaven is not all these, leave me alone in my land, the land of the little sticks."*

HELL

Canada has one hell of a way to name places. Think of Backside of Hell Cove in Labrador, Hell Fire Pond in Newfoundland, Hell Rackets in Nova Scotia's Mahone Bay, Helldiver Lake in Saskatchewan, Hells Gate in the canyon of the Fraser River in British Columbia. A French version is Porte d'Enfer Rapids on the North Thompson River. And Hell Roaring Creek runs into the South Nahanni River.

Ontario has Hades Islands in Lake of the Woods, while Québec offers warmth at Lac Hades. The tang of old slang brightens the Parry Sound area at Hellangone Lake. My fave is a pond near Windsor, Nova Scotia, Helluva Hole.

ISLES OF THE DEAD

Many islets in the coastal waters of British Columbia have the local name, Mamaloos Island. *Memalost* was Chinook Jargon for 'dead or die.' They were places set aside solely for burial, and many taboos surrounded visiting these islands. Off Stanley Park in Vancouver is a *mamaloos* place called Deadman's Island.

KOSEKIN

Kosekin is one of the first utopias created by a Canadian fiction writer. James de Mille was a professor at Acadia and Dalhousie universities who wrote Victorian potboilers on the side. Nowadays such enterprise might cost an academic his or her tenure, but not in 1888 when de Mille penned *A Strange Manuscript Found in a Copper Cylinder*. Kosekin is an imaginary country located under Antarctica where everything is topsy-turvy. Darkness is better than light; poverty beats wealth. Perhaps it is better to call it a dystopia. De Mille is still worth reading for his adventurous debunking of Christianity and British mannerisms, and, just to balance the satire, he takes a few potshots at the evolutionary theories of Darwin, too.

LA LONGUE TRAVERSE

La Longue Traverse, the Long Trail, was a synonym for death in the early days of fur-trappers, before local policing was common in the north. Anyone caught stealing from one of the posts of the large fur companies might be forced to leave the settlement with no food or weapons and try to make it to the next habitation over miles of barren tundra or inhospitable forest. The Long Trail was an almost certain sentence of death.

Traverse also had a specific meaning in Canadian English, borrowed from Canadian French where *la traverse* was a fur-trapper's term for any open expanse of water in which canoes had to paddle away from the protection afforded by the shoreline. It was also an exposed stretch of prairie or the trip made across such an area.

NIRVANA

When the Buddhist term *nirvana* became popular in English during the mid-nineteenth century, it almost immediately became a slangy synonym for heaven, and so a verbal candidate for use as a place name by immigrants looking for a new wondrous home. Thus Canada sports Lac Nirvana in Québec, Mount Nirvana in the Northwest Territories, and Nirvana Pass in British Columbia's Pantheon Range. The word is a past participle in Sanskrit, an ancient language of India, directly related to most of the languages of Europe as a member of the huge Indo-European linguistic family. Nirvana means 'blown out like a candle.' *Nirva-* is a Sanskrit verbal root that signifies 'be extinguished,' and its components are *nis* 'out' + *va* 'blow.'

In Buddhism, nirvana is the release from earthly troubles that comes when a knowing Buddhist dies. The state may also be attained by a living person who has succeeded through meditation in achieving enlightenment. In Hinduism and Jainism, nirvana can mean the spiritual bliss of reunion with Brahma after death, after the blowing out of the candle of life, but not of course the flame of being. Of course. My skepticism in the face of the spiritual elegance of nirvana as a concept was shared by European intellectuals like Freud, who understood nirvana but could only equate it with his *death-wish*. He coined a technical term in psychoanalysis—the nirvana principle—and like all such terms it is metaphorical and poetic, not scientific. Freud's current enemies seem blind to the fact that he was a poet of the psyche, and no mere clumsy prober. Freud's nirvana principle described the mind's tendency to keep psychic tension to a minimum. But such a passive state was abhorrent to European thought, and Freud could only equate this yearning for psychic entropy to the action of the death instinct, the pining of living things for a return to the peaceful stasis of inorganic things.

Snapshot of nirvana, from the personal collection of the author

NOKOMIS

Nokomis is a hamlet in central Saskatchewan and there is little Nokomis Lake farther north in Saskatchewan near Reindeer Lake. Nokomis is the Earth Mother in Algonquin myth. From *Nokomis* 'grandmother' flows the water of life. From her breasts flow the vital liquid that feeds plants, animals, and humans. And in the heavily thumping verses of Henry Wadsworth Longfellow's poem, "The Song of Hiawatha" (1855), Nokomis is the grandmother of Hiawatha.

PARADISE

Casselman's Devout Travel Service informs all wayfarers that Paradise is a few miles east of Bridgetown, Nova Scotia. If it's booked fully, try Paradise, Newfoundland, just west of St. John's. Or the Paradise, Newfoundland, that's north of Grand

Falls. The more adventurous pilgrim can stop at the community of Paradise River, about 120 miles from Happy Valley, Labrador. There are dozens of place names using the word across Canada.

My own amblings 'midst the ferny dells and heavenly boscage began at Coote's Paradise, a marshy ramble near Dundas, Ontario, under the excellent supervision of Hamilton's Royal Botanical Gardens. This paradise is named after Thomas Coote, an ardent hunter of wild fowl who as a British officer was garrisoned nearby in the 1780s.

SAND HILLS

Sand Hills is literally a bit of heaven in Alberta. To the local Blood Indians, the sandy hill country south of Lethbridge is their happy hunting grounds, where the spirits of their warriors go after death. And in popular speech some Albertans use "gone to the sand-hills" as a synonym for dead.

SKY PILOT

This vivid synonym for a preacher or a missionary was made popular by migrant wheat workers and others on the Canadian prairies at the turn of the century. Such a Gospel-grinder often handed out "soul-grub" to anyone who listened.

CHAPTER 16

And we have called ourselves *the people*

More than half of all the world's tribal and national names contain a root that signifies "the people." For example, Inuit and Innu mean 'the people.' Dene, the name of the Athapaskan-speaking peoples, means 'the men' or 'human beings.' When people of different races speaking different languages meet in history, there is territorial animosity, war, and rarely, peaceful co-operation. There is also name-calling, mutual mangling of tribal names, and odd labels for newly encountered groups.

When the Anishnabeg—the people our history calls Algonquin or Algonkian—met their first whites along the St. Lawrence and in the Ottawa valley, they were very startled by French priests with wooden crucifixes. So the Anishnabe word for the French is *wa-mit-ig-oshe* 'men who wave wood over their heads.'

But white immigrants to North America were less kind in what they called the first peoples. We've seen how the Huron may have been given the name as an insult, from an Old French word for wild boar's head or lout. White invaders also had the clumsy habit of asking tribes what they called their enemies who lived near them. The Athapaskans, for example, never called themselves by that appellation, for the good reason that it means 'strangers' in Cree.

We have seen earlier how Eskimo may be derived from an Anishnabe insult that means 'eaters of raw meat,' the insult implying they were so primitive they had not discovered the art of cooking meat. This misunderstanding would occur when an Anishnabe wandering north saw Inuit eating certain parts of fish and mammals raw but freshly killed.

This chapter provides a selection of tribal names plus nicknames, like blue nose for a Nova Scotian. Optimists hope the human mixture here might be a crisp Canadian salad of peoples, but realists know it as a dish that has not always been palatable to bigots who sit down at the feast that is our country.

BLUE NOSE

There are as many derivations of blue nose as a term for a Nova Scotian as there are Nova Scotians. A Maritime potato once had a blue nose. There are the blue noses of fishermen coming into harbour after the cold Atlantic winds have coloured them. In the War of 1812, there was supposedly a Nova Scotia privateer with a cannon in her bow painted bright blue. She preyed on Yankee ships, and they called her The Blue Nose. And now we have the famous symbol of Nova Scotia, the Blue Nose schooner, which has adorned the obverse of the Canadian dime since 1937. Over the years, many other supposititious origins have surfaced and sunk in the Bay of Improbability. Truth is, nobody truly knows this origin.

DENE NATION

Dene Nation is the new name (since 1978) for the Indian Brotherhood of the Northwest Territories. Dene is the original name for the northern Athapaskan-speaking peoples of the Mackenzie River valley and the Barren Grounds. It means 'the men' or 'the people' or 'human beings.' The Dene never called themselves Athapaskans. Southern enemies and now friendly neighbours, the Cree, called them *Athapaska*, which means 'strangers' in Cree. The Dene Nation has the political clout to negotiate with the federal government about land claims, and also sponsors programs to improve Dene health, education, and development of resources on Dene lands. Spokesperson-presidents of the Dene Nation have gained national prominence through television—for example, Mona Jacobs, Georges Erasmus, and Stephen Kakwfi. From the perspective of Canadian words and place names, the Dene consistently press for a return to the original names of Northwest Territory features. The Mackenzie River in one Na-dené tongue is *Deh-cho* 'big river,' an apt descriptive for the second-largest North American river system. Only the Mississippi is bigger. And Alexander Mackenzie did *not* discover the river.

ERIE

Lake Erie takes its label from a tribe of native Americans who once lived on the south shore of the lake. Their totem animal was the bobcat or puma. They wore its tail as a ceremonial headdress. *Erie* means 'long-tailed' in their Iroquoian language. Early French explorers dubbed Erie *Lac du Chat* 'Cat Lake.'

LILLOOET

The village of Lillooet lies on the Fraser River at the feet of the mighty Cascade Mountains in B.C.'s southern interior. The town takes its name from the Lillooet people in whose interior Salish language *lillooet* means 'wild onions.' The town was founded during the gold rush of 1850 when it served as a provisioning stop on the way to the Cariboo and Fraser River gold fields. The name became widely known across Canada in the 1950s and 1960s when Margaret "Ma" Murray was the feisty editor of the *Bridge River–Lillooet News* and her editorials were quoted on the national wire services and on television and radio.

MÉTIS

At first Métis meant a person of mixed parentage, usually aboriginal and French. When first applied, Métis was scornful and dismissive. It's a continental French word for mongrel or half-breed, arising from Old French *mestis*, in turn derived from Latin *mixtus*. In the street Latin of the Roman soldiers who conquered ancient Gaul, a *mixtus* was usually the child of a Roman father and a Gallic native. The same Latin root found its way into Spanish as *mestizo*, which also means a person of mixed blood. Métis is now a term of pride and identity in Canada.

MICHIF

Michif is a creole, that is, a dialect of Cree with French and Ojibwa words added, spoken by a few Métis in Manitoba and Saskatchewan. J.S.H. Brown in *The Canadian Encyclopedia* gives a sample sentence:

Li pwesoon nimiyaymow = 'I like fish.'

- *Li* = Cree 'I'
- *nimiyaymow* = Cree 'like'
- *pwesoon* = *poisson*, French 'fish'

Most Métis speak French or English, and know Cree only if they have needed to speak it in their particular community.

NISHGA

The Nishga or Nisga'a people still occupy their ancestral lands in the valley of the Nass River in northwestern British Columbia. *Nass* means 'abundance' or 'food depot' in their language which is called Nass-Gitksan and is a member of the larger Tsimshian language family. *Nisga'a* means 'people of the Nass.' The food depot is the river itself, which every March churns in the run of oolichan fish, so abundant that they bring seabirds, seals, sea lions, and other animals to the mouth of the Nass River and sometimes right up the river. The Nishga carve cedar totem poles, traditionally live in plank houses, hold potlatch ceremonies, and belong to maternal phratries or clanlike descent organizations.

REDSKINS

The racist notion that all North American native peoples had red skin was first expressed in published reports concerning explorer John Cabot's encounters in 1497 with the Beothuk tribes on the island that was later called Newfoundland. The Beothuks, victims of systematic genocide by whites and other native peoples, were extinct by the late eighteenth century. Beothuks ornamented their skin with red ochre for ceremonial

and spiritual purposes, hence appearing red-skinned to Cabot and his men.

A common error about Cabot, the man who named Canada, is that he was French. Cabot was born Giovanni Caboto in Genoa, Italy. Seeking financial backing for a voyage to find a western sea route to Asia, Caboto finally found it among merchants in Bristol, England. Before sailing, he became a naturalized British subject and Englished his name.

Who will lift the cat's tail, if the cat won't?

I mmigrants to northern Ontario from Finland brought us this injunction to stop being lazy and get to work. It's word-for-word from Finnish. In this glance at several "pop" occupational names coined by Canadians, I have not delved into the hundreds of specific-task names that occur in the technical jargon of most complex industrial processes. Here I picked two job names from mining and some others I thought colourful, and added one political term from Saskatchewan with evocative history and etymology.

Persistent remnants of colonial vocabulary sometimes linger like sagebrush in a prairie fence. Saskatchewan has a term, unique in Canada, for a citizen who owns property and pays local taxes. A burgess is the equivalent to what is called a

BURGESS

A man who watches the clock remains one of the hands.

He could work all day in a bushel basket and still have room to move.

Avoir le trou de cul endessous du bras 'to have your arse under your arm,' 'to be dead-tired.'

Advice to the lazy: Donkeys go best loaded.

Canadian folk sayings about work

ratepayer elsewhere in Canada. Burgess harks all the way back to 1066, when the Normans invaded and conquered England. It is an Anglo-Norman transformation of *bourgeois*, whose prime meaning was 'citizen of a burg, a fortified town,' from Late Latin *burgus* 'castle or fort.' *Burgus* traces its lineage to the Vikings, who spoke Old Norse. To them a *borg* was a wall, then a wall around a town, then a town. This wall was at first made of wooden boards, and the related Old Norse word for that, *borth*, eventually gives the English term for a piece of lumber, a board. Germans used the root to mean fortress, e.g., in Martin Luther's great hymn, *"Ein feste Burg is unser Gott"* 'A mighty fortress is our God.' The root is a fertile seed for words in European languages, giving among others, the English words *borough*, *burglar*, *burrow*, *hamburger*, and the German noun *Bürgermeister*.

CRADLE-ROCKER

Placer mining searches for valuable minerals, especially gold, in surface deposits that are alluvial or glacial in origin. In placer mining, a cradle-rocker is a trough on a wooden or metal rocker used to separate gold flecks from sand and earth by washing and shaking the muddy gravel in water, and then, if necessary, using mercury to collect the gold. The prospector who performs such a task may also be called a cradle-rocker.

DEPOT FARMER

A depot farmer grew and supplied food to lumber camps, often after the gruelling work of clearing a few acres in the bush for tillable land. Potatoes for the lumbermen and oats for their horses were the main crops. Outbuildings on the farm might be used by the lumber company to store equipment and supplies. Such a depot farm was often owned by the lumber company itself, and the shanty farmer was its employee.

DONKEY PUNCHER

Donkey puncher? Oh no! Are we in for some gruesome enormity involving animal abuse? Rest easy, you lovers of the domestic ass. A small, auxiliary engine was first called a donkey in the British navy. From ships it spread to mean any of the small engines used in the British Columbia lumber industry. The lumberman who operated these log-pulling engines was the donkey puncher or donkey jammer or donkeyman. For his perpetual safety, let us bray.

DRAEGERMAN

In the technical jargon of Maritime coal mining operations, a draegerman is a specially trained rescue worker. A draeger was a gas-mask that permitted descent into tunnels where poisonous seepage had occurred. A.B. Dräger, a German physicist and engineer, invented the mask, originally to protect German soldiers during gas warfare in the trenches of World War I. But canny Canadian soldiers brought the idea back to their mines after the war.

FIELD PITCHER

A field pitcher in a prairie harvest is one of the threshing hands. He's the guy who forks sheaves up onto the hay wagon to make a load. Sometimes he's called a stook-pitcher. He's not to be confused with the spike-pitcher who pitchforks sheaves from the load into the separator.

HOG REEVE

Hog reeve was a historical municipal official in Nova Scotia and Prince Edward Island, whose stern duty it was to collect stray pigs and tote up any damage to property done by the swine. The job definition was never extended, unfortunately, to encompass damage done by municipal officials.

ROCK DOCTOR

Geology abounds with technical terms not generally known to lithic laypeople—jawbreakers like geognosy, *Wiesenboden*, and orography. At the other, more playful end of geological jargon is this nugget of Canadian mining slang. A rock doctor is any geologist.

Oh-oh! Caught me mapping, did you?

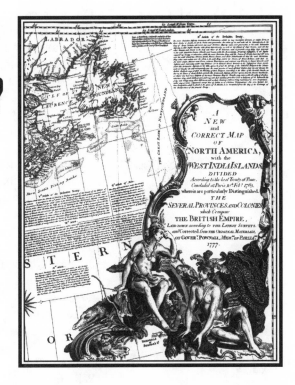

A NEW and CORRECT MAP OF NORTH AMERICA, with the WEST INDIA ISLANDS DIVIDED According to the last Treaty of Peace, Concluded at Paris 10.th Feb.y 1763. wherein are particularly Distinguished. THE SEVERAL PROVINCES AND COLONIES which Compose THE BRITISH EMPIRE. Laid down according to the Latest Surveys, and Corrected from the Original Materials, of GOVER.r POWNALL, MEM.r of PARLIA.t 1777.

H ere is our second jaunt across Canada to pluck nifty toponyms from the map. Is Dildo in Newfoundland our only naughty place name? Why is Lake Huron an insult to the first peoples whom the French called Huron. The people so named never called themselves by the term *Huron*. They called themselves *Wendat*.

We garner the Gaelic of Beinn Bhreagh in Nova Scotia and find that Ontario's Bracebridge and Gravenhurst have a literary origin, as does Flin Flon in Manitoba. Early on in their name game, fastidious inhabitants of Rat Portage, Ontario, summoned the Pied Piper of toponymy. Fort Vermilion, Alberta, literally paints the town red. And British Columbia honours an early premier who changed his name so it would

---

Coeur-Très-Pur-de-
la-Bienheureuse-Vierge-Marie-
de-Plaisance

This village in Québec has the longest Canadian place name known to the author. Contenders are invited to write and tell us if they've got a longer one— a longer place name.

more exactly reflect his philosophy of "universal love." Fulda in Saskatchewan has religious roots, and Regina was once a pile of bones. And we offer a new origin for the most whimsical of Ontario's place names, Punkeydoodles Corners.

NEWFOUND-LAND
DILDO

Do place names of obscene provenance dare to besmirch the pristine cartographical expanses of Canadian mappery? Alas, there are few tacky toponyms, chiefly due to the dreary drudges who make up geographic name boards across our pious Dominion. Before any place name gets official approval, these academic old maids of both sexes carefully winnow any off-colour chaff from the pure kernels of Canadian toponymy. With glee I report that Dildo, Newfoundland, is still there. Of course, the learned tomes assure us that it does not derive from the rubber or leather penis substitute. Oh dear no, dildo is a word used in the refrain of ancient ballads, a glass cylinder, a long 'arm' of water, a form of the doldrums. Why do we know this? Because no Newfoundlander ever had a sense of humour. If you believe that, you may side with those etymologists who think *dildo* was the refrain in an ancient ballad. Say, maybe we did used to sing that one, on feast nights out behind the castle. How did that refrain go? "With a hey nonny nonny dildo nonny nonny." And then again, perhaps it did not go like that. No one will ever know. And we may cherish Dildo as the pert upstart of Canada's place names.

NEW BRUNSWICK

New Brunswick could have been Pittsylvania in compliment to William Pitt (1759–1806), the British statesman and prime minister who opposed crazy old King George III's policies toward the American colonies. Pitt did not, however, support independence for any North American colony. New Ireland was another suggestion. After the American Revolution, cartloads of Loyalists spewed into Nova Scotia, and soon the northern area had enough new population to encourage political pressure on Halifax to split Nova Scotia. In 1784 it was officially sundered and the new northern province was named New Brunswick to honour—guess who?—the demented monarch King George III, who was a descendant of the House of Braunschweig in Germany. Glancing merely at the surface of the German roots, Braunschweig (Englished to *Brunswick*) appears to mean 'brown silence.' While that would describe the Teutonic vacuum of George III's brain, it is perhaps not the correct derivation. *Schweik* may have been borrowed into

German from a Slavic personal name, and the Braunschweig dynasty may be named, as many families are, after the nickname of a putative founding ancestor, "Brown Schweik."

Beinn Bhreagh near Baddeck, Nova Scotia, is Gaelic for 'mountain beautiful.' Alexander Graham Bell, inventor of the telephone, summered in the Maritimes, and after 1890 worked there on experiments with high-speed boats called hydrofoils and with airplanes like the Silver Dart. Bell first gave this bonnie name to his Nova Scotia home.

NOVA SCOTIA
BEINN BHREAGH

The prize naughty name also belongs down east. Do visit Kejimkujik National Park in Nova Scotia, from Mi'-Kmaq *koojumkoojik*, which means chafed testicles, caused by rowing so long across the lake to get there. Thomas J. Brown in *Nova Scotia Place Names* says it is Mi'-Kmaq for 'attempting to escape'! I suggest Thomas J. Brown was.

KEJIMKUJIK NATIONAL PARK

Places whose names give delight on Prince Edward Island include the nautically sonorous Cascumpec Bay, from the Mi'-Kmaq *kaskamkek* 'sandy shore.' Crapaud took its stark amphibian bluntness from the French name for the nearby river, *Rivière aux Crapauds* 'Toad River.' An apocryphal anecdote gave rise to Devil's Punch-Bowl Provincial Park. John Hawkins, an early pioneer of the area, claimed that Old Horny himself made him jettison a whole cargo of rum. Rustico and North Rustico derive from a 1724 Norman emigré named René Rassicot. And the charming town of Summerside grew up around the site of Summerside House, a Victorian inn built in 1840.

PRINCE EDWARD ISLAND

Canada's longest legitimate place name appears to belong to the village of Coeur-Très-Pur-de-la-Bienheureuse-Vierge-Marie-de-Plaisance, which in English makes the pious but clumsy-sounding Very-Pure-Heart-of-the-Blessed-Virgin-Mary-of-Plaisance. It is most often called Plaisance, or, at the end of a hard day, "*icitte*." *Plaisance* or pleasure in English is perhaps a remnant of the phrase *maison de plaisance* 'country house.'

QUÉBEC

The most common naming element in Québec places is *Saint* or *Sainte*. Explorer Jacques Cartier began the hagiological hooey quite early by bringing with him across the Atlantic a Roman Catholic calendar of saints' days, which lists the saints born on each day of the year and tells which saint each

particular day is meant to honour. If it's Tuesday, this must be St. Honoré day! But things very rapidly got out of hand—there were ten places called Sainte-Anne. Thus, a second element had to be added, giving us the melodious delight of Sainte-Anne-de-Beaupré 'Saint Anne of the beautiful meadow,' and her holy sister communities of Sainte-Anne-du-Lac, Sainte-Anne-de-Bellevue, Sainte-Anne-de-Kent, Sainte-Anne-de-la-Pocatière.

In all this flurry of onomastic sanctification, a few unscheduled canonizations were bound to happen, and they did, early in the game, too. The explorer Champlain's wife was Hélène Boulé. After her is named l'Ile Sainte-Hélène. She was never made a saint by the Church; she was made a saint by the map. Ditto for that sterling damsel Sainte-Hélène-de-Kamouraska. Other worthies who never graced a saint's calendar include Sainte-Eugénie-du-Lac-Chaud and Saint-Théophile-du-Lac-à-la-Tortue. I am certain, however, that Theophilus of Turtle Lake was one heck of a swell guy. My personal favourites among the place names of Québec suggest the problems of travelling in pioneer days, places like Brise-Culottes, Pis-Sec, and Vide-Poche!

ONTARIO
CALEDON HILLS

The gentle undulance of these hills north of Toronto recalled home to an early Scottish settler who named them after Caledonia, the Roman term for northern Britain and part of southern Scotland. Caledonia is also the name of a pleasant little town on the banks of the Grand River in southern Ontario. In the eighteenth century, Caledonia became a popular first name among American female slaves, and resulted in a jazz song of the same name early in this century.

GRAVENHURST & BRACEBRIDGE

Both these Ontario resort towns take their name from an American work, *Bracebridge Hall* (1822), a collection of short stories and essays by New York State writer Washington Irving (1783–1859). His best known stories include *Rip Van Winkle* and *The Legend of Sleepy Hollow*. Both town names were assigned when the Department of the Postmaster General needed names for two central Ontario post offices. The official, who may have been perusing Washington Irving's book, was a W.D. LeSueur. No sweat, *monsieur*.

KENORA

This community on Lake-of-the-Woods was first called Rat Portage, because of its position on the migrating route of muskrats who annually decamped from Lake-of-the-Woods to down near the Winnipeg River. Early settlers found the honest name Rat Portage to be unseemly and faintly repellant. So in 1899, they renamed their fair hamlet, by taking the first two letters of Keewatin (a former territory in northern Canada), plus the first three letters of Norman (a nearby town), and the middle letter of rat, thus achieving the sonorous splendour of Kenora.

LAKE HURON

Paddling toward the origin of the name of Lake Huron, we touch shore in Old French where *une hure* is 'a shock of hair.' It also meant the head of an animal, and then was applied to any human head that was animal-like. An augmentative suffix is something one adds to the end of a word to make the root meaning bigger. A common augmentative in Romance languages is *on*. For example, in Spanish, *hombre* means 'man.' Now add *on*, to get *hombron*, which means 'a big man,' a real bruiser. Thus sixteenth-century French has *huron*, the augmentative of *hure* 'a big clump of hair.' In older French it could also mean wild boar, or a bumpkin, a gross lout who never cut his hair.

LAKE HURON

French explorers first named the great lake La Mer Douce 'The Calm Sea.' But by 1790 it was Lac des Hurons 'Lake of the Hurons.'

A North American legend says a French soldier saw a group of Indians with their hair shaved on the side and long on top in what we would today call a mohawk, but in what that French soldier or explorer called *huron* because it was bristly like the hair on a wild boar's head. But there is also the distinct chance that Huron was an even more derogatory, racist epithet, "the lout."

The name *Huron* was applied to a confederation of some Iroquoian tribes that once inhabited the area between Georgian Bay and Lake Simcoe, quite early called Huronia. Huron was a French label, never one used by the confederacy. Their own name for their people was *Wendat* 'island dwellers,' either because of the many lakes and rivers with islands in Huronia, or because in their mythology the earth is one vast island resting on the carapace of the primordial turtle. Compare the name of Awenda Provincial Park in Ontario. When they fled their Iroquois enemies in the seventeenth-century, they were called Wyandot, a version of *Wendat*.

In 1615, when Samuel de Champlain and his crew of fur-seekers, a missionary priest, and adventurers first saw Huronia they found, though they did not recognize it, an expertly balanced economy among the Wendat that included fortified villages and cleared land for agriculture with three staple food crops—corn, beans, and squash—being deftly grown at the northern limit of their botanical range in North America. The Wendat were such successful farmers that they could use surplus food supplies to trade with northern neighbouring peoples who trapped and hunted beaver, deer, moose, and bear. Most of the Wendat lived in towns. They were close together in longhouses that held four or five families, and were thus highly vulnerable to the diseases brought by the French—smallpox, measles, and tuberculosis—to which the Wendat had no immunity whatsoever.

Lest one imagine it was only frowsy voyageurs from whom the native peoples contracted disease, it must be recalled that Champlain soon had Huronia crawling with Jesuit missionaries who piously passed on every spirochaete they had carried in their bodies from France.

One Jesuit-inspired custom of the French traders in the New World was that firearms could only be traded to native peoples who had converted to Christianity. Neat. That way, one could inveigle even peace-loving groups to take up arms, naturally on the French side, and fight whichever of their neighbours the French happened to be slaughtering that season. Then add the pious imprimatur of whatever semiliterate priestlet was attached to the "trading" mission.

The basic missionary impulse is an obsession that intelligent human beings of any century must wonder at. What kind of blind arrogance would drive a European to think that the nature religions of first peoples needed to be replaced by Christianity? Why foist the petulant, vengeful desert god of ancient Palestinian shepherds upon the Wendat?

In the Jesuit *Les Relations*—a series of diairies and records detailing the enormities inflicted on native peoples in the name of the Christian God—within the myriad of self-congratulatory, self-pitying lines penned by Jesuit priests, there is not a single expression of kindly humanity that stood up in a priestly conscience and screamed out, *But what are we doing to these people? Are we saving their souls only to destroy their lives?* The *Relations* is a torrential spew of smug piety. After spending hours perusing this literature of religious self-justification and blindness to common humanity, one begins to think that Brébeuf and his "black robes" got just what they deserved. Hawaii, South America, Africa: there has been no dot on earth's map unsmudged by the missionary hand.

Fifty years after Champlain met the Wendat, half of the entire population had died due to European diseases. And the Wendat lost more of their people through incessant warfare by neighbouring Iroquois tribes. In 1650 the last few Wendat, 300 people, who had numbered perhaps 15,000 when Champlain first encountered them, fled to a refuge at Lorette near Québec City, where a community survives to this day. But the last speaker of the Wendat language died in 1912.

The use of Huron to name an aboriginal people would not be the only example of insults made into names. Consider that notorious French trapper slang that became the official name of a people for many years, the Loucheux. A Dene people speaking one of the Na-dené languages, they lived in northwest Canada and Alaska. *Louche* means 'cross-eyed, squinty-eyed, shifty, shady, suspicious.' Now this couldn't be the French trappers projecting their own traits onto the native peoples with whom they traded, could it?

PUNKEY-DOODLES CORNERS

This wee hamlet near Kitchener sports one of Ontario's most whimsical but official monikers, and no one knows why—for sure. It was a stagecoach stop in the nineteenth-century, run by a local German-speaking innkeeper who was fond of bellowing out the song "Yankee Doodle." But he was just learning English, and always sang Punkey Doodle instead of Yankee Doodle. Maybe. But punkeydoodle was also a Victorian nursery word that meant 'to fool around, to fritter away one's time.' Now only the punkeydoodling originator can say with certainty, and he has gone to his lackadaisical reward.

MANITOBA
FLIN FLON

This mining town in Manitoba on the northern Saskatchewan border took its name from a dime novel called *The Sunless City* written in 1905 by J.E. Preston-Muddock, an English writer of pulp fiction. In the fantasy, a certain Professor Flonatin, whose nickname is Flin Flon, uncovers a subterranean city of gold. A Canadian prospector who staked the area had been reading a copy of this novel when he came to name his claim.

KOMARNO

Never mind Nevil Shute's *A Town Called Alice*. Consider instead Canada's very own Komarno, Manitoba, a town called mosquito, named by Slavic settlers after an early summer plague of mosquitoes beset their arrival. *Komar* комар, is Russian for 'mosquito.'

THE PAS

The Pas in Manitoba sits high on the banks of the Saskatchewan River just where it narrows. *Opa* in Cree means 'the narrows.' French traders tried to squeeze in a reference to Easter by jumbling it as *Pasquia*. But *Le Pas* and The Pas won out.

ROSENFELD

Rosenfeld is a Mennonite community founded in 1875, and the name means 'field of roses' in German.

WINNIPEG

Every Manitoba public school student knows that Winnipeg means 'murky water' or in Cree *win-nipi*. 'Tain't so. *Nipi* means 'water' or 'lake' but *win* makes the phrase mean 'bigger water,' that is, a lake much larger than usual. So that makes Lake Winnipegosis mean literally 'smaller bigger than usual lake.' Is that clear, class?

Fulda, Saskatchewan, was named by a pioneer who had visited the famous Benedictine abbey in Germany. Fulda is on a river of the same name, northeast of Frankfurt. There in a crypt under the cathedral lies buried St. Boniface, called the apostle of Germany. St. Boniface was murdered on a priestly mission in 754 A.D. He held up a codex of the Bible to protect himself against his assassins, says the legend. The symbol of St. Boniface is a book cut in half. And his original slashed codex is there in Fulda. So is another important relic—his severed head. St. Boniface in Manitoba is named in honour of the same saint.

SASKATCH-EWAN
FULDA

Pile o' Bones was the original name of the site of Regina, Saskatchewan. The Cree Indians called it Wascana, 'pile of bones,' because it was one of their seasonal buffalo pounds, a sort of stockade into which herds of buffalo were stampeded and then shot with rifles or arrows. Early white settlers thought Pile o' Bones was not a name to induce further migration. So they honoured Queen Victoria instead, calling the community by the Latin word for queen, Regina.

PILE O' BONES

Fort Vermilion on the south bank of the Peace River in northern Alberta near Wood Buffalo National Park was founded in 1798 as a trading post by the North West Company. Its name was a French translation of a native term for a nearby deposit of an iron ore that could be used as red ochre. Native people powdered the red vermilion stone, mixed it with fish oil, and used it to decorate and dye deerskin clothes and snowshoes.

ALBERTA
FORT VERMILION

Veldt is a village near Castor, Alberta, named after the Afrikaans Dutch word for 'field' or with reference to South Africa 'a high grassy plateau.' Nearby is Botha, named for Louis Botha who commanded forces at several famous battles in the Boer War and was later the first premier of the Union of South Africa (1910).

VELDT

Amor de Cosmos Creek in British Columbia celebrates one of Canada's most engaging, true eccentrics of the nineteenth-century, a man who shunned the common reclusive habit of most eccentrics and instead led a public life, becoming the second premier of the young province of British Columbia from 1871 to 1874. Born in Windsor, Nova Scotia, William Alexander Smith headed west early. By 1854 he was in

BRITISH COLUMBIA
AMOR DE COSMOS

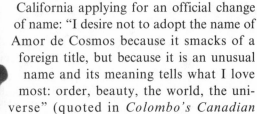

California applying for an official change of name: "I desire not to adopt the name of Amor de Cosmos because it smacks of a foreign title, but because it is an unusual name and its meaning tells what I love most: order, beauty, the world, the universe" (quoted in *Colombo's Canadian Quotations*, p. 143). In a wacky hybrid of Latin, French, and Greek, Amor de Cosmos means 'love of the universe.'

By 1854 there was already a Californian spiritual giddiness to his letters, as reported in the fascinating biography *Amor de Cosmos* by Roland White (1958). De Cosmos dabbled in the founding of communal paradises in the wilderness, but was also a practical and fervid "free Canada" advocate, promoting Canada's independence from Great Britain. After serving as premier of British Columbia, de Cosmos continued as a federal member of parliament for Victoria until 1882. Also located on Vancouver Island near Nanaimo is Mount De Cosmos.

THE TRUE NORTH

It is somehow typical that the august Canadian Permanent Committee on Geographical Names decreed in 1992 that the most northerly point of land in Canada, on the arctic tip of Ellesmere Island, at latitude 83°06′41.35″, shall be known as Cape Columbia. British explorer Sir George Nares first suggested Columbia, to honour a poetic name of the United States of America.

A new Latin tag for Canada: *per lacunas ad paupertatem* 'through deficits to poverty'

To get me out of the doggerel house, let me add a pleasant motto in Latin, which the English essayist William Hazlitt found on a sundial near Venice: *horas non numero nisi serenas* 'I count only the happy hours.' Canadian mottoes are made of sterner stuff, as we discover in this chapter while examining provincial, local, and institutional mottoes affixed to coats-of-arms and sundry heraldic bric-a-brac.

The motto of Canada, official since 1921, was suggested as early as 1866 by Sir Samuel Tilley, New Brunswick politico, and a father of Confederation. He drew it from the Old Testament, Psalm 72. In St. Jerome's Latin version of Holy Writ, called the Vulgate, the passage reads *et dominabitur a mari usque ad mare*. The King James version is "And he shall

O Latin is a dead tongue,
As dead as it can be.
It killed the ancient romans
And now it's killing me!

Old rhyme of British public school boys

A MARI USQUE AD MARE

have dominion also from sea to sea." As nitpickers, we may note Elizabethan scholars' mistranslation of the Latin adverb *usque* as 'also.' It is a particle placed before the preposition *ad* to give a kind of poetic emphasis to the meaning of the preposition, which results in the more appropriate English translation 'from sea yea onto sea' or 'from sea all the way through to sea.' Based on the same biblical passage, Tilley said the new country should be not the kingdom of Canada, but rather the Dominion. And so it is in the text of the British North America Act. However, in these politically correct and nervous nineties our Ottawa overseers, of every political hue, have thought best to suppress the use of the word as too redolent of imperialist might. Or perhaps they are merely twittery in the presence of a word like dominion that reminds them of the other word to which they have resort on weekends, namely, dominatrix? Do let's have Dominion Day back. Enough of the palely loitering, the bland, the wan and drab Canada Day.

PROVINCIAL MOTTOES

QUAERITE PRIME REGNUM DEI

The pious motto of Newfoundland is found in the Vulgate, St. Jerome's Latin version of the New Testament, in Matthew 6:33. "Seek ye first the kingdom of God," Matthew quotes Christ as saying near the end of the sermon on the mount, "and his righteousness, and all these things shall be added unto you." *These things* are bodily necessities like food and clothing.

PARVA SUB INGENTI

Modest of motto is the province of Prince Edward Island whose heraldic slogan means in Latin 'a small place next to a vast place,' but is also sometimes translated as 'the small under the protection of the great.' A somewhat Uriah Heepish maxim, it nevertheless has the virtues of clarity and plain speaking.

MUNIT HAEC ET ALTERA VINCIT

'One defends and the other conquers' states the rather Delphic phrase that often bestraddles the escutcheon of Nova Scotia. And if you've ever had your escutcheon bestraddled, you know how painful it can be, especially if the Latin is vague.

Does the motto mean that native peoples defend their land but the French and English conquer it? I can find no cogent explanation and so beg any reader who knows to enlighten me.

SPEM REDUXIT

New Brunswick's motto means 'She restored hope.' *She* is England, presumably performing this upbeat restoration job when the British defeated the French, officially recognized in the 1763 treaty ending the Seven Years' War. *The Canadian Encyclopedia* and the *Canadian Global Almanac of 1992* state incorrectly that the motto means 'hope was restored.' Why do reference book editors permit writers ignorant of Latin to translate it?

JE ME SOUVIENS

Naturally Québec's provincial motto is not Latin but French, chosen by Eugène Taché, the Québécois architect who designed the provincial coat of arms in 1883. Officially what is being remembered are cozy habitant customs of yore, the French language, and the Roman Catholic religion. But in street conversations, ordinary Quebecers tell the enquiring visitor that 'I remember' is a shortened form of 'I remember all the wrongs done to me.' It is thus a most appropriate catch phrase for the end of the twentieth century, which seems about to conclude in a mighty choral hymn of whining, victimhood, and cry-baby recrimination whose plaintive strains may echo into the next millennium.

UT INCEPIT FIDELIS SIC PERMANET

'As she began loyal, thus she remains' cooes the ingratiating motto of Ontario, as it crawls up to you and nuzzles into your mackinaw like some abandoned puppy. The loyalty is that of the United Empire Loyalists who helped settle early Ontario, after fleeing the American War of Independence. Their plight may be summed up tersely: *Stay in America, fight for King George, try to establish independence from these British tax bullies. You will probably get shot in the head. Or, there is free land in the Ottawa Valley and elsewhere.* The overnight loyalty to His Britannic Majesty was touching in its breadth and ubiquity.

FORTIS ET LIBER

'Strong and free' expresses the optimistic candour of Albertans. The compact motto is only slightly tarnished by the ambiguity of what looks like simple Latin. *Liber* is an adjective meaning 'free,' but *Liber* was also the Roman name for a fertility god of wine like Bacchus, and *Liber* can also mean 'wine';

fortis et liber can be translated as 'and a good, stiff drink.' Then, of course, *liber* also meant 'the bark of a tree,' and later 'a book or scroll,' from which ultimately English gets the word *library*. Sometimes, when coining mottoes, it is useful to check how semantically expansive Latin words are—they are notorious for the many meanings they may carry.

It is interesting that *liber* meant 'the bark of a tree' and then came to mean 'book,' because the same metaphor lies buried in the English word *book*. Its Germanic root is *Buche*, which still means 'beech' tree in German. *Buch*, the word for book in German is related. So is the English word *beech*. The German etymologist M. O'C. Walshe put forward an intriguing hypothesis that explains the connections this way: *Bücher* and, in Gothic, *bokos* were "beechwood sticks on which runes were carved" by early Teutonic peoples. But, were runes never written down? Perhaps on scrolls of beech bark?

SPLENDOR SINE OCCASU

British Columbia's motto beats not about the bush. 'Unfailing shining glory' is an appropriate translation. Or one may choose the official translation 'splendor undiminished.' In both cases, the motto celebrates the natural beauty of the sea and mountains and valleys of the west coast.

NO OFFICIAL MOTTOES

Manitoba, Saskatchewan, the Yukon, and the Northwest Territories have no official mottoes. There are, however, folksy tags appended to their names, and these include "Home of the Bay" and "The Prairie Province" for Manitoba; "Wheat Province" and "Home of the RCMP" for Saskatchewan; "The New North" for the Northwest Territories; and "Home of the Klondike" for the Yukon.

HUDSON'S BAY COMPANY

PRO PELLE CUTEM

Chartered in 1670, the Hudson's Bay Company selected its official motto shortly thereafter. The seventeenth-century writer of this motto was actually acquainted with literature in Latin, and so the motto reverberates with a satisfying Latinity not found in recently fabricated Latin mottoes.

Pro pelle cutem echoes a phrase from the Book of Job in the Vulgate, *pellem pro pelle*. In Job 2:4 God and Satan chat about how best to tempt the piety of the ever-faithful, never-blaspheming Job. God proclaims Job an upright man. But Satan chuckles, adding, "Skin for skin, yea, all that a man hath will he give for his life." This is truly an outrageous source for the self-serving motto of a fur company!

Another possible influence on the writer of the Hudson's Bay Company motto was the Roman satirist Juvenal who in his *Satires* 10.192 has *pro cute pellem* 'a hide in place of a skin.' But this citation seems a mere coincidence of similar words being used. Although most reference texts say the HBC motto means 'a skin for a skin' a better translation takes into account the generality being expressed, where—as in many languages of the world—the singular may suggest general plurality. The obvious meaning intended by the writer of the Latin was 'hides for fur.' Latin admits of this meaning. Why Canadian reference texts do not says more about their lack of Latin than the original motto-writer's skill. Sometimes an ironic translation is offered, viz. 'animal skins at the cost of human skins.' Although that may have historical validity, it is nonsense as a rendering of the Latin. Now, while this cauldron of controversy seethes, let us tiptoe quietly from the room in search of a hot toddy.

DESIDERANTES MELIOREM PATRIAM

THE ORDER OF CANADA

The Order of Canada, begun appropriately in 1967 during centennial celebrations of Confederation, is among the highest civilian honours a Canadian citizen may earn. The badge of the Order of Canada is an artist's conception of a snowflake, a severely stylized, brutally geometric, militaristic, nasty snowflake. This is a snowflake that would make Frosty the Snowman goose-step to the nearest sex change clinic and demand to be made into a scarecrow.

Circumscribed in a border around the central maple leaf is the drab motto couched in biblical Latin. Now some worthy named Carl Lochnan, who wrote the entry for "Order of Canada" that appears boldly in *The Canadian Encyclopedia*, states that *desiderantes meliorem patriam* means 'they desire a better country.' No, Carl, it does not. And you, Carlkins, will be sent to bed without supper tonight, but with Allen and Greenough's *New Latin Grammar*.

"They desire a better country" is best put into poetic Latin this way: *patriam volunt meliorem. Desiderantes* is not the third person plural, present indicative, of the first conjugation Latin verb, *desiderare*. It is the nominative plural of the present participle used as an agent noun, and can thus be accurately translated as 'those ardently wishing for a better country' or in a stretch 'their hearts' desire is a better country.' *Desiderare* in Latin does not suggest a mere polite desire for something. The semantic force of this verb is an urgent yearning, a desiderative impulse far stronger than the pipsqueak English verb *desire*. In fact, the Latin verb is misused here. The full meaning of *desiderare* is 'to long or pine for something once possessed but now lost.' Surely that is not what the originators of the Order of Canada had in mind?

Desiderantes meliorem patriam was taken from the New Testament in Latin, from Paul's epistle to the Hebrews, Chapter 11, Verse 16. The King James' English is "But now they desire a better country, that is, an heavenly: wherefore God is not ashamed to be called their God: for he hath prepared for them a city." So the better country spoken of is a post mortem heaven. Therefore, the motto of the Order of Canada implies that its recipients desire to die and go to heaven! That is the precise meaning of the biblical phrase. Of all Canadian mottoes, of all botched Latin tags, this surely is a world's record of inappropriateness, even for the Ottawa dimwits who picked and approved it.

MISCELLANY OF MOTTOES

ABEUNT STUDIA IN MORES

One abiding fallacy of liberal humanism puts on the toga here, in the motto of what was Victoria College (its official title is now Victoria University) at the University of Toronto. The Latin means 'studies pass into character.'

CHRISTUS VERA VITIS

The arms of Christ Church Cathedral in Montréal carry this priestly rewrite of a noted biblical passage from John 15:1 in which Jesus consoles his disciples with the parable of the vine, saying, "I am the true vine, and my Father is the husband-man." The Latin means 'Christ is the true vine.'

E SILVA SURREXI

This stirring Latin is the municipal motto of Grand Falls, Newfoundland, whose pulp and paper industry render it an apt slogan indeed, meaning 'I arose from the forest.'

EGO PORTA MUNDI

Moi, je suis la porte du monde 'I am the door of the world.' So boasts Dorval, whose main commerical airport brings the world to Montréal.

FELIX QUI POTUIT RERUM COGNOSCERE CAUSAS

The crest of Sutton District High School in Sutton West, Québec, says, "Fortunate is the person who can know the reasons for things."

IN MEDIA SILVA MANEO

Bishop's Falls in Québec presents this proud motto on its coat-of-arms, 'In the centre of the forest I stand.'

INITIUM SAPIENTIAE TIMOR DOMINI

Concordia College in Edmonton, Alberta, sets Christian hearts athump with the severe Old Testament thought that 'fear of the Lord is the beginning of wisdom.' St. Hilda's College at the University of Toronto echoes this in its *timor Dei principium sapientiae* 'fear of God is the foundation of wisdom.'

KAMISTIATUSSET

The motto of Labrador City is not Latin, but I include it here because I am fond of the phrase in the Montagnais language of the Naskapi, which may be translated as 'land of hardworking people.'

ΜΕΤ' ΑΓΟΝΑ ΣΤΕΦΑΝΟΣ

Hellenic spice adds zest to the crest of Trinity College at the University of Toronto, whose Greek motto means 'after the struggle, the victor's crown.'

QUAECUMQUE VERA DOCE ME

Saint Joseph's College at the University of Alberta puts into its coat-of-arms the words of the eternal student, 'Teach me whatsoever things are true.' No mean feat of pedagogy, that.

QUARE VERUM ET VIRTUTEM

Okanagan College in Kelowna, British Columbia, directs its students to 'seek truth and excellence.'

RECTI CULTUS PECTORA ROBORANT

Bishop's College School in Lennoxville, Québec, thunders in thong-consonanted Latin that 'learning what is right makes the character strong as oak.' Now this is Latin that Cicero, the Roman orator, might stoop to copy!

REMIS VELISQUE

The United Church College of St. John's, Newfoundland, rings the nautical bell with a phrase any ancient mariner would find yare. 'By oars and sails' reads the motto, while on the coat-of-arms a double-masted galley flies a pennant from her foremast, emblazoned with the words *Floreat Nova* 'May the New Land Flourish!'

TERRA PROGREDIMUR

The town of Wabush in Labrador West District, Newfoundland, has this Latin motto that means 'by the earth we prosper.' Wabush is Naskapi for 'rabbit place.'

VELUT ARBOR AEVO

The University of Toronto's motto means literally 'as a tree with age,' but in translation the English must be plumped up to a more pleasing amplitude, something like 'just as a tree branches as it grows, so does the university expand, its leaves of wisdom ever burgeoning in the sunlight of knowledge.' Though perhaps a tad overdone, that is the general import of this good terse Latinity.

The eternal grab bag

One is supposed to disguise it, to relabel it, to slide it in surreptitiously, and never, never admit that it has been included in a book. I mean the dreaded "chapter with no theme or focus." To include such chapters in tomes more pregnant with Deep Thought than this offering, Beethoven-browed academics have been known to perform feats of intellectual torsion that would daunt Elasto, The Rubber Boy of Borneo. Yes, here's the verbal grab bag of Canadian historical terms I found interesting but could not wedge in anywhere else. But any alcove of words that holds treasures like the Harold Ballard Effect, misery fiddle, and the phrase "chanting the cock," has at least the charm of diversity. I did try to knit these frayed strands into a coherent quilt, but, as Canadian folk speech, highlighted in the next chapter, puts it, "Went up pumpkin, came down squash."

BALLARD EFFECT

The Ballard Effect was a gruesome nineties reminder of the play-for-keeps attitude of Canadian stock investors. Harold Ballard was an owner of Maple Leaf Gardens and Toronto's NHL hockey team. He bad-mouthed his own players whenever they screwed up, thus reducing Maple Leaf morale to a level not found since inhabitants of the black hole of Calcutta were last polled. In the early 1970s, Mr. Ballard went to prison for fraud and theft. Among his other enormities, he once called CBC Radio's Barbara Frum a . . . a . . . "broad" on the program *As It Happens*. Alas, for some transgressions, there is no forgiveness. As Ballard lay dying, and dying, and dying, through the winter and spring of 1990, the share price of Maple Leaf Gardens stock shot up each time he seemed near death. This ghoulish rollercoaster of stock prices became known as the Ballard Effect.

BASTARD CANOE

Bastard canoe was borrowed into English from the voyageurs' French *canot bâtard*, whose slang meaning is 'one hell of a big canoe.' It referred to the largest canoes that could carry ten paddlers and two tons of freight. The less robust French designation was *canot de charge*.

The earliest citation in the *Dictionary of Canadianisms* for black ice is 1829, but then it referred to new ice on bodies of water, which appeared dark because of its clearness and solidity. The first use of black ice to mean a winter hazard on roadways was in British Columbia, whence use of the phrase spread across Canada.

BLACK ICE

Blowdown may refer to a single tree blown down by the wind, but is more often heard as an encompassing noun describing a wide area of wind damage that has cut a swathe through a forested area. Ontario has its very own Blowdown Lake in Algonquin Provincial Park.

BLOWDOWN

A boucan is a naturally burning bed of surface coal. Certain exposed seams of coal, like lignite, can catch fire as the result of lightning or a forest fire and then smoulder for decades, perhaps for centuries. In 1909 Agnes Cameron published *The New North—Being Some Account of a Woman's Journey through Canada to the Arctic*. She reported encountering boucans in the North that had been smoking continuously since the explorer Alexander Mackenzie had spotted them in 1789 and thought them aboriginal peoples' fires.

BOUCAN

The verb *boucaner* was in continental French by 1546 meaning 'to dry and smoke meat or fish.' French explorers in the Caribbean made forays into the valley of the Amazon River in South America where they met an indigenous people called the Tupi. The French found Tupi who prepared meat and fish in a way new to them, by smoking it over an open fire on a wooden frame or grid which in Tupi was a *mboukem*. French heard this as *boucan*. First *boucaner* meant to smoke meat in this way. Then by 1670 the verb developed the meaning, particularly on Santo Domingo, of hunting wild cows to provide meat to be smoked. By extension, the verb came to mean to hunt on the sea for booty, as a pirate or *boucanier*. British colonists in the Caribbean Englished this word to give *buccaneer*. In Daniel Defoe's *Robinson Crusoe* of 1719, the hero even calls himself by the word: "having been an old Planter at Maryland and a Buccaneer into the bargain."

BUCCANEER

Meanwhile in Québec, *boucaner* stayed in the active folk vocabulary, and developed some new senses—'to be smokey, to smoke (food).' *La boucane* can mean 'smoke, steam,' or 'homebrew whiskey.' *Hareng boucané* is 'smoked herring.' *Les lunettes boucanées* are 'sunglasses.' When the Acadians were expelled from Nova Scotia, some travelled to Louisiana where Cajun (Acadian) French has *boucane* for 'smoke.'

CAMP X

From 1941 to 1946, British secret agents trained at this spy camp near Whitby, Ontario, operated by Bill Stephenson's British Security Co-ordination. Among the British agents trained at Whitby in spy techniques was Ian Fleming, who went on to write the James Bond novels after the war. Deeds of high derring-do were whispered nightly into the top secret communications network there that connected security operations in Britain, the United States, and Canada. This network was named Hydra, after the nine-headed monster of Greek mythology. One of the labours of Hercules was slaying the hydra, no mean feat because every time he lopped off one of the heads, two new heads grew up in its place. And so every time Nazi sympathizers uncovered a Hydra communications station, a new one was quickly opened elsewhere.

CANADIAN BROAD-CORPING CASTRATION

Former CBC announcer Rex Loring claims he really did utter this chestnut, long cherished in the annals of CBC bloopers. "This is the Canadian Broadcasting Corporation" is a network cue that is not a tongue-twister for agile-larynxed staff announcers at CBC. The most mellifluous Canadian English I have ever heard spoken has issued from CBC Radio announcers like Ken Haslam, Pat Patterson, deB. Holly, Lamont Tilden and Harry Manis. Before audiotape though, many network cues and station breaks were broadcast live. After identifying the CBC eighty times a day, even the supplest tongue slipped once in a while. Ol' Mother Corp. has also contributed many words and phrases to the archives of our radio and television memories.

L FOR LANKY

L For Lanky was a popular CBC radio serial during World War II. Each episode happened on board a Lancaster bomber, and was loosely based on actual RCAF exploits in the early years of the war.

POC-DOC

A playful term that originated at CBC Radio in Toronto in the sixties, a poc-doc was a pocket radio documentary—a short piece (7–15 minutes) with location sound, on-the-spot interviews, and often an interwoven narration by the reporter. The word *documentary* meaning a nonfiction film story was first applied to a film by John Grierson, the first commissioner of the National Film Board of Canada in 1939. Grierson, a Scot, applied it to Robert Flaherty's *Nanook of the North*, a pseudo-biographical epic—*pseudo*, because Flaherty staged and restaged many of the Inuit action sequences.

On September 8, 1952, CBC television signed on in Toronto, with the CBC logo upside down and backwards. Among the early CBC-TV shows I remember with great affection was an evening puppet show that featured the madcap Uncle Chichimus and his femme fatale, Hollyhock, along with their genial human companion, actor Larry Mann. The dialogue was zanier and more imaginative than other contemporary puppet efforts, such as the irretrievably sappy "Howdy Doody Show."

UNCLE CHICHIMUS

"The Voice of Doom" belonged to the CBC Radio newscaster who tirelessly reported the war news over the old Dominion network during the Second World War. Particularly in the early years of the conflict, when the Allies lost battles and casualties mounted, the deep-voiced announcer was listened to with apprehension. His name was Lorne Greene, a young Toronto actor, who went on to become a millionaire playing Pa Cartwright in the long-running NBC-TV western series, *Bonanza*.

THE VOICE OF DOOM

Their names were among the most powerful Canadian words I knew, when I was six years old. They danced in my child's mind—Gene Kiniski, Whipper Billy Watson, Yukon Eric, Killer Kowalski. Unlike Hercules or Superman, these giant heroes might possibly be summoned to destroy my enemies (e.g., kids who threw iced snowballs at me during public school recess). Then, I ruined it all. At the age of 12, I paid my once-in-a-lifetime visit to a professional wrestling match at the Welland-Crowland Arena, and found out they were just big, sweaty guys earning a living with thumps and arm-twists and headlocks that required some athletic prowess, but sadly had been thoroughly rehearsed. The sleazy showbiz of some aspects of professional sport tainted all further pleasure I could take from such spectacle. I left that arena a sadder but wiser wimp.

CANADIAN WRESTLERS' NAMES

Canuckiana was a nonce variant of the word *Canadiana* and used in 1888 as a column heading for items of light, humorous news with a Canadian setting. It might well apply to the humble nuggets presented in this prospector's pan. Let's revive it.

CANUCKIANA

CHANTING THE COCK

Voyageurs picked a fight by chanting the cock, often no doubt simply to alleviate the tedium of long hours of hard paddling in canoes laden with furs. Bristling with machismo, one of these rough men would stand up in the canoe and crow like a rooster. The phrase is a direct translation of voyageur French *chantant le coq*. The crowing was usually directed at a specific other person. If the cocky challenge was accepted, a bout of stress-relieving fisticuffs followed.

CONCESSION

You won't find concession roads, so-called, anywhere else in the world except in Ontario and Québec. In medieval French *une concession* was a grant of land. The term was first used in Canada for parcels of land that a seigneur rented to tenants. Now, in Ontario and Québec, concessions are parallel lots of 200 acres each. The word also refers to the survey lines and roads that delimit such lots. The familiar rural sign, e.g., Concession Road #3, often indicates a country lane of gravel, built on the road allowance between concessions.

DROKE

Droke or drogue or drook is heard in the Maritimes to designate a clump of evergreens, a copse, a thicket, a grove, a bluff. In Nova Scotia lumbering, it also denotes a treed-out area of stumps. In origin, droke is the word *draw* with a fine Gaelic guttural tacked on its end.

FROST BOIL

Frost boils are those queasy-to-drive-over bumps on a paved road caused by the expanding of moisture in the pavement during freezing weather. Spring repair of frost boils is a feature of Canadian municipal road maintenance.

GREENPEACE

Greenpeace was founded in 1971 in Vancouver by members of an antinuclear protest group called the Don't-Make-A-Wave Committee, originally convened the previous year to disrupt American nuclear testing near Amchitka in the Aleutian Islands off Alaska. Greenpeace then evolved into a worldwide keeper of ecological common sense, though some of its outrageous publicity stunts could not be said to come under the same rubric.

HUDSON'S BAY HYMN BOOK

HBC. The letters stand for Hudson's Bay Company, the usual name for the Company of Adventurers of England trading into Hudson's Bay. These stalwarts received their charter from Charles II in the year of our lord 1670. Trappers, traders, and indigenes who often had no choice but to deal with the monopoly and with the not-always-honest factors of HBC posts had their own interpretation of the initials: Here Before Christ. The Hudson's Bay hymn book was a bit of brusque irony from the days of the fur trade in northern Canada, when the factor of a trading post would record in a ledger (the hymn book in question) the debt owed to the company by trappers going out on the line. If they had a record of bringing back to the post good commercial fur, the company would provision their trip by lending the value of goods taken against the value of furs brought in later.

Manitoba Bridge is in Bruges, Belgium, with two giant iron buffaloes at one end of the bridge. In 1944 Bruges was liberated from the Nazi occupation by Canadian troops led by the 12th Manitoba Dragoons.

MANITOBA BRIDGE

Misery fiddle is Canadian loggers' slang for a cross-cut saw, the type with a man on each end. Its use was hard, sweaty work in the pioneer lumbering days of British Columbia, before the invention of power saws.

MISERY FIDDLE

The Newfie Bullet was the jokey nickname of the slowest passenger train in Canadian history, which the CNR ran across Newfoundland until 1968. Just how slow was the Bullet? Well, it was quicker to get off the mainland ferry, sit down on the highway, and fart your way to St. John's.

NEWFIE BULLET

The word *prehistoric* was coined in 1851 by Sir Daniel Wilson, while professor of History and English at the University of Toronto. It appeared in the title of his book, *Prehistoric Annals of Scotland*. The adjective refers to any time before written historical records, before 6000 B.C., an arbitrary and now former date for the invention of writing.

PREHISTORIC

Pour la Patrie was Canada's very first separatist novel. The year of publication? 1895. Jules-Paul Tardivel, a reactionary journalist, a Rome-hating but pious Catholic, wrote of a future Québec in which humble habitant farmers were ruled politically by Roman Catholic bishops. Earlier, Tardivel had helped fuel hatred against franglais and *les maudits anglais* in his 1880 pamphlet "L'anglicisme: voilà l'ennemi!"

TARDIVEL

"I've seen more brains in a sucked egg."

This chapter looks at Canadian folk sayings and comic figures of speech, some fetched here by pioneers from every coign of old Mother Earth, others minted fresh as circumstance required. Some you may share with the most austere dowager, though she may afterward view you with disdain through a tortoise-shell lorgnette. And some are so pure of heart they would not besmirch the lily chastity of a vestal virgin. Others are rough and rural, like the one from Aylesford, Nova Scotia used to indicate surprise—*There he stood, winkin' and blinkin' like a toad under a spike-toothed harrow.*

Snappy sayings seem most at home when they criticize the behaviour of others. Why this quite uncharitable turn should infect so many of the pertest figures of our common speech is

THE FAULTS OF OTHERS

not clear. Maybe Jean-Paul Sartre, the French existentialist, was correct in his drama *Huit Clos* (No Exit) when he has a character say, "*L'enfer, c'est les autres*" 'Hell is other people.'

She went up in the air like a home-sick angel.
I learned this folk expression from a correspondent in Hanna, Alberta. It describes someone who became angry very quickly.

That boy never did grow up. One day he just sorta haired over.

He had a smile on him like poison come to supper.

I've seen more brains in a sucked egg.
I heard this as a farmer near Morrisburg, Ontario, was scolding a young hired hand who had made an error operating a tractor. The practice of sticking a finger through the top of a fresh egg and sucking out the yolk and the white has largely disappeared from rural eating habits, although I have been told it is an excellent home remedy for a hangover.

If brains were leather, you wouldn't have enough to make spats for a louse.
Nancy MacEwen of North Rustico, P.E.I., sent that gem along. Spats covered Edwardian shoes, protecting them from dust and rain.

Because the getting of food required more energy and time from our pioneer ancestors, a thin person was looked on as a nutritional failure, not a fashionable bean-pole, hence the following folk sayings—

Poor dear! He'll have to shake the sheets to find her on their wedding night! (of a new bride not sturdy enough)

He's so thin he has to stand twice in the same place just to make a good shadow.

She's so skinny, if she turned sideways holding a glass of tomato juice, she'd look like a thermometer.

Thin? Seen more meat on a hockey stick!

Other bodily faults—

Well, she wasn't behind the door when the feet were handed out, was she?

He's got a face long enough to eat oats out of a churn.

Buck teeth? Only man I ever met could eat grass through a picket fence.

She was pure as the snow, but she drifted.

Nervous as a cat in a room full of rocking chairs.

He's so crooked he has to sleep on a warped board.

Her ass moves like two rabbits in a bag.

He's stunned as Tom's dog—put his arse in the water to get a drink.

He'd talk the hind leg off a mule, and whisper in the socket.

He's so low he'd have to climb a ladder to kiss a snake's belly.

If a newly married couple don't get on well, neighbours used to say—

They'll never comb their grey hair together.

He's tight as white on rice.

Stench? Drive a buzzard off a dead cow.

Charity begins at home, and usually stays there.

No use keepin' a dog and barkin' yourself.

If she had as many stickin' out of her as she's had stuck in, she'd look like a porcupine.

CHEAPSKATES

There are plenty of Canadian folk expressions to describe penny-pinchers and skinflints. They are salty sayings because they were uttered with real passion. But we can't censor them, and tart them up in Sunday-go-to-meetin' clothes, for that robs them of their power.

He's tighter than a bull's arse in fly time.

He was so tight you couldn't drive a flax seed up his ass with a mallet.

She's so tight she'd skin a louse for the tallow.
That one, from the days when tallow fat was used to home-make candles.

Why, he'd squeeze a cent 'til the Queen cried.

Guy's so cheap he'd pick the pennies off his dead granny's eyes.

ODDS & ENDS

She's so butch, she kickstarts her vibrator.

I'll hit ya so hard, you'll starve to death bouncin'.

Jealous as two undertakers in a one-hearse town.

That smell would gag a maggot on a gut wagon.
A term that recalls the Ottawa valley of a hundred years ago, the gut wagon was the conveyance in which dead farm animals rode to the glue factory—hopefully not to the abattoir. The collagen in their bones and tissues was the basis for many commercial glues. Of necessity a humble vehicle, it is also the germ, so-to-speak, of a potent folk expression from eastern Ontario. If one detected an unpleasant odour, one might say, "That smell would gag a maggot on a gut wagon!" Or again, one might not.

I hate you so much that, when you pass my gate, I wish you'd run.
Gay Kurtz, who lives in Woodrow, Saskatchewan, sent me that Canadianism.

They got nothin'. Poor as Job's turkey. Couldn't raise more 'n three feathers, and had to lean against the barn to gobble.
Correspondent Steve Melnick, of Port Morien, Nova Scotia, has sent me over the years some of my personal favourites in the tangy Canadian sayings sweepstakes. Two gems collected by Mr. Melnick follow.

That fellow's loose as a pan of soot.

It harks back to dirty days of cleaning the coal-stove first thing in the morning. And the next one speaks for itself:

They were so poor there was nothing on the table but elbows, and the mice in the cellar had tears in their eyes.

Here's an insightful folk expression from Québec, said of men who drive expensive sports cars—

FROM QUÉBEC

Grosse corvette, p'tite quéquette
Literally 'big car, little dick.'

Avoir les deux pieds dans la même bottine
It means to have no get-up-and-go, to be lazy, literally 'to have both feet in one boot.'

Reçu comme un chien dans un jeu de quille
In playful Québécois this might be rendered as not welcome, or 'received like a dog in a bowling alley.'

Être une tête à Papineau
A Québécois folk saying that means to be smart as a whip, very clever indeed, recalls one of the heroes of French Canadian history, literally 'to be a Papineau brain (head).' Joseph-Louis Papineau (1786–1871) led a group of radical reformers in Lower Canada. Their grievances against the government of the day came to a head in the Rebellion of 1837, fomented by Papineau in Lower Canada, and William Lyon Mackenzie in Upper Canada.

È s'mouche pas avec des pelures d'oignons.
In Québec slang, to indicate a pretentious woman, one might say—*She wouldn't blow her nose on an onion peel.*

Un vrai flique-flaqueur
This is a Québec doctor who rushes patients through his office, making a flick-flack noise with the machine that processes plastic health insurance cards offered by patients at payment time.

Avoir des bébites dans la tête
To be a bit crazy, literally 'to have bugs in the head.'

Ferme ton gorlot!

Shut up! literally 'stop your sleigh-bell.'

Se faire virer la boîte à lunch

This is the extremely vulgar street expression that means 'to have a hysterectomy,' literally 'to have one's lunch-box turned over.'

Se donner un up 'n down

To masturbate, literally 'to give oneself the old up-and-down.'

Tirer une botte à l'oeil

To masturbate, literally 'to milk out a shot in the eye.'

Se passer un jack

To masturbate. The English name Jack can mean 'penis' in Québec French.

Baise-moué l'ail

Kiss my ass, literally 'kiss my garlic.'

Avoir mal aux cheveux

To have a severe hangover, literally 'to have a hair-ache.'

Chanter la pomme à une fille

To ingratiate oneself with a girl by trying to sweet-talk her, literally 'to sing the apple to a girl.'

Un char de Crisses quate par bancs

One of many colourful curses from Québec, it means 'a wagonload of Christs, four to a bench.'

Le diâble est aux vaches.

Bad weather's coming, literally 'the devil's in the cows.'

IN ANOTHER NECK OF THE WOODS

Livin' with him's 'bout as much fun as having a shit hemorrhage in a hurricane.

This musing on domestic harmony comes from Haldimand County in Ontario.

She's a hurricane on a ten-cent piece.

Here's a peppy saying from the rural interior of British Columbia, as used in writer-politician Paul St. Pierre's 1966 novel, *Breaking Smith's Quarter Horse*. It is said of a wife angry with her husband.

I'll tow that alongside for a bit before I bring it aboard.

From the South Shore of Nova Scotia comes this saying that conveys doubt about what one just heard.

Low man on a totem pole

This expression denotes the least important person in a group or business. It began on our west coast. But it was popularized by the American comic writer H. Allen Smith as the title of his 1941 collection of humourous essays. Smith meant the bottom figure, figuratively, on a totem pole. But some west coast native people who know their history remember that in days of yore, before the Bill of Rights, a captured slave was sometimes buried alive in the pit into which the giant totem pole was then sunk. This raising of a totem was, after all, a festive occasion to honour ancestors and spirits important to the tribe, and offing an unimportant slave added skookum medicine to the power of the occasion.

Faster than the mill-tails of Hell.

So one might say along Nova Scotia's South Shore, according to Lewis J. Poteet in *The South Shore Phrase Book* (1983). Poteet adds that this "proverbial way of describing speed...owes something to the nineteenth-century water-wheels and mill-races in the rivermouths of the South Shore."

He was wearing Full Nanaimo.

Are B.C. yachtsmen a trifle snooty? They seem to pay finicky attention to how their fellow mariners dress. Full Nanaimo is a sportive insult that applies to a chintzy outfit worn by a boating parvenu. Whitebuck shoes, white belt, polyester pants, and a blue blazer with a spurious yachting crest brand the wearer as a floating yutz of the first water. In Ontario, it is heard as a Full Oakville. A similar chop is FDAM, pronounced to rhyme with ram. The acronym stands for **F**irst **D**ay **A**t the **M**arina.

Have you more pungent folk sayings, used in your family— cherished dinner table proverbs passed down from grandmother or great uncle? Share them. If you know some I don't, drop me a line at the address given in the preface.

See you when the ice worms nest again!

S cientists have dubbed humankind variously: *Homo sapiens*, the knowing human; *Homo ludens*, the playful (creative) human. An anthropologist suggested *Homo denominator*, the naming human, for we are the only creatures who label a world in order to know it. But because we have named a thing, we must never be under the illusion that we have understood it. At the same time, as my grandfather used to say, "A name is not nothing, either." Names are little lighted safety beacons that let us navigate a ship of thought through rock-strewn shoals of perception. A sage of linguistics at whose feet I once sat did not approve of my interest in word roots. "Always remember, Casselman, etymology is the toyshop of linguistics," he intoned whenever my quest for word origins became too fervid. He felt that Chomsky's generational grammar was the only avenue of contemporary linguistics worth study.

On the contrary, globally inclusive, computer-assisted, comparative etymology is opening fresh vistas into the beginning and spreading of human speech. For example, the scholars Joseph H. Greenberg and Merritt Ruhlen in *Linguistic Origins of Native Americans* have found exciting correspondence in root words in languages once thought to have no relationship whatsoever. The ancient root **M-L-Q* whose meanings hover around a semantic nexus that includes 'swallow-throat-suck-milk-breast' shows up in languages all over the world. There is no chance that the following similarities are accidental! The English word 'milk' has surprising cognates in Arabic *mlj* 'to suck the breast,' in Hungarian *mell* 'breast,' in Tamil *melku* 'chew,' in Latin *mulg-ere* 'to milk,' in a Salish language of British Columbia, Halkomelem, where *melqw* is 'throat,' in Chinook *mlqw-tan* 'cheek,' in the Kutenai *u'mqolh* 'to swallow,' and, among others, in the Andean Quechua *malq'a* 'throat.' This supercomparative etymology will be one of the great contributions of the next century to the study of words.

Of learning from languages and of languages, there is no end. There are still unstudied human tongues in the remote places of the earth. Sweet vowels and airy syllables in accents unrecorded drift through rain forests. Unparsed shouts make geckos scuttle into crannies, somewhere. In linguistics, we can stay with the fellow in Henry Fielding's *Tom Jones*:

> *There is still much to be done, and great things to be seen,*
> *Before we go to paradise by way of Bethnel Green.*

Bethnel Green was the location of a well-known cemetery in eighteenth-century London.

Even this morning, completing this book, I find a new Canadian word in the *Globe and Mail*. The Canadian Alliance Against Software Theft warns in an advertisement against "softlifting," the unauthorized copying of software, softlift being formed on the analogy of shoplift.

So, my valedictory advice is: be a word-nut, for whom the English poet William Cowper spoke in his poem "Retirement," when he described:

. . . Philologists, who chase
A panting syllable through time and space,
Start it at home, and hunt it in the dark,
To Gaul, To Greece, and into Noah's ark.

BIBLIOGRAPHY

Akrigg, G.P.V., and Helen B. Akrigg. *1001 British Columbia Place Names.* 3rd ed. Vancouver: Discovery Press, 1970.

Avis, Walter S., C. Crate, P. Drysdale, D. Leechman, M.H. Scargill, and C.J. Lovell, eds. *A Dictionary of Canadianisms on Historical Principles.* Toronto: Gage, 1967.

Bergeron, Léandre. *Dictionnaire de la langue québécoise.* Montréal: VLB Éditeur, 1980.

Canadian Encyclopedia. 4 vols. Edmonton: Hurtig Publishers, 1988.

Cameron, Agnes. *The New North: Being Some Account of a Woman's Journey Through Canada to the Arctic.* London: D. Appleton, 1909.

Carr, Emily. *Klee Wyck.* Toronto: Oxford University Press, 1941.

Chambers, J.K., ed. *Canadian English: Origins and Structures.* Toronto: Methuen, 1975.

Clark, Lewis J. *Wild Flowers of British Columbia.* Sidney, BC: Gray's Publishing, 1973.

Cochrane, Jean. *The One-Room School in Canada.* Toronto: Fitzhenry and Whiteside, 1981.

Colombo, John Robert, ed. *Colombo's Canadian Quotations.* Edmonton: Hurtig, 1974.

Davies, Robertson. *Fifth Business.* Toronto: McClelland & Stewart, 1970.

———. *The Rebel Angels.* Toronto: Macmillan, 1981.

de Mille, James. *A Strange Manuscript Found in a Copper Cylinder.* (Anonymous). New York: Harper, 1888. Toronto: McClelland & Stewart, 1969.

Denys, Nicolas. *Description géographique et historique des costes de l'Amérique septentrionale.* Paris: Claude Barbin, 1672.

Desruisseaux, Pierre. *Le livre des expressions québécoises.* Montreal: Hurtubise HMH, 1979.

Dickens, Charles. *Barnaby Rudge.* Ed. Gordon Spence. Harmondsworth, Eng.: Penguin, 1973.

Douglas, Robert. *Place Names of Manitoba.* Ottawa: King's Printer, 1933.

Downie, Mary Alice, and Mary Hamilton, eds. *"And some brought flowers": Plants in a New World.* Toronto: University of Toronto Press, 1980.

Dulong, Gaston. *Dictionnaire correctif du français au Canada.* Québec: Les Presses de l'Université Laval, 1968.

Ferguson, Mary, and Richard M. Saunders. *Canadian Wildflowers.* Toronto: Van Nostrand Reinhold, 1976.

Franklin, John. *Narrative of a Journey to the Shores of the Polar Sea in the Years 1819, 1820, 1821, and 1822.* London: John Murray, 1823.

Garland, G.D. *Names of Algonquin: Stories Behind the Lake and Place Names of Algonquin Provincial Park.* Algonquin Park Technical Bulletin No. 10. Whitney, ON: The Friends of Algonquin Park, 1991.

Gesner, Abraham. *A Practical Treatise on Coal, Petroleum, and Other Distilled Oils.* New York: Baillière Bros., 1861.

Grinnell, George Bird. *Blackfoot Lodge Tales.* New York: Charles Scribner's Sons, 1916.

Hamilton, William B. *The Macmillan Book of Canadian Place Names.* Toronto: Macmillan, 1978.

Hearne, Samuel. *A Journey from Prince of Wales' Fort in Hudson's Bay, to the Northern Ocean in the Years 1769, 1770, and 1772.* Ed. J.B. Tyrrell. Toronto: Champlain Society Publications, 1911; first published, London: Strahan and Cadell, 1795.

Holmgren, Eric J., and Patricia M. Holmgren. *Over 2000 Place Names of Alberta.* Rev. ed. Saskatoon: Prairie Books, 1973.

Jack, Donald. *Rogues, Rebels, and Geniuses: The Story of Canadian Medicine.* Toronto: Doubleday, 1981.

Jenness, Diamond. *The Indians of Canada.* 6th ed. Ottawa: National Museum, 1963.

———. *The Ojibwa Indians of Parry Island.* Bulletin No. 78. Ottawa: National Museum of Canada, 1935.

King, W. Ross. *The Sportsman and Naturalist in Canada.* London: Hurst and Blacknell, 1866.

Lewis, Charlton T., and Charles Short. *A Latin Dictionary: Founded on Andrew's Edition of Freund's Latin Dictionary.* Impression of 1st ed. 1879. Oxford: Oxford University Press, 1958.

Lewis, Walter H., and Memory P.F. Elvin-Lewis. *Medical Botany: Plants Affecting Man's Health.* New York: John Wiley and Sons, 1977.

Liddell, Henry George, and Robert Scott. *A Greek-English Lexicon.* 9th ed. Oxford: Oxford University Press, 1953.

Lotz, Jim, and Pat Lotz. *Cape Breton Island.* Vancouver: Douglas, David and Charles, 1974.

Mardon, Ernest G. *Community Names of Alberta.* Lethbridge: University of Lethbridge, 1973.

McConnell, R.E. *Our Own Voice: Canadian English and How It Is Studied.* Toronto: Gage, 1979.

Montgomery, Lucy Maud. *Anne of Green Gables.* Boston: L.C. Page Company, 1908.

————. *Emily of the New Moon.* Toronto: McClelland & Stewart, 1923.

————. *Prince Edward Island. The Spirit of Canada: A Souvenir of Welcome to H.M. George VI and H.M. Queen Elizabeth.* N.p.: Canadian Pacific Railway, 1939.

Moodie, Susanna. *Roughing It in the Bush.* Reprint of 2nd ed. Afterword by Susan Glickman. Toronto: McClelland & Stewart, 1991.

Moore, Christopher. *The Loyalists: Revolution, Exile, Settlement.* Toronto: Macmillan, 1984.

Murphy, Emily Gowan (Ferguson). *The Impressions of Janey Canuck Abroad.* Toronto: Thomas Allen, 1901.

Nader, Ralph, Nadia Milleron, and Duff Conacher. *Canada Firsts: Ralph Nader's Salute to Canada and Canadian Achievement.* Toronto: McClelland & Stewart, 1993.

New Shorter Oxford English Dictionary. Oxford: Oxford University Press, 1993.

O'Grady, William, and Michael Dobrovolsky. *Contemporary Linguistic Analysis: An Introduction.* 2nd ed. Copp Clark Pitman, 1992.

Orkin, Mark M. *Speaking Canadian French: An Informal Account of the French Language in Canada.* Rev. ed. Toronto: General Publishing, 1971.

Oxford Companion to the English Language. Ed. Tom McArthur. Oxford: Oxford University Press, 1992.

Oxford English Dictionary. Ed. James A.H. Murray et al. Oxford: Oxford University Press, 1884–1928; corrected reissue, 1933.

Oxford English Dictionary. 2nd ed. Ed. R.W. Burchfield et al. Oxford: Oxford University Press, 1989.

Partridge, Eric. *Origins: A Short Etymological Dictionary of Modern English.* 4th ed. London: Routledge and Kegan Paul, 1966.

Pinker, Steven. *The Language Instinct.* New York: W. Morrow, 1994.

Pinsent, Gordon. *John and the Missus.* Toronto: McGraw-Hill Ryerson, 1974.

Poteet, Lewis. *The Second South Shore Phrase Book.* Hantsport, NS: Lancelot Press, 1983.

Pratt, T.K. *Dictionary of Prince Edward Island English.* Toronto: University of Toronto Press, 1988.

Rayburn, Alan. *Naming Canada: Stories about Place Names from Canadian Geographic.* Toronto: University of Toronto Press, 1994.

Reavley, Gair et al., eds. *A Literary and Linguistic History of New Brunswick.* Fredericton: Goose Lane Editions, 1985.

Robert, Paul. *Dictionnaire alphabétique et analogique de la langue française.* Paris: Société du Nouveau Littré, 1973.

Rogers, David. *Dictionnaire de la langue québécoise rurale.* Montréal: VLB Éditeur, 1979.

Rudnyckyj, J.B. *Canadian Place Names of Ukrainian Origin. Onomastica 2.* 3rd ed. Winnipeg: Ukrainian National Home Association, 1957.

———. *Manitoba: Mosaic of Place Names.* Winnipeg: Canadian Institute of Onomastic Science, 1970.

Scargill, M.H. *A Short History of Canadian English.* Victoria: Sono Nis Press, 1977.

Shakespeare, William. *The Oxford Shakespeare.* Ed. W.J. Craig. London: Oxford University Press, 1966.

Shipley, Joseph T. *The Origins of English Words: Discursive Dictionary of Indo-European Roots.* Baltimore: Johns Hopkins University Press, 1984.

Skinner, Henry Alan. *The Origin of Medical Terms.* 2nd ed. Baltimore: Williams and Wilkins, 1961.

Stearn, William T. *Botanical Latin.* New edition. Toronto: Fitzhenry and Whiteside, 1983.

———. *Stearn's Dictionary of Plant Names for Gardeners: A Handbook on the Origin and Meaning of the Botanical Names of Some Cultivated Plants.* London: Cassell Publishers, 1992.

Stegner, Wallace. *Wolf Willow: A History, A Story, and A Memory of the Last Plains Frontier.* New York: Viking, 1955; reprinted 1966.

St. John, Molyneux. *The Sea of Mountains: An Account of Lord Dufferin's Tour Through British Columbia in 1876.* 2 vols. London: Hurst and Blackett, 1877.

Story, G.M., W.J. Kirwin, J.D.A. Widdowson, eds. *Dictionary of Newfoundland English.* Toronto: University of Toronto Press, 1982.

Symons, R.D. *Many Trails.* Toronto: Longman, 1963.

Traill, Catherine Parr (Strickland). *The Backwoods of Canada: Being Letters from the Wife of an Emigrant Officer. Illustrative of the Domestic Economy of British America.* London: C. Knight, 1836; Toronto: McClelland & Stewart, 1966.

———. *Canadian Wild Flowers Painted and Lithographed by Agnes Fitzgibbon with Botanical Descriptions by C.P. Traill.* Reprint of first Montréal edition 1868. Toronto: 1972.

Turenne, Augustin. *Petit dictionnaire du "Joual" au français.* Montréal: Les éditions de l'Homme, 1962.

Webster's Third New International Dictionary of the English Language. Springfield, MA: G. & C. Merriam, 1976.

What's in a Name? Travelling Through Saskatchewan with the Story Behind 1600 Place-names. 2nd. ed. Saskatoon: Western Producer Book Service, 1974.

ILLUSTRATION CREDITS

pp. *ix* and 151, Jim Harter, *Music: A Pictorial Archive of Woodcuts & Engravings*, Dover Publications • pp. 1 and 2, Jim Harter, *Hands: A Pictorial Archive from Nineteenth-Century Sources*, Dover Publications • p. 7, detail from National Archives of Canada (hereafter NAC) / C61055 • pp. 8, 140 (top), and 153, Edmund V. Gillon, Jr., *Picture Sourcebook for Collage and Decoupage*, Dover Publications • pp. 11 and 14, Harold Hart, *Dining & Drinking*, Hart Publishing • pp. 13 and 91, Jim Harter, *Women: A Pictorial Archive from Nineteenth-Century Sources*, Dover Publications • p. 15, detail from NAC / C48790 • p. 17, detail from NAC / C121011 • p. 20, detail from NAC / C125264 • p. 23, detail from NAC / C68270 • p. 31, detail from NAC / C48647 • p. 34, detail from NAC / C1279 • p. 37, detail from NAC / C30043 • p. 45 (top), detail from NAC / C30045; (bottom) detail from NAC / C30044 • p. 49, detail from NAC / C48515 • p. 51, detail from NAC / C99255 • p. 52, detail from NAC / C82783 • p. 55, detail from NAC / C48694 • p. 57, detail from NAC / C20484 • p. 59, detail from NAC / C72734 • pp. 63, 66, 68, and 119, Jim Harter, *Animals*, Dover Publications • p. 69, detail from NAC / C58613 • p. 70, detail from NAC / C124729 • p. 75, NAC / C99321 • p. 76, detail from NAC / C6257 • p. 80, detail from NAC / C82950 • p. 81, detail from NAC / C2396 • p. 83, detail from NAC / C7162 • p. 85, detail from NAC / C2411 • p. 100, detail from NAC / C82867 • p. 102, detail from NAC /

C44236 • p. 108, detail from NAC / C23447 • p. 117, detail from NAC / C25700 • p. 118, detail from NAC / C2397 • p. 120, detail from NAC / C2170 • p. 121, detail from NAC / C31184 • p. 122, detail from NAC / C27697 • p. 133, detail from NAC / C77268 • p. 135, *Holidays*, Hart Publishing • p. 136, NAC / C2383 • p. 138, detail from NAC / C48601 • p. 140 (bottom), NAC / C82788 • p. 143, detail from NAC / C72985 • p. 145, detail from NAC / C62594 • p. 147, detail from NAC / C24937 • p. 154, detail from NAC / C76943 • p. 155, detail from NAC / C82910 • p. 161, detail from NAC / C48584 • p. 164, detail from NAC / C17922 • p. 165, detail from NAC / C85373 • p. 166, detail from NAC / C38557 • p. 169, detail from NAC / C36126 • p. 172, detail from NAC / C82799 • p. 174, detail from NAC / C85378 • p. 176, NAC / C82955 • p. 178, detail from NAC / C72064 • p. 179, NAC / C46332 • p. 180 (top), detail from NAC / C63537; (bottom), detail from NAC / C39756 • p. 181 (top), detail from NAC / C46244; (bottom), detail from NAC / C63533 • p. 182, detail from NAC / C63536 • p. 187, detail from NAC / C82974 • p. 188, Jim Harter, *Transportation: A Pictorial Archive from Nineteenth-Century Sources*, Dover Publications • p. 190, detail from NAC / C99255 • p. 195, detail from NAC / C48791 • p. 196, detail from NAC / C48588 • p. 197, detail from NAC / C62680 • p. 199, detail from NAC / C5462 • p. 200, detail from NAC / C48538 • p. 203, detail from NAC / C7866

INDEX

CANADIAN FOLK SAYINGS & PHRASES

rare comme d'la marde de pape, 94
reçu comme un chien dans un jeu de quille, 199
rough as a dogfish's back, 63

se donner un up 'n' down, 200
se faire virer la boîte à lunch, 200
se passer un jack, 200
se pèter les bretelles, 94
she was pure as the snow, but she drifted, 197
she went up in the air like a home-sick angel, 196
she's a hurricane on a ten-cent piece, 200
she's so butch, she kickstarts her vibrator, 198
she's so skinny, if she turned sideways holding a glass of tomato juice, she'd look like a thermometer, 196
she's so tight she'd skin a louse for the tallow, 198
sly as a lynx, 63
soit sur le plancher des vaches, 66
stench? Drive a buzzard off a dead cow, 197
sure as there's cold shit in a dead dog, 93

that boy never did grow up. One day he just sorta haired over, 196
that fellow's loose as a pan of soot, 199
that smell would gag a maggot on a gut wagon, 198
that's as easy as stuffing soft shit up a wild cat's ass with the narrow end of a toothpick, 93
the fartin' horse will never tire; the fartin' man's the one to hire, 94
the fox smells his own hole, 94
there he stood, winkin' and blinkin' like a toad under a spike-toothed harrow, 195
they got nothin'. Poor as Job's turkey. Couldn't raise more 'n' three feathers, and had to lean against the barn to gobble, 198
they were so poor there was nothing on the table but elbows, and the mice in the cellar had tears in their eyes, 199
they'll never comb their grey hair together, 197
thin? Seen more meat on a hockey stick, 196

un vrai flique-flaqeur, 199
up the well-known stream without the necessary means of conveyance, 93

va pèter dans le trèfle, 94
vous vous faites aller la marde de tête, 94

water's flatter 'n a plate of puppy pee, 95
well, she wasn't behind the door when the feet were handed out, was she? 197
went for a dump and the gophers got him, 103
who will lift the cat's tail, if the cat won't? 165
Why, he'd squeeze a cent 'til the Queen cried, 198

SUBJECT INDEX